靴 四 足

FOUR PAIRS OF BOOTS

A 3,200 KILOMETRE HIKE
THE LENGTH OF JAPAN

by

CRAIG McLACHLAN

YOHAN PUBLICATIONS, INC.

FOUR PAIRS OF BOOTS

Published August 1996

Photographs by Craig McLachlan

YOHAN PUBLICATIONS, INC.
14-9, Okubo 3-chome, Shinjuku-ku, Tokyo, Japan.

Printed in Japan

For my lovely wife, Yuriko,
and our boys, Riki and Ben.

Andrew Brokenshire
some friendly button-pushers and a tripod

A special thanks to
David, Robin, Tomoyo, Yuriko, and to all those
who supported me on my Journey.

CONTENTS

CONTENTS

INTRODUCTION

This book is about my search for the "Real Japan", wherever that may be.

I was inspired by the feats and writings of an Englishman, Alan Booth, who walked the length of Japan in 1977. I treated Mr Booth's book, "The Roads to Sata" like a bible in preparing for my trek. I am only sorry that I did not have the opportunity to meet him before his death.

In 1977, when Alan Booth walked the length of Japan from north to south, I was starting High School and my first Japanese language classes. One American dollar was worth 270 yen.

During my walk in 1993, from south to north, I turned 31, and the American dollar hit an all-time low of 101 yen. Without doubt, Japan is a country that has undergone tremendous economic change. But what of the people?

This book contains experiences I had in 99 days of walking the 3,200 kilometres from Cape Sata at the southern tip of Kyushu, to Cape Soya at the northern tip of Hokkaido. This is what happened to me. As much as possible, I have tried to stick to my experiences, and not generalize about "the Japanese".

Television, I feel, tends to give us a biased picture of Japan. We see crowded trains, cramped housing, and industrial smog. 43% of Japan's 125 million people live in the three main urban areas of Tokyo, Osaka, and Nagoya, it is true. But it should also be noted that 70% of Japan's land area is covered with forests and fields. I am often surprised by comments from Japanese who I am showing around New Zealand's South Island, surely one of the most beautiful places on Earth.

"It's almost as beautiful as Japan!" I am told.

All conversations in this book took place in Japanese, unless otherwise noted. There is a glossary of Japanese words used after the final chapter.

I would like to re-emphasize that these were my experiences. I encourage anyone interested to go out and have their own. Japan is a fascinating country!

1. ISLANDS IN THE FOG

The beer was cool and refreshing. While chewing on a grilled squid, I contemplated what lay ahead.

Being an "ideas man", I often come up with somewhat crazy schemes that tend to get filed away into the "do later" part of my brain. For some reason I couldn't quite pinpoint, the idea of walking the length of Japan kept popping out of that file. I had discussed it so many times with friends that it was now a case of having to do it just to prove my credibility as a "doer" and not just a "talker". If the truth be told, I would have been happy to finish my beer, wander out, and hop on a flight back to Osaka, back to the security and warmth of my waiting family.

"Ready to go" from Cape Sata

But there I was at Cape Sata, not quite the end of the world, but definitely the southernmost end of mainland Japan, contemplating the idea of 100 days of sore feet, blisters, and the unknown.

I was staring at the lighthouse on the small island off the end of the Cape, feeling a little lonely and insignificant, overawed by the magnitude of my plans.

"That foreigner is going to walk to Hokkaido!" I turned and saw the gold-toothed woman who had sold me the beer talking with a middle-aged couple. It was a Thursday afternoon in late May, and there were few tourists about.

"You're kidding! Walk! I'll bet he's going to hitch-hike!"

"I'm going to walk," I said. "It's 3,200 kilometres to Cape Soya, and I'm going to walk every kilometre!"

This stunned him. "He speaks Japanese!" he informed his wife, who had been listening, and who seemed to have figured this out for herself.

"Where does he come from?" the man asked the beer vendor, who I had had quite a chat with, and looked ready to spill the beans.

"I'm from New Zealand," I replied. The beer vendor looked upset. I had stolen her thunder. We continued a stilted conversation in this vein — a kind of four-way conversation about me. The husband would ask the woman a question about me, which I would answer directly to him, and he would comment on, back to his wife. We finished up with a photo session, in which the vendor took photos of me with the couple, who came from Nagoya, "in case he becomes famous!" I couldn't wait to get out the door.

As I was leaving, he said it was marvellous I was going to walk the length of Japan, and "would I like a ride to Kagoshima?"

So at 2:30 pm, May 20th, 1993, I was jolted into action, with five hours of sunlight left, and hit the road. I strode aimfully up the path, through the lush tropical undergrowth, away from Cape Sata, latitude 31 degrees North, and headed for Hokkaido.

The first seven kilometres was on a toll road that I had specifically been told I was not allowed to walk. On my way to the Cape, I had had quite a battle convincing the bus driver that I only needed a one-way ticket, and I intended to walk back! He took a lot of convincing, but when I finally had him on my side, he helped me semi-convince the official at the Cape. Rules are not made to be broken in Japan, but I took it as an OK when he only glanced up from his comic as I walked by and out onto the sealed road.

The question of "can I walk for 100 days?" was still bothering me, when I discovered that I had already broken my sunglasses! A few expletives made me feel better, and then I was into it.

In a few kilometres I found a shortcut that took me off the toll road, and then, around a corner, the tiny fishing village of Odamari came into view. Nestled in a cove below green rugged mountains, its harbour was protected by a huge concrete breakwater, the sea sparkling in the bright sunshine. It didn't take me long to get there, and into the local shop for a drink.

I knew what was coming when I realised I had been spotted by a group of schoolchildren on their way home. Sure enough I was followed into the cool air-conditioned shop.

I could hear the whispers.

"Do you think he can speak Japanese?"

"Look at his long legs!"

"He's so tall!"

"What is your name?" I asked one little girl who reacted with an excited squeal.

"He can! He can!" This signalled an onslaught, and I spent the next fifteen minutes explaining that no, I was not an American, measuring children's height against my 188 cm body (I am considered a giant in Japan), and hoisting my 20 kilogram pack on and off tiny backs that sagged with the weight. Few foreigners visit such remote parts of Japan as this, but while the children gleefully showed their interest, the woman owner showed commendable restraint in treating me as a normal customer. Since I had no idea how far I would get on that first afternoon I thought it prudent to buy supplies.

The children's interest perked me up considerably, and on leaving, I felt confident in what I was trying to achieve. Their encouraging banter made me feel that my personal search for the real Japan would be successful.

Route 68 wound up into the hills, high above the coast, and until I reached the town of Sata three hours later, I had only passed the occasional cluster of houses. The beer woman from the Cape had stopped to offer encouragement on her way home.

"You've got this far already! You've got such long legs! It won't take you long to get to Hokkaido!" She grinned. "Are you sure you don't want a ride?"

Then at 6:30 pm as I wandered down out of the hills, the magnificent volcanic cone of Kaimondake came into view, far in the distance on the other side of Kagoshima Bay. At 922 metres, it is hardly a monster, but rising directly from sea level, and being such a perfect shape, it dominates the horizon. Kaimondake is known as Satsuma Fuji. Satsuma is the old name for the Kagoshima area, and Fuji refers to the mountain's resemblance to Mt. Fuji. Japan, on the Pacific "Rim of Fire", is an incredibly volcanic land and many cones resembling Fuji are nick-named in this way.

As I walked past the school in Sata, I couldn't help but notice the shoes in the open doorless lockers outside the gym. There is obviously not a great crime problem in Sata as about fifty pairs of gym shoes sat there available for anyone who might want to take them. At the school bus stop, four young guys sat smoking, one playing a guitar. There were whispers as I passed and then they all burst out laughing. I thought of asking them what they found so funny, but thinking better of it, wandered into the town which now seemed to be rather uninviting. There were few people around and in a few minutes I found I had gone right through the town and was out again on the main road, this time on a narrow strip of land with the coast on my left and forested steep hills towering above on my right.

The lights of the resort town of Ibusuki shone brightly on the far side of the bay. By seven-thirty it was dark, with me out in the middle of nowhere. The adrenalin must have been pumping, as I had walked right through my intended destination, and on my first night out, was stuck with nowhere to pitch my tent. I eventually found an uncomfortable spot amongst some banana trees and spent a hot and sweaty night wondering why I hadn't used my brains and gone for a bit of comfort, staying in Sata.

"Sniff! Sniff! Sniff!" A sizeable animal was inspecting my tent! By the sound of it, less than a metre away through the nylon. "Sniff! Sniff!" There was only one thing I could do. I jumped and yelled at the top of my voice.

"Aaaarghhh!" Whatever it was, it was definitely more afraid of me than I was of it! It scurried away through the bushes. A monkey? A fox? A badger?

May 21 was my 31st birthday and I celebrated by clambering down over the boulders for a swim in the calm, clear sea. It was 7 am and the sun was already high in the cloudless sky. Away to my right a fisherman was casting off the rocks, and I took my time, enjoying the bright warm sunshine, inspecting my feet which had carried me 23 kilometres in five hours on my first day! I am a keen sportsman and in good condition, but the prospect of 100 days of walking had dumbfounded me as to a training program. Consequently, I hadn't had one and was trusting my body's adaptability and a strong mind to carry me to Hokkaido.

I spent the morning wandering up the coast, past farmers digging potatoes, old women tending their rice paddies, and friendly roadworkers along the road.

"Okuni wa?" What is your country?

"New Zealand."

"Ah, toi desu ne!" You're a long way from home! Big smiles under broad-rimmed hats, protecting swarthy faces from the strong sun.

There were untended stalls selling a variety of vegetables, vending machines selling hot and cold drinks, and every few kilometres, white crosses marked with names and dates of people who had died in traffic accidents. The latter were usually accompanied by signs encouraging safe driving, and by flowers, food or alcohol left for the loved ones who had passed away there.

Just before midday I stopped at a small noodle shop for lunch. It had been a hot morning. Despite the fact that I was the only person in the place, the middleaged couple running the shop looked run off their feet. As the clock struck midday, I saw why. The owner donned a white hard-hat and headed out with a large metal bookcase-like container filled with bowls of noodles. I could hear his motorbike whirr into life, and he was off with the noodles suspended from a high hook attached to the back of his bike, so that they'd stay level when he raced around corners. The lunch hour rush was not slow in coming.

"We spend all morning preparing for lunchtime, and all afternoon recovering," joked the woman, left on her own with a shop of ever-increasing customers.

The midday news was on the TV and the news of the day came from the United States. A male employee was claiming sexual harassment against his female boss. The Japanese announcer and everyone in the shop were totally incredulous. The next item concerned the first sexual harassment case in Japanese courts. From the reaction among the customers it was obvious the woman did not have too much sympathy from the male public for coming forward with the case.

I looked for a reaction from the woman owner, but there was none. As I left she said "It looks like rain. Ki o tsukete (take care)."

I continued up the coast under cloudy skies, past rundown weathered wooden buildings, past an old lady working in her garden who wanted to know if I was lonely, and past an old rusted out minivan being used to store firewood. Sakurajima, the massive active volcano that towers over Kagoshima came into view mid-afternoon, and even from about 30 kilometres away, it completely dominated the view ahead. The coast was littered with concrete breakwaters.

"It's calm at the moment," said an old man with gold front teeth, "but you should see it in a typhoon. Typhoon season is only for a month or so in August and September, but when they come it's terrible!"

I congratulated myself on having started in the south, heading north. If I had gone the other way, I would have hit Kyushu in typhoon season, which was obviously not a good idea.

At about four and with sore feet I spotted an old rusty sign for a "minshuku" — a small family-run homestay. In times past, before the arrival of fast cars and freeways, minshuku were in every village, but this was the first I had spotted since Cape Sata and I couldn't help myself.

I knocked and entered to find a tiny 94-year-old being tended by her fortyish and rather attractive "helper" as she described herself. A guest, and especially a tall blonde one, was obviously not expected. The old lady burst into her own version of the local dialect which frustrated me totally. I had thought I had a reasonable grasp of "Kagoshima ben" as it is called, but obviously not!

During World War II, while the Americans used Navajo Indians speaking their native language for radio communications, the Japanese used speakers of the Kagoshima dialect to keep communications secret. To me, it sounded like a different language. When my face was blank, thankfully, the helper came to my rescue and translated the old lady's questions into standard Japanese. I was astounded when my answers had to be put back into Kagoshima dialect for the old lady who, the helper explained, couldn't understand my standard Japanese!

"She even has problems understanding TV. We use so many foreign words nowadays! She can't keep up. She still watches though. There's little else she can do."

She had been born, married and lived all her 94 years in the tiny village of Hamada without leaving! I could only understand two words she uttered. They were "American" and "telephone".

"But I'm not an American," I tried to explain.

"There's no point in telling her," the helper said. "She thinks all gaijin are Americans. And I doubt if she's ever heard of New Zealand."

As for the word "telephone", it turned out that there was no way to telephone the old lady's family, who would be working in the fields until 5 o'clock, to find out if I could stay the night. The problem wasn't that they were full, but that I was the first guest for weeks, and since I didn't have a booking, the family might be too surprised to find me there! So we sat there drinking green tea, chatting as best we could, until the 5 o'clock siren rang, signalling the end of the day's work to the villagers and those out in the fields.

"Well I've had six children. And about fourteen or fifteen grand-children," the old lady told me through her helper. "But I'm not sure how many great grand-children I've got." She tried counting but gave up, rubbing her temples and complaining of a headache.

One of her daughters, who was seventy, arrived, and although surprised to find an unusual guest socialising with her mother, soon had me seated in my own room, sipping tea and watching the sumo tournament on TV, live from Tokyo.

"What did my mother tell you?" she asked, no doubt wondering if her mother had let out any family secrets to the gaijin.

"She told me she had no idea how many great grand-children she has," I replied. The elderly daughter seemed to think that was a great joke and cackled away for a good five minutes.

A hot bath followed by a delicious meal set me up for an early evening, and I was almost asleep when the daughter came in to lay out my futon at nine o'clock.

It had rained most of the night and my washing hadn't dried, so at 8:40 when I started out I was in a damp shirt and shorts. It was humid and the hills inland to the right were covered in cloud.

There were huge puddles along the side of the road and I was soon soaked as cars and trucks threw up a wall of water. It wasn't the only water flying though. I looked down a sideroad and there was an immaculately dressed man in a black suit urinating into the gutter! He started at me as I walked by, as if to say "What are you looking at?"

The top of Sakurajima was lost in the clouds, as I continued up the coast.

"From Cape Sata?" a man yelled from a factory rooftop.

"Yes."

"To Hokkaido?"

"Yes."

(How did he know?)

"Gambatte!"—the equivalent of "Good luck" or "Keep going!"

Every few kilometres I passed a signboard for the "Joybox" Casual hotel in Kanoya which had a smiling Mickey Mouse encouraging young couples to rent its rooms by the hour for a "casual" frolic. The terms "casual hotel" and "fashion hotel" have euphemistically taken over from the former label of "love hotel". The size of Japanese houses and apartments, and the fact that walls are often made of little more than paper, means that finding privacy is a problem for enthusiastic couples. The demand is adequately met by the "short-term" stay hotels that can be found all over Japan.

On the inland side I passed a public toilet that looked incredibly like a train station, and then noticed overgrown bridges and dark unused tunnels. But there were no tracks and no train line marked on my map. The answers came when I arrived in Furue and had a break at "Tetsudo Koen" or "Railway Park". In 1987 the national railways were privatised, and inefficient and unused lines were pulled up.

"Most people used cars, and only old people doing their shopping and kids going to school used the train," explained a local who was playing with his kids. "It just didn't pay to keep the trains running."

Furue had converted its station into a public park. The tracks had been pulled up and replaced with a grass area that gave the children a place to play.

It was not all flat up the coast, and where the hills came down to meet the sea, there was climbing over headlands, then the descent back down to the coast. On one such descent, a car pulled over, and a well-worn woman beamed out at me. She was fortyish with crooked teeth and white make-up, and along with her two companions was unmistakably a member of the "mizushobai" or water trade, as it is politely known. Japan's entertainment service industry is large and these "beauties of the night" looked as though they seldom saw the light of day.

"We're on our way to the hot springs," said the least attractive of them, flashing me an inviting smile and a wink. "Why don't you join us? It would be fun!" She giggled a horrendous laugh which reminded me of the "wicked witch"! Had they been sent to tempt me? I explained my mission and when they finally headed off I felt relieved to have escaped from their clutches. If I succumbed to all such temptations I'd be lucky to make it to Kumamoto, let alone Hokkaido. As the car raced away, one in the back who I hadn't had a good look at turned her head and waved. On seeing her, I thought that maybe a hot bath wasn't such a bad idea! But they had gone. I wiped my forehead and sighed!

It was after one and I was starving. I hadn't seen a "shokudo", a small eating house, for hours. There seemed to be plenty of "Cut and Perm" shops, but no shokudo. Things just seem to be few and far between when you're walking! I've whizzed around Japan by car before and been astounded by the number of shokudo, but walking, they didn't appear with much regularity. My legs were aching.

"We saw you walking two hours ago," said the only other customers when I finally found a noodle shop. "Wouldn't anyone give you a ride?" I sighed.

"It's only ten minutes into Tarumizu," one continued.

"Is that walking or by car?"

"Walking" was the answer. It took an hour!

Another lesson learnt! Ask for distances in kilometres. No-one walks nowadays, so no-one knows walking times.

With Sakurajima getting closer, I took a break, talking with a woman in her shop in the small town of Tarumizu.

"I've lost a lot of business since the trains stopped," she complained. "The old people don't come to shop here anymore. There's a bus, but it's not as convenient as the train." We both lamented the lack of young women in the rural areas of Japan.

"Even my daughter wants to move to the city," she said pointing at a spotty girl who had just come downstairs, looking ready to run when she saw me. "It's got so bad that we're not going to have a dance at the festival here tomorrow night. I guess there's no good reason for the girls to stay."

My target for the day had been a campground, marked on my map as being in the tiny fishing village of Enoshima, a few kilometres before Sakurajima. I had my first opportunity to swear at the map-makers when its nonexistence was confirmed by three locals.

"A campground? I don't know!" said the last, an old man in a fishing jacket, in English. For the second time in three days I walked well past my intended destination.

A smoking Sakurajima towers over Kagoshima Bay.

Sakurajima means Cherry Island and an island is precisely what it used to be. However, a large eruption in 1914 had spewed forth enough lava to connect the island to the mainland with a narrow isthmus about one kilometre wide. The 1,117 metre cone towered high to my left as I climbed over the isthmus and back down to the coast. At 6 pm I found a gas station but still no shops or eating houses. Four kilometres up the road, I was told, was a noodle shop. I picked up the pace, passing biwa orchards. Biwa are loquat, not particularly sweet, but very refreshing. I had been munching on them after being handed a bag by a driver who had offered me a ride.

I had a nasty feeling that, according to Murphy's Law, the noodle shop would close at 7 and I would arrive at 7:05. But when I got there, it was still open. Only just though, as there were no other customers. Running the shop were two elderly women, and one's two daughters, in their 40s. They must have been bored, as I was immediately showered with attention. Within seconds I had a large frothy beer at my elbow, and minutes later a steaming bowl of noodles with delicious pork pieces on top. Of course, I perked up with the beer, food and attention and we had quite a conversation. The front of the shop was smack up against the main road and shook when the occasional truck roared by. The shop itself was of the concrete-floor variety (easy to clean!) and had three tables with stools along the bar. There was also a tatami room where customers sit on the reed matting floor. The back of the shop was the house's living room and it was here that the girls had been gossiping when I entered.

The major problem of an empty stomach had been solved, so now my mind turned to the next worry. It was getting dark outside and I was starting to worry about a place to sleep.

"There's a ryokan about ten minutes up the road," said the elder daughter. But I had learnt my lesson!

"Is that ten minutes by car, or walking?"

"Aaahh ... by car"

"That's about two hours walking!" The girls held a private whispered meeting.

"Do you have a sleeping bag?" The elder daughter had taken control.

"Yes."

"Well ... you can sleep in the restaurant's tatami room. We'll just push the tables aside!" Problem number two solved! The short-legged tables that customers eat around were shoved into a corner and my sleeping bag rolled out in grand fashion.

It had been a long hot day and my body odors must have been a bit strong, as I was sent out to the bathroom to bathe. All the comforts of home! It got even better! When I emerged smelling sweeter than before, the shop had been closed, and my new friends were sitting down to their dinner with a huge 1.5 litre bottle of shochu, a kind of potato alcohol popular in Kyushu.

The mother, who owned and ran the shop, was in her late 60s with permed curly hair that was too black to be natural. She cackled when she laughed, and had bright smiling eyes. The daughters had inherited their mother's character and were bright and teasing. Both were good looking and it was with great enjoyment that I told them they looked like they were in their 20s. With each glass of shochu we knocked back, they looked younger and younger! The older one beamed.

"You're too young to flirt with a woman who's about to become a grandmother!" she scolded me. "My daughter got married two weeks ago and will have a baby in a couple of months," she said proudly. Hardly the answer I'd expected!

The younger one, with a long beautifully plaited ponytail and a vibrant face, laughed away, and I realised how lucky I was to be with such nice people.

Japanese are renowned for having a "public face" that is shown to the outside world, and a "private face" that few outsiders get to see. I felt deeply privileged to see the "private face" of this lovely family who were opening up and telling me family stories even though I had just walked into their noodle shop.

The shop door opened and the mother's friend, who had been helping in the shop earlier, pushed in a large girl with a video camera. The girl, who was more than a bit shy, had been summoned to practice her English which was almost nonexistent, and to record the event for posterity. She was delicately persuaded to sit next to me and was duly filmed speaking English with the foreigner. We had polished off most of the shochu by this stage, and I announced my intention to preserve the moment with a photo. This caused quite a ruckus as the ladies all departed to make themselves up for my camera which I retrieved from my backpack. Once they had reassembled, which took a good five minutes, I stood up for the event and promptly banged my head on the door frame.

I have spent a fair bit of time in Japan and at 188cm, I am used to ducking and weaving in Japanese houses. But I still cannot understand why, with the average height of Japanese increasing every year, that no-one has told the carpenters to raise the height of door frames. I usually survive these unexpected bumps, but this one put a damper on the evening as it is the last thing I can remember!

I was woken up the next morning by the 6 o'clock siren, designed to get everyone up and at it early. There is no way that a local authority could get away with a 6 am siren in a western country. The loudspeakers would be wiped out by hungover sleepers! I had a sore head and it wasn't just from whacking it.

We ate breakfast together in less riotous fashion than dinner the night before. The younger daughter was wearing curlers, and not looking as attractive as she had when I'd been under the influence of shochu. And the mother kept calling me an American when we had spent half the previous evening talking about New Zealand!

Still I was in high spirits as I thanked them for their generosity and headed out for Day 4 on the road.

It was a sunny Sunday, and wispy white smoke was pouring out of Sakurajima to my left. I passed recreational fishermen, an old woman collecting shellfish, and children playing on a beach that had pumice marking the high tide line. Still feeling a bit seedy, I scratched my sore head, and was surprised to find a big lump of dry blood where I had made contact with the door frame!

At one, I took an hour recovery nap in a small park beside the beach, thankfully taking my shoes off my now aching feet. It was hot! A pregnant mother was trying to control her toddler, a small boy who found me infinitely more interesting than the swings.

"Don't bother the gaijin!" she scolded him. "He looks so tired!" I felt tired.

The scenery was about to change as my route turned inland, and I would not hit the coast again until the northern tip of Kyushu.

I staggered in sweltering heat through the town of Kokubu and just as I was sagging, found an onsen by the road. Onsen are natural hot springs, and such spots are revered by the Japanese. Most have bath-houses that are open to the public. The onsen I had found had an air-conditioned communal room with TV, ice-cream and beer machines where one pays, and then separate bathrooms for males and females. The bathroom had eight different baths of varying temperatures, some with bubbles, one with an electric current in the water and my favorite, the cold-water bath which is great after you have been in the others. As an added treat, this one had a chair below two streams of water that cascaded from the ceiling and gave a pounding shoulder massage. I was careful to keep my tender head out of the way!

My timing was perfect and I emerged to join about thirty others watching the last few bouts on the final day of the sumo tournament. Each tournament has fifteen days with competitors fighting once a day for a total of fifteen results. Akebono, the monster from Hawaii, with a 13-1 record was leading going into the final day, but his last round was with Takanohana, 12-2, the great Japanese hope. The crowd at the onsen, including myself sucking on an ice block, was hopeful but not expectant. How could Taka, as he is affectionately known, beat the behemoth! But he did, and the crowd roared its approval. Both now had 13-2 records and a play-off was required to see who would be Grand Champion. The unbelievable happened, and Taka won again. The people in the onsen were ecstatic as I am sure was most of Japan. The smaller (160kg!) Japanese had outdone the hulking foreigner and all of Japan was happy!

I felt good too as I pulled out and started climbing up to the Kirishima mountains. Sunday traffic was driving back to Kagoshima City.

"It's all right mother—he speaks Japanese more correctly than I do!" said the waitress at a roadside shokudo. Her mother, in a white coat and scarf, had frozen at the sight of me. (It was an unexpected boost to my ego. What a compliment!) "And he can use chopsticks!"

I carried on as it got dark, shining my torch at oncoming traffic in an effort to stay alive. I passed a chicken farm and then a series of love hotels, including one called Skyrub — Japanese have problems with our letters "l" and "v". But I resisted the temptation, pitching my tent in an open field at the pass.

Early the next morning I crawled out of my tent into misty rain, and wearing my bright yellow raincoat, trudged through the town of Kirishima. I was surrounded by green paddies, and every now and then, beside the road, there was an old wooden barn with a few cows. The road climbed steadily, and just before ten I was happy to escape the rain and take a break in the Kirishima Visitors' Centre. Being a Monday, there were few visitors around, and I had the attention of the doll-like beauty of the information officer all to myself. She sat me down in front of a video on Kirishima National Park, provided me with green tea and snacks, and made me feel quite human again.

"Goyukkuri dozo," she said smiling. "Take your time!"

By the time I departed over an hour later, somewhat loathe to leave the warmth of the Visitors' Centre, the young lady had rung ahead and booked me a cabin on the far side of the mountains.

"Please be careful," she warned. "We're going to have a long rainy season this year. I hope you make it!" Her parting smile almost melted my resolve and I considered another cup of tea, but the rain had stopped and I had no excuse. I wandered out and under the high wooden "torii" or gate, marking the entrance to the shrine, and then on to the shrine itself which was shrouded in mist. The characters for the name Kirishima mean "Island in the fog" and the area around the stunningly ornate shrine certainly lived up to its name. Giant Japanese cedars towered into the mist. The shrine, which was first built about 500 A.D., is dedicated to the grandson of the Sun Goddess who, legend has it, came to Earth to found Japan at Kirishima.

"Haro! Haro! What your name?"

"Me Japanese boy!"

"This is a pen!" Suddenly I was engulfed by students in their black school uniforms on a school trip. The girls in their sailor outfits much shyer than the boys in their more austere suit-like uniforms. I was lucky as they were soon called away a few metres for a group photograph in front of the shrine by a pony-tailed photographer in a baseball cap. I made good my escape, and after confirming my route with one of the priests who was selling souvenir trinkets, headed up a mountain trail into the misty forest.

The track kept splitting, and I kept taking the right-hand fork until I found the road to Takachihogawara. The road was steep. I climbed 600 metres in altitude over six kilometres, and every now and then, a convoy of huge sightseeing buses would roll by, spitting fumes as they struggled up the road. I was struggling too, and at the top I needed a bowl of noodles in one of the souvenir shops by the final carpark before attacking the mountains. The old lady, whose four front teeth were gold, was drinking sake, recovering from a busy weekend. The prices were outrageous and I could understand how she could afford gold teeth.

"Is that Mt Takachiho?" I asked her, pointing at the volcano towering above the carpark. "Where the grandson of the Sun Goddess came to Earth?"

"I don't know much about history," was her reply. "Would you like to buy a book?" What a businesswoman!

"You should have been here yesterday," she said. "There were plenty of hikers to walk with. That carpark was full," she said, pointing at one that must have had room for a couple of thousand cars. There were only four or five cars parked.

I thanked my lucky stars I'd arrived on a Monday!

I could hear them talking on the trail behind me.

"Look at that silly American wearing shorts! And carrying that big backpack! What does he think he's doing?" I heard the man

Mt. Takachiho and flowering Kirishima azaleas.

grumble to his wife.

"Shhh, maybe he can understand Japanese!" was the reply.

"Don't be ridiculous!" the husband laughed. But the voices lowered anyway.

I couldn't resist a look back. The middle-aged couple were wearing kneesocks, plaid knickerbockers and Swiss mountain hats with feathers poking out. I couldn't help but feel that my attire was more appropriate!

The clouds had cleared from the volcanic peaks ahead of me although mist still enveloped the valley below. I was climbing above the forest line and amongst the spectacular purple azalea bushes for which Kirishima is famous. Kirishima is a string of four major volcanic peaks and I was heading towards the highest. The track was easy to follow, and in places, it was obvious that too many people had taken this path before me, as it bit deep into the land like an unnatural valley.

Ahead of me, the track turned steeply up a rocky hill and I could see about a hundred brightly-clad little bodies tumbling down it towards me. Then I could hear the high-pitched voices. I ran into one of the teachers first. Their group was of eighty primary school children from Miyazaki on a school outing with four teachers and two mountain guides.

"Gaijin! Gaijin!" A foreigner! I could hear the word being passed back.

They had climbed from the carpark to the first peak, had a picnic lunch and were now heading back. So I had eighty cheeky little children to pass. Some just stared. Some tested their limited English; "Haro, Haro!" One little girl who was at a particularly tricky spot was climbing down backwards. She looked down for her next foothold, saw my unusual face, screamed and fell off! It was lucky I was below and could catch her!

I reached the peak of Shinmoedake soon afterwards. The peak is the rim of a perfect volcanic crater. Looking into the crater, 160 metres below, I could see an emerald green lake and vents in the sides billowing steam. To add to the atmosphere, there was a pungent sulphuric smell, a bit like rotten eggs. It was a stunning view, and after finding a sheltered spot on the rim I broke out a beer from my supplies and surveyed the scenery. To the south, Sakurajima, which I had passed a couple of days before, rose out above the cloud in the valleys, and to the east Mt Takachiho, only a few kilometres away, towered majestically above Miyazaki Prefecture. The Prefectural boundary between Kagoshima and Miyazaki runs along the top of the Kirishima peaks. I was into my second prefecture. A minor milestone achieved.

Kirishima-Yaku National Park, Kyushu

The track from Shinmoedake to Karakunidake at 1,700 metres turned nasty. It was steep and slippery, and I was dirty and covered in scratches from the overgrown scrub invading the track when I eventually reached the peak, above another huge crater. This one had scoria rubble around the rim, and I was careful not to slide in. The track became rocky and rough as I descended into Ebino Kogen, my target for the day. I hadn't seen a soul since the eighty students a couple of hours before, and when I turned my ankle, I realised that wandering around in the mountains by myself was maybe not such a good idea. I could see the headlines. "Ill-prepared foreigner lost in the mountains—found with only one can of beer!"

To prevent such an embarrassment, I took it slowly and surely down into the tiny resort village of Ebino Kogen. I knew I was back in civilisation when eight huge buses roared by, with tourists staring out at the dirty, hobbling foreigner who had come off the mountains. Fortunately, the campground where my cabin had been booked had a natural hot spring bath, and I wallowed for an hour in the warmth which brought me back to the land of the living.

I needn't have worried about booking my cabin. The only other guest was a hitch-hiking Welshman who was taking advantage of the good nature of the Japanese he was meeting. He couldn't speak a word of the language, and wherever he got to, he was totally reliant on whoever he met. I mentioned that I had broken my sunglasses.

"Have these," he said, handing me his. "A guy who gave me a ride yesterday gave me them. I've got my own!"

Day Six was warm and sunny, and after a morning dip in the hot springs, my knees, ankles and feet felt a lot better. My body was still adjusting to its abrupt change in lifestyle and my feet especially were moaning about the five kilometres-an-hour, thirty-plus kilometres a day pace. In my planning, I had been over-generous in allowing for this adjustment and had actually allowed eight days for getting to Ebino Kogen, when it had only taken me five. The adrenalin was still pumping, but would I burn out if I kept up this pace? Should I slow down and preserve myself?

Another issue was that maps tend to make an area look flat, even when it is mountainous. Take for instance Day Six. There I was starting at Ebino Kogen. A couple of hours would be spent descending into the Ebino Valley, a couple of hours to cross it, and then three hours to climb the mountain range on the other side. This I could see as I started walking, but from the map alone, from which I had done my planning, the whole area looked rather flat. Maybe it was time to throw the plan over my shoulder and just walk!

The narrow winding road descended through the forest with little traffic. The cicadas were deafening. As I neared the plain, the forest ran out and I was into paddies, market gardens, and cattle in barns. It was hot, and I stopped a couple of times to change my washing. It had not dried overnight, and I had it hanging off my backpack, drying under the hot sun. Socks, underwear and shirts were what I most needed and I had a couple of each plastered on my pack. I must have looked a little like a travelling ragman!

Taking the advice of the owner of the noodle shop, where I had lunch, I headed slightly west, away from the main road into the next mountain range, and took a road that was too small to be on my map.

"Don't worry," he had assured me. "There's definitely a road. You should get a better map." But still I had worried. I was walking all the way to Hokkaido. The last thing I wanted to do was take the long way!

The road first took me to Yoshida Onsen, a tiny hot springs village. I found the run-down building marked "onsen" in the solitary street among all the other run-down buildings. There was no-one sitting in the money-collector's chair, but an old man with no hair who was changing told me to go to the shop next door. There I found two tiny old ladies having a cup of tea and a yarn who took great interest in me. They ooohed and aaahed and it took me a good twenty minutes to get back to the bath-house.

It was a hot day. The single fan was whirring away, and the windows were wide open in the changing room which meant that anyone driving up the main street had a perfect view of my white bottom which I specifically pointed in that direction. I put my gear in one of the available baskets and my pack beside it. Of course I had no security in a place like that, leaving my wallet in my pants pocket, but I have never had a problem and am full of admiration for the honesty of the Japanese.

To say I caused a stir in the tiny bathroom is an understatement. There were six little old men in a tiny rust-coloured, concrete-floored room with one big bath of hot, brown water. Anybody not

My onsen friends

yet retired is working at that time of the day, and the average age of those guys must have been about 75. As for the colour, Yoshida Onsen is recognized as having water that is good for the body—not a fountain of youth, but with a healing quality. One of the men had only one arm, while another had had a stroke and the left side of his body didn't work. A couple of them came each day, while the others came two to three times a week by car, and all swore that they felt better after each visit. We sat in the foul-smelling hot water for over an hour, and each time one old man would have to go and leave me with his best wishes for my journey, he would be replaced by a new arrival for whom all the same questions would have to be answered. The walls and roof were covered with a musty lichen-like growth.

"Try drinking the water!" the old one-armed man encouraged me. "It's good for your body. You'll need to be healthy to get to Hokkaido!" The rest agreed. So I tried it.

I just about choked. Anything would have tasted better than the foul-smelling water that was coming out of that rusty pipe at Yoshida Onsen.

"It takes a while to get used to," they all laughed.

No kidding!

"Could you understand Kagoshima ben? You must be happy to be in Miyazaki Prefecture," said one old bloke. "At least we speak understandable Japanese here!"

"Even we have trouble with Kagoshima ben!" another added.

"They're so proud! They want to be different." I couldn't decided if he was envious, or just happy to be understood.

The situation turned comic when one tiny old fellow tried to lift my pack out in the changing room. He called to his mates and six wrinkled naked old men trooped out to take turns trying to pick it up.

Eventually I had to leave my new friends and hit the road. As I was changing, the man who had had the stroke asked me, "Where is your car?" We had been talking about my walk for an hour, but when I reminded him I was walking, he just cackled with laughter for a full two minutes and had to be calmed down by some of his old cronies.

By the time the five o'clock chimes rang, I was climbing up a mountain road, and was soon gulping cool water at a spring beside the road with cups made of bamboo provided. I found a hiking track heading straight up and took it. It was obviously rarely used, as I was breaking spider webs while climbing among the trees. I reached the magnificent Yatake Kogen and had a great view over the valley I had crossed, with the Kirishima peaks towering in the background.

"Enjoy your flight," said a sign in English. On closer inspection, it turned out to be a take-off spot for hang-gliders. "Be careful not to have a mid-air collision," the sign continued in Japanese. A perfect camping spot, though exposed to the wind.

Something told me to continue. I rediscovered the deserted country road, passed a cattle feedlot, a couple of market gardens, and then had the good fortune to run into a real character.

He was standing beside his "vinyl house", which is like a glasshouse, but covered in thick clear plastic. It probably has a more technical name, but that is how it translates. He was fiftyish with a scraggly black beard, scruffy hair, wearing a black T-shirt, black sweatsuit trousers and plastic thongs.

"Nihonshu?" The word for sake, rice wine. My ears pricked up at the word.

"Eh?" I said, slightly bewildered.

"Nihonju, Nihonju?" he asked. This made more sense, meaning "Length of Japan?"

Slightly disappointed, but happy to be on the same wavelength, we broke into conversation. When he had ascertained that I was a New Zealander he indicated for me to follow, and led me into the nearest "vinyl house". In it, I was astounded to see lupins, a variety of flower common in my home country. He explained that he had a photo of Mt Cook, with the Hooker Valley in the foreground full of brightly coloured lupins, and this had inspired him to produce a smaller variety that he could sell in Japan. He had that "mad scientist" look about him, and I could picture him trying to mutate lupin seeds.

He insisted I stay the night so we could talk about lupins, and sped off in his rusty car to the farm house a few hundred metres away, at my suggestion, to warn his wife of the impending arrival of a foreigner. It would give her a chance to prepare herself, and a few minutes to scold her husband before my arrival on foot!

I needn't have worried. His wife, who had studied English at university, was delighted at the chance to use it again, while their teenage daughter fluttered her eyelashes. Grandfather was keen to have a drinking companion, so I was ceremonially placed at his right elbow and forced to drink all sorts of concoctions including one mixture of shochu and fresh cow's milk from their farm.

This was not your normal farmhouse, and it reinforced my "mad scientist" ideas. For instance, the father had designed and built his own fireplace using steel plates which were welded together. Not unusual. His fuel was though. They were burning cut up tires, old rubber shoes, and plastic fertilizer bags that they had collected from surrounding farms! It certainly produced plenty of heat! And it wasn't even cold out!

"It's a bit of a hassle really," explained his wife. "The flue goes up right in front of the TV. So when we use the fire, we can't watch the TV, and when we want to watch the TV, we can't use the fire! It's a problem in winter!"

"Why don't you move the TV?" I asked. But my question didn't get answered.

They were an interesting family. The couple had moved there from the city 24 years before in order to be self-sufficient.

"And because I hate wearing a tie!" moaned the mad scientist. I calculated back—1969. I guess there must have been a radical movement in Japan in the 60s too.

They were incredibly hardworking people. The 30 hectare farm had 30 milking cows which the husband milked each midnight as well as the vinyl houses used for growing vegetables and flowers.

"We haven't had one holiday or day off in the twenty-four years we've been here," complained the wife. I should have kept my mouth shut. But I couldn't.

"Why don't you get a manager to look after the place, and take a vacation?" I suggested. If looks could kill, I'd have been dead and buried! The mad scientist wasn't too impressed.

For not the first time on tour, I woke up feeling somewhat under the weather. I wandered out into the kitchen to find myself a hero in the wife's eyes, and not very high on the husband's list of favourite visitors. The wife was talking about holidays to all sorts of exotic destinations, while in my tender state, I almost wilted under her husband's steely stare. I was rescued by the wife who dragged me off to collect chicken eggs. Another reason she liked me was that I liked her pickles, which her husband wouldn't touch. The task of collecting eggs was more interesting than it sounds, as the chickens lived in an old rusted out minivan and station wagon in the yard. We even found an egg in the backseat of the husband's car and one in his shoe. I hadn't seen this part of the farm, and was astounded to see a collapsed barn, the result of a typhoon two years

Collecting eggs in unusual places.

before, and every possible object a junkman could collect, including six or seven abandoned vehicles.

During my walk so far, I had struck two or three "car graveyards" as I called them. A spot hidden away where old cars were simply abandoned and left to rot on the side of the road. It is cheaper for the owners than paying to have them junked. Of course the licence plates had been removed so that owners could not be identified, and windows smashed in by vandals. One graveyard I walked past was in a country road in the forest and there were at least twenty rusted wrecks abandoned and rotting. The worst kind of human littering. I had seen a used washing machine in a river, that had been thrown off a bridge, and the odd spot in the mountains where anything imaginable had been discarded. Garbage lined many of the roads I had been walking and I couldn't help but think that quite a few Japanese seemed to have little respect for their country.

By 9 am, after a cup of coffee, and waving goodbye to my hosts, I was back walking and almost immediately into the third prefecture of my walk, Kumamoto. The narrow country road was shaded by overhanging trees, but it was warm and the cicadas were out in force. The road descended into a narrow valley, and in a small cluster of houses, surrounded by rice paddies, I found Yatake Station. The train line entered the valley by a tunnel from the Ebino Valley, the direction I had come from, and wound down the valley towards Hitoyoshi. The wooden station was run-down and there were weeds growing up out of the concrete. Two old ladies stared at me as I checked out the train timetable. The first train to Hitoyoshi, which my host's daughter had taken to school had departed at 7:05 am. It was lucky she hadn't missed it, as the next one, which the old ladies were waiting for, left at ten!

Further down the valley, I found the Yatake Primary School. It was brand new with tremendous facilities, and the wife told me it had cost some incredible amount. There were however only five children, with a similar number of teachers. One of the main reasons for building it, she had said, was to encourage young families to move back to the countryside, and to encourage those there to stay. The exodus to the cities in the past few decades had been devastating to rural Japan. Young women especially had been drawn by the big city lights, away from the hard working country life. It had become so bad that some young rural men had gone so far as to "import" brides from poorer Asian countries! The wife at the farm had gone so far as to encourage me to move to Yatake. My wife and children would be well looked after, she said, and a house with a garden near the station sounded cheap enough to make it a worthwhile proposition!

A little further on, a toothless old man was hacking away at weeds with a scythe.

"You look busy," I said.

"I'm just playing. It gives me something to do" was the reply. There was more than a hint of sadness in his voice.

After midday I lost my comfortable carless country road and turned right onto Route 267 into Hitoyoshi. I had just crossed the wide Kuma River and was debating whether to bypass the town when I spotted an "onsen" sign. Two elderly ladies giggled excitedly as they escorted me the kilometre or so to the bath-house, and I so enjoyed the hot soak that I was in there for an hour and a half. Bath-houses were becoming a great source for information, and once again, I had a group of elderly men staggering as they tried to carry my pack and poring over my map giving me advice.

I needn't have listened. The route I was recommended on the "quiet" side of the Kuma River proved to be too quiet and petered out despite being marked on my map. I spent fifteen minutes swearing at map-makers and bath-goers as I clambered through bamboo, around paddies and through tall grass in an effort to stay next to the river. Fortunately I found a bridge over which to cross to the "busy" side.

Though the Kuma River was to be my friend for the next few days, we hadn't started too well. By 6:30 I had reached Isshochi, back on the quiet side of the river. The gorge was narrow with mountains rising steeply on both sides, with barely room for a train track, let alone a village. But Isshochi was at a point where the main gorge joined with a tributary valley and the tiny village could even boast a train station. Its one eating house was closed, despite having its doors open, and it was thanks to the owner of the single shop, where I bought supplies, that I was allowed to put up my tent in the carpark of the local onsen. Of course, this meant another bath that my battered body relished, and it didn't take long for me to crash once I had crawled into my tent.

The highlight of my eighth morning on the road was lancing a huge blister on the little toe of my right foot. I hadn't realised it, but the whole toe had become one big blister, and as I pricked it, the explosion brought instant relief.

I felt even better when a pretty school-teacher broke into a smile as I passed the playground while her wards yelled "Haro, Haro" at me. My mind felt better, but my stomach was growling as I walked on looking for a place to eat. There was a lot of road construction going on, and at one spot, I talked with workers who were busy concreting the side of the gorge. Twenty kilometres to the next eating house! This revelation brought me back to reality with a thud.

I needed a break and found a shady spot to eat my last orange. To my surprise, around the corner wobbled a young boy, in school uniform, on a bicycle. He looked totally exhausted and, slowing down, came to a stop beside me.

"Where are you going?" I asked.

"To visit my grandmother in Miyazaki," he replied. This was a bit of a surprise, as Miyazaki City was about 120 kilometres away.

"Where have you come from?" I was prepared for an interesting answer.

"Kumamoto." About 75 kilometres away. Considering that the boy, who turned out to be 12, had absolutely no gear with him, I wasn't too surprised when he asked me for something to eat.

I had eaten about half my orange, but handed him the rest. He mumbled his thanks, then said, "You're a foreigner, aren't you?" Without waiting for a reply, he listlessly mounted his bicycle and wobbled off. The way he was going, I doubted he would make it to Miyazaki.

I wandered past a small dam and power station. There was an incredible amount of flotsam backed up to it, including driftwood, all kinds of garbage and two soccer balls. By 1:15, I was starting to wobble too, and the ecstatic relief of lancing my toe had worn off. It was painful and I lay down for a nap in a grassy area beside the road. A construction worker had explained the lack of eating houses. A new freeway had opened a few years before between Hitoyoshi and Yatsushiro, taking most of the traffic. With it went the facilities required. Traffic on Route 219, which I was on had decreased to the point where now most of the drive-ins and eating houses were closed. This explained the signs which, from a distance, had been getting me excited at the prospect of a full stomach, but which from closer up revealed a closed eating house.

I had virtually given up on the idea of lunch, when almost unbelievably a run-down drive-in appeared that wasn't closed. I staggered in to find the owners watching TV with a leather-jacketed, tough-looking truck driver. Initially they just stared, but when I started speaking Japanese, I was treated like a long lost relative. The wife, who had dyed brown curly hair sat me in a corner, and while the husband cooked me an oversized portion of pork cutlet and curry on rice (katsukare), she and the truck driver peppered me with questions. They both spoke a rough Kumamoto dialect and I had to concentrate hard. The truck driver, who had to pull a toothpick out of his mouth each time he spoke, bought me a beer.

"You look like you need one!" We became good friends. He was fifty, but proud that he looked younger, and he had the muscular frame of a hard-working man. He was delivering timber to Yatsu-shiro and was so impressed with my walking the length of Japan that he bought me my lunch. The wife gave me some fruit, and then the husband emerged from the kitchen to say he'd booked me a room at his friend's small minshuku about ten kilometres down the road! Suddenly life seemed all rosy again. From being hungry, lonely and with no roof over my head, I was full, with new friends and a place to stay. It's amazing how quickly things can change.

They improved even more when, a few kilometres down the road, an old man who I had had a chat with as he worked in his garden, rode up on a 50cc motorscooter and handed me a can of beer. He was wearing a white helmet and broke into a wide grin as he handed me the can.

"Gambatte!"

And then, just before I reached my destination, my friend the truck driver stopped for a chat on his way home. He still had the tooth-pick sticking out of his mouth.

"Incredible! You've already got this far! Keep going! Don't forget us!"

The minshuku had a big bath and I soaked in it for ages, happy that my journey through the Kuma River Valley was almost over.

I woke to the strains of Edelweiss playing over a loudspeaker at seven. Hardly my choice of music to wake up to, but better than a siren.

I spent the morning still following the Kuma River, but it was

wider and not so swiftly flowing near the end of the gorge. I left
my pack on the side of the road and relieved myself in some bushes.
Emerging, I found my friends from the day before's drive-in waiting
for me. They had spotted my pack.

"We figured you'd come this way! Good thinking! Most of the
traffic is on the other side of the river. We brought you some
'manju'," the husband said, handing out some buns containing
sweet bean paste.

A car slowed as it passed me. The lady driver was leaning
forward over the steering wheel. As she drew level, I could see
why. A tiny baby was strapped to her back.

I could tell Yatsushiro from far off. Smog-belching funnels gave
away its position, and although wanting to dodge it, I didn't have
much choice. It was a hot, cloudless day and the plan of heading to
the station and finding an air-conditioned restaurant in which to
eat lunch seemed the best option. This I did, and found a quiet
little shop before midday.

The grandmother who was running it had been to Australia and
so had some idea where New Zealand is. She was quite excited by
my presence and took advantage of it to show off her knowledge
of Australia to another couple of customers. She had obviously
decided I was Australian, which didn't bother me as much as it
normally would. It made a pleasant change from being stereotyped
as an American.

Things got a bit out of hand however when her son arrived.
"Incredible, incredible," he said. "You're only walking!" He
decided that I was enough of an oddity to be a celebrity and was
keen to call the local TV station to interview me in his shop, or
preferably, he said, in front of his shop. He was most upset when I
wasn't interested, but still rushed off to the station to buy an instant
camera so we could be photographed together, "in case he becomes
famous!" I had heard that before! I feigned a smile for the camera
and then made my escape. Just as I was leaving he called after me.
"I'm going to Kumamoto, would you like a ride?"

I was on the flat now, not far from the coast, heading almost
directly north. The mountains were on my right and I was surrounded by fields of reeds used for making tatami floor mats.

It was hot. I stopped at an air-conditioned convenience store for
an ice cream. The little toe on my right foot felt as if it was about to

fall off, and in a moment of inspiration I whipped out my pocket knife. The shop owner looked worried at the sight of a "giant" gaijin with a knife, but relieved when I took off my hiking boot and sliced a hole in the side so my toe could breathe. For the second time in the past few days, instant relief. The pressure was off!

The walk to Matsubase was almost painless. The heat was intense and I had sweat running down my arms by the time I got there a little after five. There was a tractor filling up at a gas station where I got directions to the public bath-house (sento).

In times past, when Japanese houses didn't have bathrooms, everyone went to bathe at the sento, the public bath-house. The idea is to wash with soap outside the bath, then soak in the hot water. In this way, only clean bodies enter the bath, and everyone can use the same water. However, with economic affluence, houses came to be built with their own bathrooms, thereby bypassing the need to use a sento. Washing practices stayed the same within the home, but fewer people ventured out to bathe. In fact there is almost a stigma attached to using the sento. It implies that you don't have a bathroom at home. I, on the other hand, love going to the sento. It is a great place for social interaction, and usually has a variety of hot baths that I can uncurl my long legs in, instead of sitting in a cramped uncomfortable position in a bath not much bigger than a saucepan. My mother-in-law does not understand my reasoning.

"But we have a bath at home!" she moans, every time I go out to the sento. Modern-day sento are doing their best to disguise themselves as onsen which are popular with everybody. The sento in Matsubase was obviously suffering from either a lack of patronage, or a lack of reinvestment by its owner, as there were tiles falling off the walls, tiles missing in the bath, and no toilet. The only other bather was a completely bald octogenarian with no teeth, and even he disappeared soon after my arrival.

The old man running the place was also hairless, wearing a white singlet to cover his bulging stomach. He was quite a character, and as it turned out, ran a small minshuku at the back of the sento. After some light-hearted bargaining, I had a place to stay for the night. Part of the deal involved me using some of my beer coupons. A couple of nights before leaving Osaka, I had gone drinking with a good friend who had proudly presented me with his contribution for my walk. He had scoured his office and come up with a pile of telephone cards I could use to call my family, and even better, fifteen beer coupons worth two bottles each. While walking, these had become my most carefully guarded valuables, and here was the chance to break them out!

I had a large tatami room to myself, and I proved to be the only guest for the evening. It didn't take me long to find the lounge. The old man was waiting with an equivalent number of bottles to my contribution and I could see it was going to be a long evening. His wife produced tsumami, a variety of snacks that go well with beer drinking, and one of his daughters appeared to pour our beers for us. The only problem was that whenever customers arrived at the sento, the old man would get up and stagger down the corridor to collect their money. I should point out that at most sento, the money collector sits on an elevated chair and has a commanding view of both the men's and women's changing rooms. I am now so used to this that I have lost my shyness about getting undressed in front of staring female money-collectors.

My elderly drinking partner, however, was obviously quite keen on his work. Each customer, upon entering, would call out. If it was a male voice, he was in no hurry to go down and collect their money, grabbing a handful of tsumami on his way. He was more attentive however if it was a female voice, and one time, when giggling youngish female voices arrived, he positively rubbed his hands with glee, and didn't reappear for about twenty minutes! No wonder sento are not overly-popular with young ladies!

He was also a history fan and revelled in telling me about the area. I was struggling with his accent and also the contents of the history lesson when, thankfully, another guest arrived. He was a travelling salesman from Northern Kyushu and was obviously a regular. I could tell by the way he slapped the old man's daughter on the bottom and by the fact that he arrived with a bottle of shochu, which of course we had to drink before going to bed. The owner kept making the daughter who had had her bottom slapped sit next to the man, despite her obvious lack of interest.

When his wife arrived to scold the old man for making too much noise and take him to bed, the party broke up, and we all staggered off to our respective rooms.

My tenth day out started with a sore head and this time I knew the shochu had something to do with it. There wasn't much chatter

over breakfast—pickled plums and green tea, which the old man's
wife swore was a good cure for a hangover.

Despite the throbbing between my ears, I was in a good mood.
It was only twenty kilometres into the city of Kumamoto, where I
would be completing Stage One of my walk as I had planned it.

Unfortunately, the shortest route was due north on Highway 3.

So I set off up a main road, which I had successfully avoided
doing up to then, and found out why they were worth avoiding.
The footpath was wider than some of the roads I had been walking
on, which was good, but there was a continuous roar as cars and
trucks whizzed by. The fumes made me dizzy and the roof of my
mouth felt worse than after the shochu! The kilometres dragged
by and I found myself on a countdown to McDonald's. The first
sign was 15 kilometres out. "McDonald's in 15 km!" Then there
was a sign every 2 km until 5 km out, and a sign every kilometre
from there on in. I was so sick of it that when I finally got there, I
made a rude gesture at Ronald, who had that silly smile on his
face, and had lunch in a shokudo across the road.

It was a Saturday and the car yards on the outskirts of Kumamoto
were making the most of it. The Japanese economy was in the
doldrums, and of course, those to feel the pinch first were car
salesmen. One technique for marketing in Japan is to get an
abundance of young, pretty girls, dress them in very short shorts
or skirts and have them entice men to come in and check out
whatever you are selling. They are called "Campaign girls", and
there was no shortage of them along the road I was walking. There
was, however, a lack of customers for the girls to force their well-
intentioned attentions on. Consequently, the tall, funny-looking
gaijin walking along carrying a big backpack attracted a lot of
attention, which I revelled in. It perked me up from the foul mood
I had been in along that foul main road. All of a sudden the
kilometres were flying by and at about one I found my friend's
house. I was ready for a beer, a yarn, and a day off.

2. SLEEPING IN STATIONS

It was overcast and cool. I had had a relaxing break, yet (fool that I was) had explored Kumamoto, on foot of course, with my host, and covered 12 kilometres in 30 degree heat!

Kumamoto City is the prefectural capital with a population of about half a million. Its most famous landmark is Kumamoto Castle which was built in 1607 and is renowned as one of the three grandest castles in all of Japan. It is surrounded by nine kilometres of massive stone walls, and dodging the flag-following tour groups, we explored it at length.

But the highlight of the day for me was wandering through the shopping arcades, which were packed on a Sunday, and noticing all the pretty young women who were in abundance. It made me realise what a shortage they were in in the country!

I set out at about 9:30 with a lighter pack. The first ten days of walking had given me the opportunity to revalue the importance of some of my gear. Consequently, the not-so-necessary stuff had been sent back to Osaka. I felt like a new man!

It was a Monday morning, and fortunately there were few cars on the road. The Sannomiya Shrine, just out of town, showed the tell-tale signs of a busy Sunday. White prayer papers covered the trees in the shrine compound and tents were still set up to protect worshippers from the rain. I had gone slightly off the track for two reasons. One was to avoid the major roads marked in red on my map. The other was to visit the gravesite of one of my favourite characters from Japanese history and literature, Miyamoto Musashi. I found the famous swordsman's final resting place and enjoyed a break in the classic Japanese garden that surrounds his towering statue. There was running water, white and pink azalea bushes and tall green conifers. I was the only visitor.

Musashi, who was active in the early 1600's, was the "Robin Hood" of Japanese history. A master swordsman, he was renowned for developing a technique for fighting with two swords, for his purity of soul, and for his self-discipline in following the ways of the samurai. He lived his final days as a hermit in a cave near Kumamoto, writing the "Gorin no sho", his book on swordsmanship and strategy. It is widely read to this day and is believed by some to provide the strategy behind many business decisions in Japan.

A small white car pulled over, and a young man with thick glasses wound down his side window.

"Would you like a ride?"

"Thanks, but I'm only walking."

"To Aso?" Aso is a major volcano in Central Kyushu, famous for its hiking trails.

"No, to Hokkaido" He blinked a couple of times, then shook his head. "That's great! Great! I wish I could go! I love hiking! Here," he said, passing out 100 yen, "please buy yourself a drink! Please take it! I'd like to contribute. Great!" He drove off still shaking his head.

I passed the "Hotel Pecking", a love hotel with turrets at each corner of its castle-like building, just before turning left off the main road and heading into the hills. Looking in the entrance, I could see a couple of cars, both with the standard licence plate covers so their owners could not be identified.

The sun was out, and steam was rising off the wet road, and off the rich, black, volcanic soil in the fields. Half the fields were bright green, growing food for cattle housed in barns along the road, while the other half were freshly tilled and black. It was warm and humid. I was happy to have left the city and main road far behind, feeling at home on the small rural roads with little traffic. The houses were large, with big gardens, and I passed a coin-machine on the side of the road that was selling rice.

From about 400 metres away I could hear the drums of music practice at the Kyokushi School. The racket wafted out over the paddies, and I was glad to escape from it into the first tiny shokudo I had seen for hours. It seemed dark inside, but two elderly patrons and the owner were watching the news on TV. It was little more than a week until the Imperial Wedding and the smiling face of Masako Owada, the soon-to-be bride, was dominating the news. We sat sipping beers, and watched the Japanese media frenzy of the upcoming event. At the end of the news for the day, Masako's daily outfits for the previous two months were shown, and discussed by a panel of "experts". Every morning, as she left home to go to work, she was met with camera flashes, rolling film and squeals of excitement as all of Japan looked on. But there in that rural restaurant we decided it was all a little ridiculous. Still, it was hard not to look at Masako's smiling face!

The news finished with the weather forecast, which for Kumamoto was for heavy thunderstorms. As I walked out the door, I could see that it would probably be correct. The humidity had intensified and the sky behind and to my left was dark black. Thunder boomed in the distance, but the sky over the mountains ahead of me was bright, and being an optimist, I kept walking.

Japanese place names can often be a mystery, even to the Japanese. On maps, they are usually written in kanji—Chinese characters—that have several different pronunciations. At the restaurant, I had shown the owner my map and he had confirmed that the village I was aiming for was Ryumon. My problem was that I was on very small roads that twisted about all over the place and whenever I found someone to ask whether I was going in the correct direction, I was told to head off to the west. According to my map, I should have been heading north-east. It was difficult to know what to believe—my intuition or the directions I was being given. Of course it didn't occur to me that the restaurant owner was wrong in his pronunciation of the village's name. Luckily, I trusted my intuition and after several hours climbing and traversing carless rural roads, I arrived at the village of Tatekado (or Ryumon, as its characters can also be pronounced!). Another lesson learnt. Locals living ten kilometres away can make mistakes with village names!

Paul lives in a hamlet on top of a mountain, at the end of a road that wasn't even marked on my map. In fact, by the time I had climbed the near-vertical road and arrived in Kigo, I was surprised that the tiny cluster of houses had managed to come to the map-makers' attention at all! The road had climbed through thick forest and the clearing at the top surprised me. There were perfectly-manicured rice paddies, which I found out later, were still sown by hand, and at Paul's place, tea bushes and two hectares of land used to produce feed for dairy cattle.

I have met Englishmen in some unusual places, doing some unusual things, but Paul, the organic dairy farmer in Kigo ranks right at the top. When he arrived there, his land had been planted in pine trees by the former owners who had forsaken farming for the city. His first job was to return the land to the seventeen small productive fields it had been. Instead of rice however, Paul planted crops which surprised the locals almost as much as the arrival of a gaijin farmer! Not only that, he raised his crops without the aid of fertilizers or insecticides which are a national institution when it comes to Japanese agricultural production. But Paul wasn't as mad as the locals might have believed. His organically-grown crops are fed to five dairy cattle, producing exceptionally good milk and yoghurt. So good, in fact, that one hundred and fifty families in Kumamoto are members of a co-operative that own the dairy on Paul's farm. He delivers to them weekly and they are more than happy with his quality product. He also produces organically grown tea.

One thing I have found that eccentric Englishmen have in common is a phenomenal alcohol consumption rate. My beer coupons came in handy again as under a clear starry sky, we discussed the state of the world. And the state of just about everything else! Paul is a great believer in self-sufficiency and the idea that the social aspects of one's lifestyle should be more important than the economic. I couldn't help but agree with him that if foreign rice should be able to flood into Japan, that rural towns and villages such as Kigo would disappear. Even as it is now, young people, especially women, are leaving, and of the fifteen households in Kigo, only three have children at home.

My main discovery for the evening though, was to find out that it is not wise to walk in long grass with exposed legs or feet. New Zealanders, coming from a snake-free country, are not accustomed to worrying about such things.

"You can forget about walking to Hokkaido if you get bitten by a mamushi!" warned Paul. "In fact, if you don't get the antidote within a couple of hours, you can forget about everything else as well!" The mamushi, or pit viper, is not a snake to tangle with. I tucked away that sobering bit of information for future reference when looking for campsites!

Of course, after a late night, I wasn't in too good shape when the alarm sounded at 5:45 and Paul's children were up preparing for school. Mind you, Paul didn't look too sharp either, and he gets up at that time every morning!

Despite the early start, I didn't hit the road until 10:15. I had been hoping to continue over the hills and down the other side, suspecting that there would be a walking track, if not a road. This time, however, the map-makers were correct. There was no road, and Paul only laughed when I asked him about a track.

"You're in the age of the car!" he said. "No one around here walks anywhere anymore! If there was a track, it disappeared years ago!" So I had to backtrack five kilometres before I could even get started for the day. I tumbled down the road that I had staggered up the night before and emerged onto the main road right next to a tiny eating house.

"You must be a friend of Paul's!" the owner said as soon as I walked in, my hangover still with me.

"Oh you stayed at Paul's!" added one of the two customers. It was obvious Paul was a bit of a celebrity in those parts. A bit of this celebrity status must have rubbed off on me, as, as soon as I sat down, a beer was placed before me, and then a few seconds later, a steaming plate of curry and rice. The other customer, who, on his way to golf, was spotlessly-dressed, announced he wanted to pay for my lunch, and by the time I left around mid-day, I was feeling a lot better after my "mukaezake" (Hair of the dog!).

It was hot and I was climbing to a pass. There was a new 262 metre tunnel at the top, and halfway through it, the prefectural boundary was marked. I was in Oita, the fourth prefecture of my journey.

It had been a couple of hours since I had seen anybody apart from the odd car when I came across a "Fishing Park". Keen fishermen are almost guaranteed success in ponds that are stocked with undersized fish, and there were quite a few cars in the carpark. I used a public phone to call ahead to the Oyama Youth Hostel and make a booking for the night. Just as I was hanging up, an old man strode up and thrust something at me.

I recognized him as the rider on a scooter that had passed me going the other way just before I reached the fishing park. He had parked his bike, but was still wearing his blue helmet. My initial reaction was to pull back as he thrust his hand at me. No problems though as it contained a 1,000 yen note, not a knife, and his un-shaven face broke into a smile, revealing gold-rimmed front teeth.

"Please take this for your trip," he said. "I have been overseas! I went to Korea and China over fifty years ago."

Probably not a goodwill visit, I thought to myself.

"I like talking to foreigners. I met many Americans after the war. Do you have time?" He abruptly turned on his heels, went back to his scooter and returned with a 750ml can of beer. I took a sip and handed it back to him, along with the 1,000 yen.

"I can't drink! I'm riding! Keep the money!" he said, pushing it back at me. "Is it as good as American beer?"

"It's good," I replied. "Are you sure you won't join me?" He looked thoughtful, then turned back to his scooter and came back with a second big can. He opened that one too, and despite the fact that I had only just started the first one, handed it to me!

"Thank you! Thank you for being so kind and talking to me!" he spouted. "I have to go!" He raced off, waving as he went. I was a bit nonplussed. I had only talked to him for five minutes, yet when he left, he had given me 1,000 yen, two big cans of beer, and had thanked me for being kind!

It was a hot day. 32 degrees, according to the old man. In the shade, I polished off one can, and moving down a few gears, strolled down the valley with the other. My hangover had disappeared and I was feeling happy with life!

A few kilometres further on, a little yellow car pulled over. A lady in a pink apron wound down the window and handed me out an ice-cold can of grapefruit juice. "Good luck!" she said in English, and drove off.

Then a couple stopped to offer me a ride.

"I'm sorry," I said, "but I'm only walking." They handed me out a can of iced tea!

Of course, by this time, my bladder was working overtime. All this kindness was helping me to build up an inner-strength. How could I possibly give up when I was being given so much support from people who didn't even know what I was doing.

I spent the rest of the afternoon wandering alongside a man-made lake which looked desperately short of water. The road was narrow, with no footpath, and my only choice was whether to walk on the inside of the road and risk getting squashed up against the concrete wall, or walk on the outside and risk getting sideswiped off the edge to plummet far below. Big construction trucks raced along at regular intervals and I breathed a sign of relief when I arrived at the Youth Hostel about 5:30.

There were only two guests for the night, but my hopes for a quiet evening were dashed when the manager's husband turned up with a bottle of shochu. He ran the liquor shop down the road, and his wife had asked him to keep me company. Of course I had to be sociable!

It was raining outside as we watched the TV over breakfast.

With three days to go, excitement was starting to peak over the Imperial Wedding. All the green public telephones along the parade route had been replaced by gold ones according to a virtually orgasmic newscaster, and once again, we checked out Masako's outfit for the day. As usual, she had the professional smile of a career diplomat as the cameras flashed.

The other guest was a dam inspector from Osaka who was there on business.

"I love coming to the country," he said. "City people are like dogs! They are only concerned with themselves! People in the country act from their hearts."

As I left, the manager, her husband and three old ladies were sorting a huge pile of green plums they had collected the day before.

I spent the morning trudging the 20 kilometres into Hita in driving rain and wind. The road was narrow in places, and trucks had to slow down to pass me. I could see the drivers swearing in their nice dry cabs at the idiot out walking in the rain!

I was totally soaked when I finally got there, and headed straight for the onsen that was marked on my map. It turned out to be in a street of high-rise hotels which take daily turns having their bath open for public use. The public bath for the day turned out to be on the eighth floor of a fancy hotel overlooking the Chikugo River. The exceptionally pretty girl at reception didn't even blink at the sight of a wet dripping foreigner and welcomed me with a big smile that made me feel much better.

The bath had plate glass windows, and lying back in the hot water, I could look out on Hita and the hills that were covered with fog and low cloud. I soaked for an hour and a half in a bath the size of a squash court, and I needed that length of time to recover from my wet morning.

The woman at the Visitor's Centre at Hida Station giggled uncontrollably when I told her I was walking. I had asked her about the best route through the next range of mountains, and of course, she had pointed at the main road on my map.

"I'm walking," I said, "and am trying to avoid main roads as much as possible." From that point on I couldn't get any sense out of her at all!

On the road out of Hita for Hikosan I passed a piggery that I had been able to smell for about 500 metres, and then I found three tiny kittens, abandoned on the side of the road with a saucer of milk. But of course, I couldn't do anything except curse whoever had left them there. I worked out my anger by striding out for the next couple of hours.

A little after six I crossed into Fukuoka Prefecture, and before turning up a tiny valley road heading straight up into the mountains, I bought some supplies in a dark little shop.

"My son married a gaijin," said an old lady, my only fellow customer. "His wife is a Filipina. They live with their children in Guam. I went there once but it wasn't the same. Their children can't even speak Japanese properly. And they never come to visit me," she said sadly. "You should hurry back to your family!"

I wondered what my family was up to.

"You shouldn't walk in the mountains at night," warned the old man as he added up my purchases on an abacus. "There are foxes! And bears!" Not what I wanted to hear!

A train track wound up the same valley, and my map showed it disappearing into a five kilometre tunnel well before the pass. It grew dark and the croaking of frogs in the paddies on either side of the road was deafening. The darkness however, brought out the "hotaru" or fireflies, whipping around over the rice paddies. Tiny flecks of brilliant light that brightened me up and held my interest so that I almost missed the last station at the end of the valley.

Many people had told me that if I got stuck, country train stations were great places to spend the night. I timed it perfectly and after the last train went through at 8:48 dropping off three school kids, I had the tiny station to myself. I pushed two benches together, closed the sliding door to quieten the noise of the frogs and crawled into my sleeping bag.

Of course, the benches were hard, and too short, but I was so tired that I slept right through my alarm and was almost as surprised to see the bentover little old lady who arrived for the 6:10 am train as she was to see me.

Not wishing to startle any other passengers, I got my gear together and made an early start. I found out why I had seen so few people working in the paddies on the trip so far. It was because they were already working at 6 am and took a break during the heat of the day. The saying of "Hayane hayaoki" is popular in rural Japan. The English equivalent is "Early to bed, early to rise" and the philosophy was obviously closely followed in that area.

The road climbed and wound among some of the most carefully organised paddies I had seen. They were separated in elevation by cleverly-constructed stone walls so that water could be trapped

Early morning in the central Kyushu mountains

and used all the way down the valley. Down on the flats, the elevation difference between paddies was minimal and the paddies were large. Up there at the steeper top of the valley, the paddies were small, with sometimes 1.5 to 2 metre stone walls supporting them. Then I was into the forest, in land too steep for other use. The road snaked its way to the pass and a tunnel, before winding down the other side. The mountains were rugged, and the road was obviously minor, as I didn't see a car for the first hour and a half.

I came across a road construction area with about forty workers, a third of them women, preparing to start work for the day. I could hear them whispering as they stared at the gaijin walking out of the forests.

"Where did he come from?"

"Where did he stay?"

"Good morning! Is it far to Hikosan?" I asked.

They were all wearing hard-hats, with the women wearing

sunbonnets under their hardhats to shade their faces. Then the questions flew, and too embarassed to admit that I had slept in a station, I told them that I had used my tent.

"But it's dangerous in the mountains!" one old bloke said. "There are bears—and foxes!" Foxes are credited with being sneaky, untrustworthy and mischievous. A nasty mixture that most rural Japanese will avoid at all costs. I was more worried about the bears!

The valley widened, flattened out, and I was back among the paddies. A tiny shop by the road lured me in for an ice cream. A woman in her 60s was watching TV with her mother.

"What a pity! I haven't got any bread!" the younger one muttered as I entered. Foreigners, to those Japanese who have never met one, are stereotyped with various attributes. One is that we eat a lot of bread as we find Japanese food unpalatable. People are constantly surprised at my ability to do all sorts of simple things such as use chopsticks, sit in a kneeling position, and eat all sorts of food that they produce thinking I will balk at them.

We watched an item on TV that showed a housewife in Tokyo whose hobby was raising pet frogs in her kitchen. Her biggest problem was finding enough live flies to keep her charges contented, since she didn't like to feed them dead ones. The camera followed her on a fly-catching safari and then "the kill" as she fed them to her pets who had free access to the kitchen. This was followed by an interview with her son whose only comment was, "My mother is strange!"

After this excitement, I headed out into the heat of the day, to find that the wind had picked up. The road was following a wide river and the wind threatened to blow me into it. An old lady carrying her shopping crossed the road and asked:

"Niichan, nanji goro desho ka?" It wasn't that I was so surprised to be asked the time, but the fact that she called me "niichan". Literally, the words mean older brother, but in this context, took on the meaning of "young man, what is the time?" But it is a casual, friendly greeting that I had not been addressed with before—certainly not by someone I had never met. At the time, it made me feel great, as if I was not a 'foreigner', but a normal person. I had been treated as something different by everyone I had met since I started walking, but this greeting made me feel accepted. I have since discussed this with my wife who is sure the old lady had bad eyesight and thought I was Japanese!

By the time I reached the town of Kawara, I was hot, sticky and covered in dust that the wind was blowing around. I escaped into a small noodle shop where I discovered that the last public bath-house in town had closed the previous year. The husband and wife team were so apologetic that their town didn't have such a facility that they insisted I use the bath in their tiny apartment above the shop. The wife ran off to fill the bath while the husband and I shared a beer downstairs. Their knowledge of New Zealand was based on a trip to the "New Zealand village" in Yamaguchi Prefecture the week before. A kind of a fun park, it gives the opportunity to visit New Zealand without actually going! These "villages" have recently become popular, and there are "Dutch villages", "Canadian villages" and all sorts of other villages all over Japan.

After using their tiny bathroom, we had iced coffee and a block of New Zealand cheese they had bought at the "village". The couple's five year old daughter watched TV the whole time, and even when forced to greet me, couldn't take her eyes off the tube.

"That's all she does!" her mother complained. But looking around their limited living area, I could see that there wasn't much else she could do. There was nowhere to play, no other kids around according to her parents. Even the arrival of a strange foreigner to use the bath hadn't sparked any interest. I could see why they were worried.

I felt like a new man after the bath. Beaming a smile at a cute female gas station attendant, I narrowly avoided falling into a rice paddy, and then a woman selling watermelon on the side of the road chopped up half a melon for me. Her stall was next to a vending machine selling pornographic magazines, and next to that, a kennel of about twenty beagles who went totally berserk when they spotted me.

A tall, blonde American in a suit, waiting at a bus stop, told me I was crazy when I stopped for a chat. "Aah, so it's not only the Japanese who think so," I replied.

I had a problem. I was walking along a major road into the huge industrial city of Kitakyushu, and the further I walked, the more built up it became. The road was lined with buildings, with the unfriendly feeling of a big city, so I just kept walking. By the time I found a park where I could pitch my tent, it was well after 10, and I had walked fifty-four kilometres for the day!

The wind blew all night long, and when I got up at 5:30 the open area I had picked for my tent was like a battlefield, covered with small branches, twigs and leaves. My tent had stood up well however. An electric monorail whizzed by within one hundred metres on an elevated concrete track carrying the first keen commuters into Kitakyushu, and I realised I would be joining the morning rush.

The main road was my only choice, and when I emerged down some steps out of the park, I ran into an old man walking his dog. He didn't even blink at the sight of a foreigner coming out of the park at 6 am and we chatted for a kilometre or so.

Two words that are very important in Japanese society are "honne" and "tatemae". They are the equivalent of "private face" and "public face". As I walked, I thought about my search for the "honne", the "private face" of Japan. I wasn't there to see the side of the Japan that is presented to the world. I was there to see the real Japan, warts and all! I was down with the man in the street—with the man out walking his dog at 6 in the morning. I was lucky! Few people get such an opportunity. Most foreigners visiting Japan only get to see the "tatemae", what they are meant to see. It was a great chance. I vowed to take it.

I was soon being passed by droves of schoolchildren on bicycles, and the cars were crawling by. I had given up greeting the people I passed. In the country, especially from younger people, there was usually a hearty "Good Morning" or "Hello", but with hordes of people in the city, such nicities are impractical I suppose. I knew where I would rather have been! I was keen to get out of there.

And then came probably the worst twelve kilometres of the whole trip. I was trapped, having to choose the lesser of two evils. The two roads up the coast both coursed through the smoggy, dirty industrial strip of Kitakyushu. Forested mountains a kilometre inland meant that the smog had nowhere to go. It just sat above that horrible strip of land. I changed between Routes 3 and 199 hoping to find some relief, but I couldn't escape. The vehicle fumes made me dizzy and lightheaded, while my mouth tasted terrible. I tried to put my brain into "turn off" mode, but whilst my brain will turn off at most times, when I consciously tried to do it, it wouldn't.

I could just make out Ganryu Island in the straits between Kyushu and Honshu, where Miyamoto Musashi had won his famous duel with Sasaki Kojiro in the early 1600s. I'm sure the two famous swordsmen would have turned in their graves if they could see what had happened there. The kilometres really dragged out, but at 11, I was sitting eating an ice cream underneath the Kanmon Bridge linking Kyushu to Honshu.

I took off my shoes, inspecting my feet, which hadn't been a major problem since I had operated on the shoe. I dunked them in the salt water. The major hurdle of the island of Kyushu was over. Before starting, I had known that if I could get through Kyushu, then getting to Hokkaido would not be a problem. It was a good feeling.

Yamaguchi Prefecture beckoned from across the straits. The characters for Yamaguchi mean "the entrance to the mountains" and I could see why. There was a movement off to my right. A scruffily dressed workman was urinating into the bushes within twenty metres of a "designer toilet". The range in the quality of public toilets in Japan astounds me. From the dirty, broken-down hovel to newer ones that look like they're out to win architectural awards! Maybe the workman thought that one was someone's beach-house!

Anyway, his watering of the plants summed up my last twelve kilometres in Kyushu, and I couldn't help laughing out loud. He unhurriedly rearranged himself, scowled at me and walked off.

I took the elevator 55 metres underground to the 780 metre long Kanmon Tunnel that leads to Honshu. Halfway through, a youth on a moped whizzed past and it occurred to me that everyone who had walked the length of Japan must have walked through that tunnel. I was feeling proud, and wanting someone to share my personal triumph, I tried to call my wife in Osaka.

Of course, there was no answer.

3. THE HAGI BIJIN

I wandered out of Shimonoseki with a sore head, not from a hang-over, but from belting it on a shinzen, a small Shinto shrine that hangs on the wall in some houses. The shinzen had come off worse and was undergoing repairs when I left my friend's sister's house. I had had a relaxing day off and was leaving with a new friend. Hanging off my backpack was a small puffed-up, dried blowfish called a "fugu". Shimonoseki is famous for its fugu, which is con-sidered a great delicacy and is horrendously expensive. The only problem is that unless it is prepared correctly, it is lethally poison-ous. Cooks in "fugu" restaurants need to be specially licenced— and with good reason. Every year two or three deaths from fugu poisoning hit the news. My fugu wasn't too dangerous though. He was wearing blue sunglasses, a red hat, and a plastic walkman, and I had been presented with him just before leaving as a souvenir of Shimonoseki. He was dangling next to my "omamori", a safety charm that my wife's sister had given me before I left Osaka.

The straits between Shimonoseki and Kyushu are known for two great battles. One was the duel between Musashi and Kojiro in the 1600s, and the other, about 500 years before, the battle of Dannoura. This famous clash was between the two powerful clans of the time, the Minamoto and the Taira, who were battling for power and to unify Japan. Legend has it that one of the Ladies of the House of Taira plunged into the sea with the infant emperor in her arms instead of surrendering to the enemy.

I hit the coast at the Dannoura Memorial, turned left and headed north, with the inland sea on my right. The northern tip of Kyushu was barely visible through its industrial smog, while the mountains loomed before me. It was a warm, sunny Sunday and there was action all up the coast. Fishermen were casting off the rocks, a group of eight young men were racing radio controlled cars in an empty carpark, and golfers were pinging balls in a two-tiered driv-ing range. I passed a shop called "Ultraman Amuzone", wondering if I was worthy enough to enter, and after lunching on noodles, turned away from the coast toward the mountains.

The coastal plain was narrow, and immediately I passed under the bullet train tracks as one raced overhead, and then under the freeway. Both transport links were high above the ground sup-ported by great concrete legs that jutted out of the paddies and disappeared far in the distance.

My map showed an onsen at Kikugawa and when I dropped

into a shop for directions, an elderly woman pointed me off to the right, telling me it would take thirty minutes to walk there. She wasn't overly convincing however, and I was dubious. Outside the shop, I asked an old man—the opposite direction and fifteen minutes! The attraction of the onsen was being offset by the contradicting directions! I gave up on the idea, continuing on the road I was on, and lo and behold, within five minutes, what should I run smack into, but the onsen. In the hour I spent in the bath, only one wrinkled old man bothered to talk with me, and then only for a few minutes. He was soon back with his mates in another pool.

"He says he's from New Zealand. Walking to Hokkaido! Says he's walked from Kagoshima! Did you see the size of his pack in the changing room?" I turned off.

I was gradually climbing up a country road to a small Buddhist temple when I was spotted by three little girls. One was walking, one on a bicycle and one was cruising along on a unicycle. They decided to be my escort. It was a couple of kilometres up through the paddy fields to the temple and I enjoyed their company. They took turns on the unicycle and were so good that my walking pace was almost too slow. The only hitch we had was when they spotted a squashed snake in the middle of the road and screamed in unison. I could feel the stares of a couple working in a paddy next to the road.

"What's that gaijin doing to make those little girls scream?" I could see them thinking.

We were almost to the temple when the five o'clock siren rang. They raced back home after we took a photo at the temple gate.

From the gate it was a steady climb to the temple up worn stone steps lined with o-jizosan—small, carved stone statues wearing red bibs—that had been brought by worshippers for various reasons.

"One was brought by the family of a sick man praying for his recovery, some by people praying for a stillborn baby, and one was brought in remembrance of a pet dog!" explained the old priest.

The temple doubles as a Youth Hostel, a way of making extra income which the priest's family didn't seem to need. The large wife drove a large Volvo and told me how she loved to visit Scandinavia!

The temple itself was exquisite. The priest, who was dressed in blue sweatpants and a sports shirt, had the classic priest's haircut and proudly showed me through the wooden buildings. There had been a temple there since the Kamakura period, 800 years ago, he said, but the buildings had burned down with monotonous regularity. The last time had been thirty years ago.

"There is a saying that there are four things to beware of," he said. "Earthquakes, lightning, fires and fathers!" This was well put, as I wasn't sure if he meant to beware of fire, or to stop me casting my eye over his rather attractive daughter who helped run the hostel.

I was the only guest and the daughter served me dinner in a huge tatami mat room used to entertain visitors to the temple. The shoji (paper doors) were open, overlooking an immaculate garden with water gurgling down a well-organised course. Classic paintings hung on the walls, including one of a being with the body of a lion, and the head of a demon. Statues stood in the appropriate spots, and the simplicity of the room made it elaborate. It was the most "Japanese" room I think I have ever been in. I sat cross-legged on a cushion at a low table, enjoying my surroundings. The daughter served me a delicious, beautifully presented meal, and everything was classically, impeccably Japanese. I was sure nothing had changed since the 16th century! But then I saw him! A stuffed Mickey Mouse was sitting on a chair in the corridor! Back to reality with a thud!

The daughter, who was 22, must have suspected I was a big eater, as she brought me seconds, and then joined me for tea. The youngest of four daughters, she was a chemistry graduate who wanted nothing more than to go on and do whatever chemistry graduates do. She had been offered a job in Tokyo which her mother had declined on her behalf.

"Mother said that Tokyo was too far away. She needs someone to cook and do the washing here. She's getting old and one of us has to help her!" She sounded as if she were trying to convince herself. The other daughters were all away doing their own thing. She had been away at university for four years, but when forced to return, had found that all her friends had left. She was quite miserable. What is the point, I thought, of making sure your child gets a good education and then crushing her ambition once she's qualified to do something she's interested in?

The family had their dinner later and the priest invited me to join them for a beer. The mother, who had taken on tyrant status in

my eyes, turned out to be a great burper. In between downing full
glasses of beer in single gulps, she would belch loudly and proudly
and tell me of her experiences in Sweden.

"Belch! Don't take all the best bits! Belch!" she chastised the
priest who was carefully picking through the meal as she raved on.
"Pour the gaijin another beer! Belch! And me too!" Meals are
usually served not with one plate per person, but with a variety of
food placed in the middle of the table to be shared by all.

She obviously took a dislike to me for the way I got along well
with her daughter whom she ordered about like a slave. It was
clear who was in control in that household. I redeemed myself to
some extent by telling her she couldn't have daughters in their
mid-twenties as she looked so young herself! My standard situation-
saving comment!

When I couldn't find the futon, it was the priest who was sent to
get it for me, and I dreamed about being knocked off a road into a
paddy by a Volvo-driving, beer-burping tyrant.

The daughter made me breakfast.

"My university professor is looking for a job for me," she confided. "The economy is in recession though. He called the other
day to say that no company in my field is willing to employ a
woman. They all think that a woman will marry within a few years
and leave." She looked keen to escape from her mother's clutches
while the mother was keen to see me on my way. She knew a bad
influence when she saw one!

The daughter was ordered off to perform some menial task, but
then as I was leaving, she brought me a tomato and, with tears in
her eyes, asked me not to forget my stay at the temple. I felt very
sorry for her.

It was not quite 9 when I left, but already hot, and I passed two
ladies who were walking under sun umbrellas. The narrow country
roads meandered through river valleys and the odd tiny hamlet.
Some of the houses still had thatched roofs, and there was a
sleepiness about the area.

I dropped into a tiny shop for an ice cream. Three women in
white jackets and scarves had been nattering, but on spotting me,
two instantly disappeared, volunteering the third to serve me. She
giggled hysterically, but when I spoke to her in Japanese, she calmed
down, and the other two reappeared to interrogate me. The shop

was air-conditioned, and being hot outside, I stayed for two ice creams and a yarn.

The town of Mine didn't impress me. I spotted two huge smoke-stacks belching dirty grey smoke from a long way off, and the shokudo I found near the station was run-down and over-priced. Its "noren", the shop curtain that hangs outside proclaiming that a restaurant is open, was sun-bleached and ripped. It then took me fifteen minutes to walk past a huge cement factory on my way out of town.

The freeway to Osaka was only a couple of kilometres further on. Cars and trucks whizzed by.

"Maybe I should just stand on the verge and catch a ride to Osaka," I said to myself. "That would give my wife a surprise! And my feet a rest!" But I couldn't.

I spent the afternoon trudging away to Akiyoshidai.

The Youth Hostel there was a completely different story from the temple. It was a huge building with room for 120, but I was the only one there. There had been no shortage of foreigners through lately according to the book, and the "parents" showed no interest in me at all. Rules were plastered on all the walls and the impersonality of the place put me off completely.

I'm sure I was brought natto, a kind of sticky beans, for break-fast, as foreigners are known to find them uneatable. The lady gasped as she came to get my tray.

"You've eaten your natto! We didn't think you'd be able to eat them!" I wondered why they had brought them to me in the first place! Maybe it was to reinforce her ideas about foreigners. But I was happy—I quite like natto!

At 8:30 I was at the entrance to the Akiyoshidai cave system as it opened, and was among the first to venture in for the day. The caves extend for 10 kilometres, but only about one kilometre is ac-cessible to the public. I was almost through when I ran into a school party of forty children from Amakusa in Kyushu, who had entered via a tunnel at the far end. They were busily posing for a group photo which gave me a few minutes to chat with their teacher. After the photo, they seemed to find me more interesting than the spectacular stalagmites, and we were crowded by children praising their teacher for her English ability! But we had been speaking Japanese!

Akiyoshidai National Park is a huge, grassy, rock-studded plateau covered with hiking trails. Busloads of sleeping children on school trips roared past and I enjoyed the smiles and waves from the tour guides in the front seats. Some would point at me, jabbering away into their microphones, and all eyes would look down in surprise at the strange foreigner who was walking, as the bus sped by.

Four old women were tending fields of tobacco, and a park ranger stopped to offer me a ride. He had seen me in Mine the day before but couldn't believe I had walked all the way.

Then I turned onto the road to Hagi, and there was nothing except the occasional group of houses for twenty kilometres. I was over-joyed when I found a new toll road with a tunnel that cut the distance by six kilometres, and finally, after a long exhausting day, I rolled into the historical town of Hagi. Hagi is on a flat island at the mouth of the Matsumoto River. To the north is the sea, while in all other directions, it is surrounded by mountains. As I came out of the hills I caught my first view of the Sea of Japan, whose coast I was to follow much of the way up Honshu.

Hagi is proud of its part in Japanese history. Until 1868, it was part of the Choshu domain, ruled over by the Mori family, old enemies of the Tokugawa shogun. When the foreigners arrived in the 1860s, the Choshu, along with the Satsuma from Kagoshima, and the Tosa from Kochi, were instrumental in rebelling against the Tokugawa, restoring the Meiji Emperor to the top job, and pushing Japan into the modern world. Ito Hirobumi, Japan's first Prime Minister, came from Hagi, as did many of his fellow Meiji-era politicians. Hagi is also proud of its cultural and artistic links, and Hagi-yaki pottery is known throughout the world.

The Youth Hostel was near the ruins of Hagi Castle, which must have been quite a sight until it was razed in 1870 to show support for the Restoration of the Emperor. This time I was not alone, though I might as well have been. Two guys had arrived on motorbikes, but were asleep by 7:30! Hostels generally lock up at 10, so I found an alternate route over a back fence, should I require it, and wandered into town to explore.

Six drunk businessmen just sat and stared when I entered a little bar in the main street. Then, self-consciously, they went back to their noisy conversation. I sat at the bar sipping sake and watching baseball on TV with two middle-aged woman who ran the place. In very un-Japanese fashion, one of the pitchers threw at the batter, hitting him in the helmet. The dugouts emptied and I witnessed the first major fight I had seen in a Japanese baseball game. It was enough to capture even the businessmen's attention. But not as much as the arrival of the "Hagi bijin"—the beauty of Hagi.

She was quite exquisite—like a Japanese doll, except that instead of a kimono, she was wearing a shopkeepers apron. She had come to visit her aunt, one of the owners with whom I had been watching TV.

"Oh Mitsuko!" her aunt said, "What good timing! Come and sit next to this handsome foreigner!" I should probably point out that even my mother would laugh at the suggestion that I am handsome, although a few years back a man asked me to pose with his daughter, because, he said, I look like Paul Newman! My friends still laugh about it.

Mitsuko sat one bar stool away, and then, at her aunt's insistence, moved over next me. She had sparkling eyes and deserved the title I gave her, the "Hagi bijin". The older women cackled away, and refilling my sake pot, proceeded to serve us all sorts of local delicacies—raw tuna, squid and whitebait. The businessmen were giving me the odd glare, as if to say, "Bloody foreigners, coming here stealing our women!", but after three weeks on the road, I didn't care.

I enjoyed the female company and the teasing of the aunt and her friend. A truck driver and his wife arrived. They were all friends and the big-armed Aunt took the opportunity to point at them saying—

"What a nice couple. What about you two?"

I took time out at this stage but as I closed the door to the toilet I could hear a burst of excited conversation as the truckie was told about me.

"He's from New Zealand. He's walking from Kagoshima to Hokkaido! Can you imagine it! He just walked in here! And he's eaten everything we've put in front of him—even the raw fish! He says he can eat natto!" The chatter continued until I rejoined them.

Mitsuko was 22 and worked at the toy shop. She loved children, she said, but was keen to leave Hagi and go and see the real world. She said most of her friends had left for the Tokai, the industrial eastern coast of Japan, where most of the big cities are, and where salaries and living standards are much higher, she said. I didn't know if I agreed with her about the living standards.

I offered to walk her home on my way back to the Youth Hostel, but after all the teasing, suddenly the aunt turned serious and made sure we left separately. As we stood up to say goodbye, I was surprised to find that she barely came up to my chest in height. But she was very cute.

I had consumed a fair bit of sake and merrily wandered back through the dark streets, past Hagi's old samurai houses, and hopped over the back fence into the Youth Hostel. I had very much enjoyed my brush with the Hagi bijin.

Day 21, June the 9th, was the day of the Imperial Wedding in Tokyo. It had been made a National Holiday and there was to be continuous television coverage throughout the day.

But while the rain poured down in the capital, the Japan Sea Coast of Yamaguchi Prefecture basked in warm sunshine. There wasn't a cloud in the sky as I virtually ambled up the coast. Despite the holiday, small factories were operating, children in school uniforms rode by on bicycles, and shops were open. Japanese flags fluttered in the cool sea breeze. I put my watch and map in my backpack. All I had to do was follow the coast.

I passed snorkellers in wetsuits collecting shellfish and seaweed, fishermen casting off the rocks, and families picnicking on the beach. Everyone seemed to be enjoying the day, except a group of about twenty high school girls jogging in running outfits. A few metres behind, their coach, a man with slicked-back hair and sunglasses, followed driving an air-conditioned van.

It was hot, and whenever I stumbled across a little shop, I dropped in for an ice cream.

"How's the weather in Tokyo? Still raining?" I would ask.

"Yes, I hope it clears in time for the parade!" was the common reply.

The coastline was rugged. But while the road kept to it as closely as possible, it often ducked inland, climbing and descending before rejoining the coast. One such route had a 1,469 metre tunnel that took twenty minutes to grind through and left me spluttering and coughing from exhaust fumes.

A coin machine in the middle of nowhere was selling pornographic magazines with such unimaginative titles as "Dick" and "Command". Faded covers were displayed to the potential buyer, displaying big-breasted blondes who looked pretty scary to me.

I arrived in the fishing town of Susa in time to watch the Wedding

Parade in a small bar over the road from the station. The owner and two patrons had obviously been drinking whisky for quite a while, and together we celebrated the end of the rain in Tokyo.

"This proves the Divine power of the Imperial family!" one said excitedly. "The rain stopped at just the right time!"

I didn't like to point out that if the Imperial family were truly divine, it probably wouldn't have rained at all on the big day.

The Parade went ahead, and between us, we decided that Masako Owada made a very presentable member of the Imperial Family, despite the fact that she towered over the bridegroom by close to ten centimetres.

The other two patrons had spent the morning playing pachinko, a kind of vertical pinball, and the afternoon drinking, and were feeling very patriotic. They felt that since such an Imperial Wedding only occurs once every twenty or thirty years, they had every reason to have a good day! And I agreed with them.

They were planning to drive to the town of Masuda for further celebrations as I left. I made mental preparations to get well out of the way should I spot their car coming anywhere near me. Drunk-driving laws are extremely strict in Japan, but those two revellers weren't going to let the law restrict their fun!

I wobbled out and enjoyed the final five kilometres to the Tama River Campground, where, after setting up camp, I spent the evening with a family who were "night fishing". They were casting large lit floaters out onto the river and reeling in small fish fairly regularly. The night was very dark. The stars sparkled overhead. The frogs croaked in the paddy fields. It had been a good day.

I was woken by the 6 o'clock siren and wandered out to a pebbly beach at the mouth of the river. The water was calm, clear and cold and I enjoyed a swim before starting out.

By nine I was into Shimane Prefecture and could see the San'in Coastline stretching away before me. Western Honshu is virtually split down the middle by the Chugoku mountain range which runs east-west. San'in means "in the shade of the mountains," as opposed to San'yo for the Inland Sea coast which means "on the sunny side of the mountains."

The San'in has always been relatively inaccessible from the seats of power as compared to the San'yo. Its rocky coastline and rugged

mountainous interiors, coupled with inhospitable weather from the
Sea of Japan meant that it was virtually left behind as the more
accessible San'yo developed. It was for that reason that I had chosen
to walk along the Nihonkai, the Sea of Japan coast.

"Kureigu! Kureigu!" yelled the man who had stopped his car
on the far side of the road—unmistakably, the Japanese pronunciation of my name, Craig. It was one of the drunken parade
watchers from the day before.

"We made it to Masuda! But that's all I can remember. We
even looked for you on the way! I'm just on my way home now.
Late for work. Here, take this," he said, handing me a box of
Hokkaido cheese. "Gambatte!" He sped off to face his boss.

The last six or seven kilometres into the town of Masuda was
along a continuous concrete breakwater that fortified the land
against a "weather invasion". It was really blowing and big white-
caps were pounding in.

A windsurfer had parked his car on top of the breakwater. He
was standing on his board on the concrete, practicing, trying to
control his sail in the near gale.

"I'm only learning," he explained. "I'm not going out there
today!" he said, pointing at the waves crashing into the concrete.
A wise man knows his limits. His was a well-advised decision.

My legs felt terrible, my right foot was aching, and by the time
I reached the station, I was ready to give up for the day. A young
policeman was eating his lunch and reading the paper at the station
Koban (Police Box). He jumped to attention, and in a few minutes
I was armed with a map and directions to a restaurant, a sento and
a small ryokan (inn).

The sento didn't open until three, so I sat writing postcards in a
small restaurant, watching Imperial Wedding replays on TV. The
owner had nipped out to tell the sento-owner that she had a customer
waiting, and a few minutes before three, an old lady in her 80s
popped her head in the window.

"I'm opening now. Please feel free. You're most welcome!"
What service! Of course she gave me the full inspection as I
changed, and once I was in the bath, I could vaguely hear her
chatting with her friends on the female side of the bath-house. The
word "gaijin" seemed to be in common usage.

A young man from Okayama came for a while but soon left,

complaining the bath was too hot. He looked at me sideways when I didn't agree. Another stereotyping of foreigners is that they can't bathe in very hot water and find Japanese baths too debilitating. I enjoyed surprising him!

By the time I had spent an hour in the bath I felt much better and decided to press on. I was, however, trapped on Route 9, the main coast highway, and when rush hour came, the cars hurtled past in a continuous stream. The sun became a magnificent red ball inching its way down to the horizon.

After a quick dinner at a drive-in, in fading light, I ran into a high school student on his bike.

"Is there anywhere around here I can pitch a tent?" I asked him. He thought for a moment.

"What would be best, a schoolground or a beach?" I opted for the beach. The idea of being surrounded by schoolchildren should I wake up late didn't really appeal.

"There's a spot not too far away," he said. "I'll take you. It's on my way home." He hopped off his bike and we wandered together in increasing darkness. He was on his way home from school in Masuda.

"I have soccer practice every day after school. Then I cycle home. It's about fourteen kilometres."

"This is one fit kid!" I thought to myself.

"I get home about 8:30. Then I have dinner and study till about midnight. I want to go to university in Hiroshima, but the entrance exams are very hard! I don't know if I'll make it."

Fireflies were whipping around on that warm evening. We ran into one of his friends, and the two fifteen year olds showed me to a great camping spot overlooking a beach.

"This is more interesting than studying!" they both agreed.

The second boy raced into his home to fill my waterbottle and came back with two cans of coffee.

"My parents wish you the best of luck!" he said politely.

There were two cars at the point overlooking the beach, and I could see glowing cigarettes in the dark. Maybe this was "lovers point". The sight of a gaijin pitching his tent with the help of a torch must have been too much though, as both soon drove off. And I was left alone, listening to the waves crashing onto the beach below.

A siren rang at 5 am, and a few minutes later two cars drove up, parking on either side of my tent, despite the fact that the area had room for at least a hundred or so cars. I crawled out to see what was going on.

"Oh, it's a tent!" one fisherman said in surprise to another. What else could it possibly have been? "A gaijin in a tent!"

Camping on the Sea of Japan coast, Shimane Prefecture.

It was a beautiful morning, already warm. I lay on my sleeping bag in the sun eating rice balls and cookies and watching a fishing boat out in the bay. The sea was calm.

After a brief stint back on Route 9, I found a small local road that stuck to the coast. People were on their way to work, and their greetings were hearty. Friendly country folk.

"Ohayo gozaimasu!" and even its English equivalent "Good Morning" from a beautiful, immaculately-dressed woman outside a station. A mother was biking her son to school. His yellow primary school hat bobbed up and down on the back of the bike as he struggled to keep me in view. An old lady was digging up potatoes, while bunches of onions lay drying on the footpath. Then an old man on a motorbike rode by, and staring at me, almost crashed off the road as he narrowly avoided missing the next corner. The Matsubara Post Office presented me with a gift pack of a hand towel and some plastic bags, and a car with loudspeakers on top raced back and forth advertising horse racing in Masuda.

It was a very enjoyable few hours, but I was soon back onto Route 9. At a point high above the coast I passed a car grave-yard. Piles of rusted wrecks, and even a BMW on top!

Well before mid-day I found a noodle shop where the women laughed at my long legs.

"You'd only take one step to my three!" one joked to the delight of the others. It was twenty kilometres to Hamada they said, though one was sure that she had walked it in an hour and a half. My map indicated it was only about six kilometres away, and I laughed to myself that the Japanese, renowned around the world for their "exactness", could be so inexact!

"Your wife is very kind to let you free for such a long time!" one said, smiling. "She must be very strong!" It was my turn to tease them.

"Like all Japanese women, she was very kind before we got married," I said. "But once we married she changed! And when we had a baby, she got even stronger! Now, she's totally in charge!"

"My wife was like that too!" chirped in one of the customers who had been quietly eating his noodles. Everyone laughed.

"We're all like that!" said the woman owner, grinning.

I'll never forget a conversation I had once with a friend in Tokyo. He was complaining about not having enough money. He, like many Japanese workers, adhered to the practice of taking his salary home and giving it to his wife. She was in charge of running the household and administering money matters. In return, she would give him pocket money for his everyday needs.

"My wife doesn't give me enough money each week," he was complaining. "She wants me to stop smoking, so she only gives me enough for lunch. None for cigarettes, or going out drinking."

"What do you do?" I asked. "Do you ask her for more?"

"Oh no! I couldn't do that! I go and ask my mother. She's much more understanding!"

A run-down love hotel on the coast was trying to increase its potential earnings.

"Accomodation for fishermen" read the sign. "Cheap overnight rates." Lovers during the day, fishermen at night. What a combination! I couldn't help wondering which was their best market.

An hour later I was in the weather-beaten town of Hamada asking directions at a gas station. There were six staff, three of them sitting in deckchairs, and no customers, so I had plenty of advice on how to find the sento.

One of Japan's little mysteries is why gasoline prices are so high, despite the phenomenal rise in value of the yen over the past fifteen years. The yen has tripled in value since 1976, whilst the US$ price for oil is still about the same. I can't understand how gas prices have actually gone up! But no one complains. Especially not the six staff sitting in that little gas station doing nothing.

The west end of town, near the port, smelt of fish, and along with six old ladies I waited for the sento to open at 3. They were teasing and friendly. I enjoyed their company immensely. It was a bit of a different story inside though. I was alone in the men's side until three swarthy, curly-haired men turned up. I wasn't surprised to see them covered in elaborate tattoos. The yakuza are the Japanese version of the mafia and are easily recognizable by their tattoos, and on the odd occasion, missing fingers which they chop off as a token of loyalty to their boss.

I didn't bother to get close enough to check out their fingers though, as they gruffly showed their disapproval of my presence. I felt much happier once they left after about fifteen minutes.

"Oi! Oi!" An old man came out of his house on the side of the road. He handed me a natsumikan, a summer orange—large, slightly bitter, and with heaps of pips.

"Gambatte!"

By seven I had found the Iwami Seaside Park which advertised its auto-campground. It had a beautiful sandy beach, and for 3,300 yen, campers were allocated a small area for their vehicle and tent. It was a Friday night and only a few spots were taken.

I quickly made friends with a family from Osaka, a couple with a three-year-old daughter who had driven their huge four-wheel-drive sports truck the 350 kilometres in search of a good wind-surfing spot for the husband. They had racked up 8,000 yen in road tolls on the way! They had all the gear imaginable including a barbeque, table and chairs, and an umbrella. We sat around chatting as the red fireball of the sun dropped below the horizon.

"Autocamping is booming because it's so cheap," he said. "You can go anywhere. There are so many places to explore in Japan.

We don't need to go overseas. I'd rather go away each fortnight for a couple of days than work all year and go overseas for a week! The only problem is driving back to Osaka on a Sunday night. The traffic jams are terrible! But we're used to it."

Saturday morning was windless and my friend the windsurfer was sitting in a deckchair at his portable BBQ table dejectedly staring out to sea in search of a gust. I had rolled over when the 5 o'clock siren sounded, but when I crawled out of my tent at least an hour later it was all action. Children were playing soccer, swimming and riding bikes, while their parents were preparing breakfast.

The windsurfer's wife had trotted off to use the "200 yen for two minutes" showers and came back grumbling.

"There was no hot water!" It was clear that autocamping really wasn't too high on her list of favourite activities. We breakfasted together, and when I left, her husband was still praying for wind.

It was hot as I continued up the coast. At Gotsu, I watched rugby players labouring in the heat on a grassless ground that looked as hard as concrete. It probably was, as during the five minutes I was watching, two players were carted off with injuries after crashing to the ground.

At a run-down concrete-floored drive-in, a toothless old woman grinningly rubbed the blonde hair on my tanned arm without saying a word.

I spent half the afternoon gingerly creeping through dank dirty tunnels trying not to be squashed as the traffic roared by. Every now and then there was an o-jizosan, a small statue beside the road marking a spot where someone had died in a traffic accident, and gritting my teeth, I crept through the next tunnel hoping my children would continue to have a father!

If I walked 3,200 kilometres, and I averaged 1,500 steps each kilometre, then I would walk a total of nearly five million steps! It was a long, hot day!

The new J-league Soccer was on the TV in a small roadside resthouse where I stopped for a break. Soccer had never been really big in Japan, but with the massive 1993 launch of the J-league and its accompanying marketing and promotions, the country was going soccer-mad. The standard of play couldn't match European or South American levels, but big names from overseas had been signed, and soccer players had become instant heroes. Or so it seemed from the throng of screaming girls in the stands!

At Nima, I found the Kofukuji Temple Youth Hostel on top of a hill a couple of kilometres off the main road. It was a beautiful wooden building that looked as if it could still be in another century. Once again, I was the only guest.

The priest's wife, who ran the hostel, was running around with a mobile phone that seemed to be ringing constantly. She prepared me a delicious sukiyaki dinner and together we watched the news in between her phone calls. The day's headline on the Shimane News was that a bear had come out of the woods in Hamada where I had been the day before. Great!

"Beware of bears!" the announcer warned before signing off.

"Please visit our Sand Museum," said the wife bringing out brochures. "We have the biggest sand timer in the world! It goes for a full year and is turned over each New Year's Eve. It's very exact. They counted each grain of sand when they made it!" She wasn't kidding!

And then just before bedtime, a 30-year-old student from Kyoto arrived on a moped. She marvelled at his amazing trip. He had travelled 300 kilometres in a day on his little bike! How amazing! He refused to believe that I was celebrating my 24th day of walking and had covered about 800 kilometres. I went to bed furious!

The biker left before me in the morning, on his way back to Kyoto. Before I hit the road, the priest showed me around the temple, which had all the qualities of a classic temple except for the Coke machine by the main doors!

After I had been walking for an hour, the biker pulled up.

"You'll never believe it!" he said, embarrassed. "I turned left instead of right when I got back to the main road!" He had gone the wrong way! He must have gone thirty or forty kilometres the wrong way and I didn't like his chances of becoming the lawyer that he planned to be. "Hoko onchi" is one of my favorite terms in Japanese and aptly describes someone who is hopeless with directions, and has no idea where they are. It described him perfectly and I doubted if he could find Kyoto, although basically, all he had to do was keep the sea on his left and mountains on his right.

The Izumo Peninsula gradually came into view as I marched up the coast. There were quite a few tunnels, and my left arm was dirty from scraping against filthy tunnel walls while trying to stay alive.

I passed a group of old women with numbers plastered on their upperbodies, front and back like ski racers who were playing gateball, a Japanese version of croquet popular among the elderly. It can get quite vicious, and one particular old girl who was bent over from too many years working in the fields seemed to be taking great joy out of slamming her opponents balls all over the place!

An old bath was being used as a goldfish pond in someone's front garden, and a truck, with Nagasaki licence plates was stopped on the side of the road, engine running, curtains pulled around the cab window, and a pair of feet lounging on the steering wheel.

I lunched at the "Ramen Daigaku", the Noodle University. It was a franchise of a fast-food noodle shop chain, but I didn't feel I'd bettered my education when I walked out the door.

Emerging from a soak in Oda Onsen, I found that the humidity had risen sharply. It was positively sticky and I could tell that rain wasn't far off.

When it rained, it rained like there would be no tomorrow. The heavens opened and it bucketed down, while I, out in the middle of nowhere, trudged on. And on. And on.

And then salvation. I turned a corner to see the bullet train. Well it wasn't really the bullet train, but a noodle shop with a couple of fake facades to make it look like the bullet train. And even better, it was a noodle shop specialising in chashumen (noodles with pork slices on top), my favorite! So I sat eating noodles and reading the newspaper as customers came and went. All stared at the soaked gaijin in the corner as the puddles grew larger outside. As I stared out the window wondering what to do next, my eyes focused on a sign advertising the local "Kokuminshukusha", or government-run Lodging House, a kilometre away and I knew all would be OK!

I rearranged my dripping gear and ventured forth, past the "Hotel Venus" fashion hotel to the Koryo Onsen kokuminshukusha where I was greeted a bit disdainfully at the Reception by a young bloke who was obviously not impressed by my dripping all over place.

"Do you have a booking?" he asked. Oh no! Just my luck. They were bound to be full!

"No. Do I need one?"

"No, we've plenty of rooms." Whew!

I was given a private room with a view of Lake Kaminishi, and spent an hour or so recovering in the onsen. Fortunately there was a drink-machine dispensing cups of sake, and I spent the evening in my room watching baseball on TV, happy to have escaped the rain!

"Stand by Me" was the piped music as I ate breakfast. It was cloudy and humid once I got going, but thankfully not raining outside.

The large flat river plain I had to cross before reaching Izumo Taisha was covered with vineyards. The vines were protected from birds by netting, looking as if the grapes were growing in blue net cages.

I had my first clash with the rather abrupt sounding Izumo dialect.

"You're walking! Where's your bicycle?" an old lady laughingly questioned me. "Good luck!" But she had gone before I had figured out what she had said!

I wandered through the town of Taisha which relies on visitors to the Izumo Taisha, famed as the shrine where all the Shinto gods go on vacation. They apparently leave their shrines throughout Japan and visit for a month in October. It is reputed to be one of the two oldest Shinto shrines in Japan.

Dodging the tour groups at Izumo Taisha.

It was a Monday and there were few people about. Under the huge concrete "torii" marking the entrance, a taxi driver was trying to convince two attractive young women to take "his tour" of Taisha. Among the spectacular pines before the Taisha itself, I was surprised to find big groups of red-faced, rowdy elderly Japanese having group photos taken. Such groups aren't usually red-faced and rowdy, but on talking to a few, I found that they had just come from a wine-tasting session at the Shimane Winery!

So with the prospect of an interesting afternoon ahead, I enjoyed my visit. I spent most of the time watching tour groups arrive, line up before the Taisha, have their photo taken, and then rush off following their tour guides who were waving tour flags in an effort to keep their people together. The photographer was so busy that he had a walkie-talkie which he was using constantly between groups, and there were officials whose job it was to get the groups from the bus to the photo stop as quickly as possible without losing anybody. It made great viewing!

One tour escort was so cute I couldn't help but follow and listen to her explain the Taisha's history to her group of forty. Her poker-faced commentary was like a recording and I am sure she must have been doing it for about the two thousandth time. Her group was from Hyogo Prefecture and seemed more interested in me.

"An American! Look! An American!" Oh no! Not again! On this note I left, heading east. The road ran at the foot of the mountains past huge empty parking lots. And I thought it had been crowded! I'm glad I hadn't been there on a weekend.

I stopped for an ice cream, but the tiny shop fooled me. The standard ice cream freezer was full with fishing bait, even though "ice cream" was written on the side. The smell put me off altogether.

Then a Spanish-style building, complete with red roof and arches came into view. The Shimane Winery! The carpark was packed with buses and I soon found out why the tourists at the Taisha were so red-faced.

Japan does not have a long tradition of wine-making. As with beer, wine was introduced by Europeans and there is an "exoticness" associated with it. The visiters were obviously keen to make the most of it. They poured off the buses into the souvenir shop and tasting area, congregating around the eight huge "punch bowls" full of different wines. Each bowl had its own pile of plastic cups for tasting and was regularly restocked by attentive staff in blue aprons. After checking out the full range of options, most "tasters" were already red-faced, and headed off to squander their money in the souvenir area. The walls were lined with bottles and the options were virtually unlimited. Wine jellies, wine cookies, wine cake and wine everything else! All perfectly packaged for presenting to relatives and friends. There was even a desk for sending the stuff all over Japan so they didn't have to carry it.

It was interesting to see Japanese domestic tourism in action. Twelve million Japanese may be going overseas each year, but domestic tourism is alive and well. The buses poured in and disgorged their loads of visitors, who wilfully emptied their wallets before clambering back onto the buses to head for the next attraction, the Taisha. All to the benefit of the local economy.

I wasn't much of a benefit though! I got a good view of what was going on as I sat on a bench in the corner writing postcards and "tasting". I had a bit of trouble deciding which wine was best, but after I had gone through the selection a few times, my writing was becoming unreadable and I decided to get back on the road while I still could!

I have to admit to being a bit naughty at the winery. I took advantage of a weakness sometimes known as "gaijin fever". Whilst the tasting area was carefully attended by vigilant staff, I only received smiles and giggles each time I went up to refill my cup. I knew that no one would approach me, as few rural Japanese would be confident to come up to me and speak English. The idea that I might speak Japanese would not occur to them. Hence I didn't let on that I could speak their language. I knew that I could probably have spent all afternoon "tasting" and writing postcards.

This "gaijin fever" was something I was stuck with throughout the walk, and it was nice, if a bit naughty, to take advantage of it for once. Because in most cases, it was a disadvantage. Few people would talk to me first. Once I spoke to someone in Japanese, they would visibly sigh with relief, and with the fever subsiding, I would be treated like a reasonably normal person. On entering a restaurant, a comment in Japanese about the weather was usually enough to restore normality. After all, no one expects a tall gaijin in shorts carrying a big backpack to enter a tiny country shokudo!

Later in the trip, once the rains started, this fever would become quite a problem when seeking accommodation, but at that stage it was simply an inconvenience I had learned to contend with.

Foreigners have a checkered history in Japan, a country populated almost entirely by one race. First came the European traders
in the 1500s, followed closely by the missionaries. The Christians
were relatively successful in spreading their word, especially in
Kyushu. In the mid 1600s, however, the Tokugawa Shogun decided
that the disease had spread far enough. Christianity was banned. The
Christians were virtually wiped out, and the country was "closed" to
the barbarian influence. It remained this way for over 200 years until
the Americans arrived in the 1850s and forcibly "opened" Japan.
The Japanese resisted, but finding that their isolation had left them
technologically far behind the rest of the world, had to face reality
and submit to foreign pressures. Japanese society underwent a
huge upheaval with the military Shogun removed from rule and
the Emperor Meiji restored to the top job. Japan was playing catch-
up and scholars were dispersed all over the world to learn what
was going on and to "modernize" the country. Japan learnt quickly
and all aspects of society changed dramatically. The military were
also learning and in 1905 surprised the world by defeating the
Russians, when only fifty years earlier, they had been unable to
defend themselves. The military influence became stronger, and
with the economy dependent on imported raw materials, expansion
became the name of the game, leading into World War II. Before
the war, there were few foreigners in Japan, but defeat brought an
influx with the invading forces. Most were Americans and they
brought baseball and later McDonalds with them. They lived "on
base", lived an American life as much as possible, and made few
attempts to interact with the locals. Few learnt Japanese or
bothered to take much note of local customs. Hence "gaijin fever",
and the image of a foreigner being someone unintelligible and
lacking knowledge of Japanese ways. Of course foreigners from
many countries now live in Japan, but few venture forth into the
countryside to challenge this image. In most cases I made an effort
to prove my normality, to show that I can be "partly Japanese", but
in this case, at the Shimane Winery, I acted as a local would expect
me to act, as a useless foreigner with no understanding.

So I wobbled back out onto the road, grinned at a squashed
snake, and narrowly avoided being knocked into a paddy field by
a huge tour bus from Nara. The urge to walk quickly subsided, and
I was glad it wasn't too far to my friend's place in Hirata. I was
looking forward to a rest!

4. GOAT TRACKS

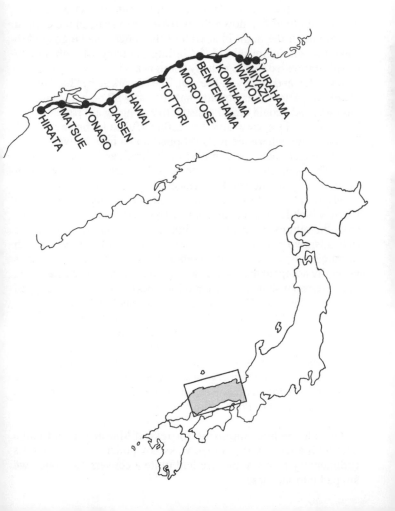

HIRATA
MATSUE
YONAGO
DAISEN
HAWAI
TOTTORI
MOROYOSE
BENTENHAMA
KOMIIHAMA
IWAYOJI
MIYAZU
YURAHAMA

I really enjoyed my day off in Hirata. One reason was that I sat inside for most of the day staring out at the pouring rain and congratulating myself on my great timing. Another was that my friend's mother must have thought that I was looking a bit skinny, as she filled me up with all sorts of delicacies. And she was right. I had weighed myself the morning I left Osaka—a trim 88 kilograms. But here in Hirata, after 27 days walking, I was down to 82 according to the scales! I was feeling fit, but my feet were sore, partly from tumbling down the narrow, steep stairs in the dark in the middle of the night in search of the toilet. I had managed to wake the whole household, including the baby who obviously wasn't impressed by the clumsy foreigner.

It was hot and muggy as I set out. The carpark at the "Las Vegas" Pachinko parlour was already half full at 9:30 on a Wednesday morning, and I could hear the distinctive clanging as I passed. Lake Shinji came into view and I was thankful to be on the "lazy" northern side where the hills dropped down into the water with barely enough room for a single railroad track and an uncongested road. The lake, although the sixth largest in Japan, has a maximum depth of only six metres. Its surface was calm under the clear sky.

My friend's sister-in-law had made me an obento, a packed lunch, which I devoured on a grassy spot beside the lake. She must have thought me a bit underweight also, as there were six huge riceballs: two covered in nori, dried seaweed; two plastered with sesame seeds; and two with umeboshi, pickled plums, inside. It is generally accepted that gaijin can't eat umeboshi, but she had been so impressed with my eating natto for breakfast, that she had slipped them in. I thought about saving some for later but stuck with the "Winnie-the Pooh theory". If my memory serves me right, Pooh was about to go on a picnic when he said, "Why don't we eat all our provisions now, so we don't have to carry them!" That was a smart bear! I hope A.A. Milne will forgive me if the quotation isn't exact! Since I was carrying all my gear on this 3,200 kilometre adventure, it certainly made sense to carry as little as possible, and I strictly adhered to Pooh's theory.

Outside the huge imposing fortress of Matsue Castle I had a chat with a lean, wiry, tanned rickshaw puller. He tried out his rudimentary English, but we had quite a conversation once we slipped into Japanese.

"You can go anywhere!" he said. "I would like to walk the length of Japan too, but I have to work!" Then, strangely, he commented that walking is a luxury! I disagreed.

"But only someone with spare time can walk," he persisted. "Most people don't have the time!" And I suppose he was right. My feet didn't feel like they were participating in some extravagant exercise, but he had a point.

No wonder he looked so fit. He must pull his "jinrikisha" up the steep stone pathway to the castle countless times each day.

I wandered down to the modern business area around the station thinking what a nice city it was. Matsue, Shimane Prefecture's capital, has thankfully missed out on the shabby industrialization that has spoilt so many of Japan's cities. Banners were advertising the new train link to Osaka taking exactly three hours and three minutes. I wondered how many days walking it would be. And what were my wife and family doing?

I watched the news on High Definition TV in a department store and then wandered back out into the dark to meet some friends, sharing their tiny two-room apartment for the night.

My friend's room-mate was training at a women's college to be a kindergarten teacher, so at 9:30 the next morning I was dragged off to English conversation class. There seemed to be an endless supply of giggling girls riding by on bicycles as we entered the college. On the third floor of a large building overlooking four tennis courts, I was stuck with fifteen eighteen-year-old girls for an hour. I wasn't quite what they expected to find in their classroom, and one actually squealed in surprise when she came in late. Their regular teacher, an Englishwoman who spoke with her hands, like many foreign language teachers, seemed happy to have me as a diversion for the day. I told them about New Zealand, my family and my walk. To finish, each of the girls had to ask a question in English.

We went around the room. The first few girls were happy to get their questions out of the way, and the standard simple ones were asked.

"How old are you?"

"How tall are you?"

About half way around the room I sensed panic among the shyer ones who hadn't volunteered earlier. The easy, obvious questions were being used up!

One tiny pimply girl who seemed on the verge of tears finally came up with the best question of the day.

"How do you do your washing?!" But I had put on a clean shirt and socks and everything for the visit!

For the final few minutes, I asked the girls to explain to me how I should get back to the road to Yonago. There was quite a variety of contradictory responses, and after the bell had rung, I was left with one girl who tried to draw me a map. Her sense of direction was about as good as the motorcyclist's who I had met a few days before. By the time I departed she was more confused than when she started. I went out the gate, straight down the road for about 200 metres, turned right, and lo and behold, I was on the road I wanted!

It was very hot. Road workers in full protective gear were trimming the scrub beside the road and staring at me at the same time. I came across a drive-in with about fifty vending machines selling everything from soft drinks, to noodles, to dirty magazines. The parking lot was full, and businessmen in suits took up about half the positions around video game machines. Cigarette smoke hung in the huge "play room" and I got out as quickly as I could. These places upset me. It seemed like social interaction was disappearing. No wonder the small friendly country shops were less and less in number. Everyone was buying everything out of a machine! Do we exist just to exist? Or is there something more to life than eating, drinking, sleeping and being kept amused by machines? What has happened to that famous Japanese culture? Or did I have to buy a portion in a can from a vending machine?

I spent my 29th night in a small business hotel near Yonago station. An acquaintance had arranged it for me, and his "old girlfriend" who ran the place looked after me like a lost relative.

My name was witten in katakana, the phonetic script used for foreign words and names, on a card beside my breakfast when I came down the next morning in my yukata, a cotton, summer kimono provided for guests' use. The rest of the guests were wearing suits and ties, and one sniggered at the sight of a gaijin in a yukata. I smiled back, thinking the same about him in his suit!

Mt. Daisen, my target for the day, came into view soon after I started out. The magnificent volcano, known as "Hoki no fuji," the

Mt. Fuji of Tottori Prefecture, was wearing a white hat of a cloud on its peak, and was hazy in the distance. It gradually drew closer as I plodded past paddies and fields with impeccable rows of white onions.

The attendant in a post office at the foot of the mountain seemed surprised to see me. He weighed each of my three postcards separately. Finding that they all weighed the same, he took ages to find that a postcard overseas cost 70 yen, even though I had told him this before he weighed them. Maybe I don't have an honest face.

At 1,729 metres, Daisen is not a huge mountain, but from sea level, it loomed large ahead of me. I passed the Love Hotel "123". Should it be "123 Bang!" I wondered. The road climbed steeply up the forested lower slopes. At a horse-riding centre, three women riders were being led at a pace well below my walking speed around a small track.

It was hot and I could feel the sweat running down to the ends of my fingers. And still the road climbed. There were marks on the road where tyre chains had bitten into it in the winter. The cicadas laughed at my tired efforts. Would it never end? My calves ached. The road seemed to get steeper and steeper. But finally I made it to the Daisen Visitors Centre, 757 metres above sea level.

I had a good map of the area but was keen to get some up-to-date information on the trails, and also a local's thoughts on the weather. At the Visitors Centre I was introduced to a scruffy, unshaven old bloke who was known as "Sensei" or teacher. He was shown great respect by the others.

"Sensei knows everything about Daisen!" I was told.

"Not a problem!" he said. "That trail is good. It might be a bit overgrown, but you should make it over to the Tottori side easily."

Most climbers of Daisen ascend from, and then descend back into the village. My plans, however, had me going up and over to continue on my planned route without any backtracking.

After a meal of hot noodles and a spree of ration-buying at a tiny over-priced shop, I set out climbing with a much bigger pack. The village was preparing for a summer influx of visitors, and even the temple and shrine that most people come to see were undergoing a facelift. A long skinny snake slithered off the trail just ahead of me.

Suddenly the trail narrowed and I was on my own in dense forest on the rugged volcano. It was steep and tough-going until I reached a ridge line and could look down on the village far below.

Dong! Dong! The gong at the temple boomed out and reverberated around the mountain. The track was covered in roots, and on the ridge the wind whipped through the trees chilling the sweat I had generated. There were some gnarled spots where the track skirted around, or through areas where landslides had dropped down into the valley and there was a spectacular view to Yonago, which seemed to be too far away to be the place I had started from that morning, and out to the coastline. But the view quickly disappeared as I entered the clouds that clung to the sides of the mountain.

I was climbing in the clouds until finally the interestingly-named Utopia hut appeared from out of nowhere. It was a concrete box precariously stuck on a ridge and provided welcome respite from the wind. Any thoughts of reaching the summit of Daisen were well-abandoned by this stage. The weather wasn't up to it, and the last thing I wanted to do was wander off a cliff. Eating my heaviest rations, I took a well-earned break.

Branches has been grabbing at my pack the whole way, and dismayed, I found that my fugu, the blowfish that had been hanging off my backpack, had been ripped off in the climb. I can imagine someone finding it in a hundred years and wondering how a puffed up blowfish wearing sunglasses and a walkman could possibly be halfway up a volcano! Was the mountain once under the sea? Fortunately I hadn't lost my mamori.

It was almost four when I left the hut. The forecast was for rain the next day, and I thought it best to get off the mountain via the route I had been advised was OK. I had an inkling of what was to come when I found the signpost lying in bamboo scrub with all the paint peeled off by sun, wind and rain. Initially the trail was identifiable, but it turned into a goat track that most goats would have trouble sticking to! I was dirty, tired and scratched all over when it disappeared altogether, and I was stuck, swearing at the Sensei at the Visitors Centre. "No problem," he had said! There wasn't even a track!

So there I was, by myself, stuck in heavy forest, with no track, and the bad weather due to come in. Not the best of situations! I found a spur and followed it down through the steep bush, occasionally sliding down on my backside, and wondering if, like my fugu, I would be found on Mt. Daisen in a hundred years! I have a history of broken ankles, and it was not the time for a re-occurance.

I reached a dry creekbed and turned downhill. It was pretty rugged stuff, but thankfully I came across a track, and then a rudimentary hut that I could use to identify my position on the map.

It was 6:30 at this stage, and my tent being a more attractive proposition than the grubby hut, I virtually jogged the final five kilometres to a road. Emotionally drained and physically beaten I finally arrived at the Ikkondaira camping area. It had great facilities but not a soul was there. I wanted to call my wife, but the pay phone only took 10 yen coins and of course, I didn't have any!

It was drizzling when I woke up. I didn't want to get out of my tent. I was stiff, sore, and dirty from my clamber over Daisen.

The place was deserted. Some crows had busily gone through food scraps from my dinner that I had left under the cooking shelter. Caw! Caw! They made quite a racket.

There were about thirty sheep in the paddock next door, the first I had seen on my walk. The crows cawed as I started out into the rain in my bright yellow raincoat, and within a couple of kilometres I had passed two big cattle feedlots and was climbing in clouds on a narrow road. I still hadn't seen a human for the day.

I finally came across a tiny hamlet after entering a long narrow valley. It must have been garbage day, as there was a huge pile of plastic garbage bags beside the road, and an even larger heap of second hand goodies such as a fridge, a microwave, two televisions and a table with chairs. Japanese garbage piles often harbour a hove of treasures, and during a stint in Tokyo, my apartment was partly furnished by the neighbourhood's unwanted goodies. I even have some friends who had plans to export good quality electrical goods they found on garbage days.

The road wound down the valley towards the coast past huge country mansions with perfectly manicured gardens. An old woman was sitting on the ground in her garage beside the road peeling rakkyo, shallots. She looked up in surprise as I passed.

"Gokurosama," she murmured. "Thanks for taking the trouble."

At Nishitakao, which wasn't even big enough to be on my map, the shop owner apologized for still having the locks on his ice cream freezer outside the shop. He was wearing a white singlet and confirmed what I had already guessed.

"A shokudo? No, there are none around here."

"Rain? Yes, it's going to rain all day."

So the rainy season had finally caught up with me. On my second day walking, the TV had announced the arrival of tsuyu, but miraculously, I had escaped the rains for the first month. Any Japanese will tell you that Japan is a land of four seasons, but there are actually six definable seasons. Besides the standard four, there is tsuyu, the rainy season before summer, and akisame, the season of the rains after summer.

Television weather forecasters take great pride in predicting the exact arrival of each season, but the summer of 1993 was going to stump them all. The tsuyu rains hadn't really come, and some people were predicting little rain, while others thought tsuyu would be longer than usual. Of course, the weather was of great importance to me, and my eyes were glued to any forecast I came across.

"Of course the San'in is the real Japan!" the man told me. "The Tokai is just a copy of America!"

I was sitting on the ground eating an ice cream outside a convenience store. It had stopped raining, but I was drained of strength.

"Yes, you made a good choice in walking up the San'in. The scenery is great, but the weather is lousy, especially in rainy season!"

How encouraging!

"Would you like a ride?" he finished lamely, obviously forgetting our conversation about my walking.

It was a long trudge to a temple that was doubling as a Youth Hostel. The huge imposing concrete temple was clearly visible over the paddies a couple of kilometres before I got to it. The priest's wife was totally disinterested as I registered, but I didn't take it personally. She was disinterested in everything. She was watching the news, and even the announcement of general elections for the following month didn't shake her, as it did most of Japan.

The priest was much more interesting. He was fully decked out in his priestly gear waiting for some visitors. We shared a coffee, and while he chain-smoked, he told me about the dank, concrete temple, of which he was very proud.

"The wooden one we had before burned down twelve years ago. It was over 200 years old!"

"What a shame," I said.

"Not really. It was old and run down. We needed a new one!" He smiled, lighting a cigarette in a way that made me think his lighter might have had something to do with the old temple's demise.

Of course I was the only guest. It suited me fine as I could spend an hour in the bath with no feelings of guilt.

The priest's wife scolded me for not doing my dishes the next morning. I felt like scolding her for not emptying the "long-drop" toilet which had become a short-drop. We hadn't hit it off, and when I called good-bye three or four times as I left, there was no reply.

The forecast was good, but it was cloudy. I enjoyed pottering around the back streets before hitting Route 9 on the coast. It was a Sunday, and at the Hawai Seaside Park a large group of middle-aged women on bicycles rode by, somehow managing to avoid catastrophe. Most of them were staring at me as they rode by not looking where they were going. There were fishermen out on the rocks and at one spot, three van loads of snorkellers were collecting seaweed and shellfish.

A grey Subaru pulled over and a bespectacled man in his fifties indicated for me to get in.

"I'm only walking," I said. "Thank you anyway."

"You're walking? Where to?"

"Hokkaido"

"You're walking to Hokkaido! Unbelievable! Will you go through Tottori City?"

"Yes, I plan to be there tonight," I replied.

"Please stay at our house. You would be most welcome. What do you like to drink?"

This was a pretty difficult invitation to turn down!

"We have a daughter," he added.

It was getting even better. So we arranged to meet at Tottori Station and he drove off waving as he left. The prospect of a soft futon, a few beers with this congenial man, and some feminine company was too much to decline.

The roadside stall didn't sell ice-cream. It had an amazing selection of seafood though, including oysters, squid and a few frozen crabs. The couple running it were friendly, though pessimistic about business.

"People are much more careful with their money," the husband said, "The economic bubble has burst, and what with the elections next month, people aren't buying." The Japanese use of the English word "bubble" always intrigues me. It comes out as "bubburu".

"You're lucky! Tsuyu isn't strong on the San'in this year. They're having a terrible time in Kyushu though." Not a worry! I was finished with Kyushu!

His wife gave me a green tea ice cream she kept for herself in the freezer, and as I left, she ran after me with some snacks called "Calorie Mate" and an energy drink.

"Good luck," she said with a warm smile.

A man was playing with his naked children on a beach a little further on, and a group of about fifteen surfers were struggling to get up on some small swells. It's a bit tough on a keen surfer when he has only one day off a week and there are no waves!

The clouds had cleared to reveal a spectacular blue sky. It was a lovely Sunday. A jet-ski roared around, and a young couple asked me to take their photo at a particularly scenic spot overlooking the coast. The "Hotel Camel" sported a camel with two humps. Was it symbolic?

At Hamamura Onsen I avoided the big hotels and was directed by a taxi driver to a tiny local onsen. The old man collecting money was wearing headphones and watching TV, and was startled by my entrance. The single bath was about the size of a double bed and exceptionally hot. I felt like a boiled lobster after only a few minutes.

One of the locals, who was quite a character, opened a window out onto the main street and proceeded to have a conversation with a friend outside while he sat naked, washing himself on his stool. From the bath I had a fairly good view of a woman having tea in her house over the road!

"I come here twice a day," he said. "For my health!" But he was grossly overweight and didn't look too healthy. Maybe a bit of exercise was a better option.

"When does it rain around here?" I asked.

"Whenever I forget my umbrella!" was his reply. When he left he shouted "Gambatte" through the open window as he rode past on his bike.

Who says that Japanese live in crowded conditions?

I passed Tottori Airport on the way into town and saw the most innovative housing I have ever seen. An aircraft fuselage was on an open lot, wings and tail detached, slightly rusty, but with a TV aerial on top and a mailbox outside the door!

The road into central Tottori was lined with neon signs, flashing lights, pachinko parlours, car yards and gas stations. Colonel Sanders beamed at me. Eric Carmen was singing "All by Myself" over the loudspeakers at one place, and an advertisement pasted to virtually every pole encouraged patrons to the Pro Wrestling which was coming to town, starring "The Terminator" and "The Head-hunters".

I duly met my new friend at Tottori station and received an interrogation on the way to his house. He had obviously been scolded by his wife for inviting me home.

"Can you sleep in a futon on the floor?"

"Can you use chopsticks?"

"Can you eat fish?"

"What time do you go to bed?"

"What time do you get up?"

"Are you married? Oh of course not! No wife would let her husband do what you're doing!"

When I surprised him by saying I was married he was instantly disappointed. I found out why when I was introduced to his attractive, divorced daughter for whom he was searching for a new husband. We had a nice evening, but after two beers, they all looked at the clock, announcing that the family went to bed at 9 each night. I found out why. Everyone was up at 5:30 the next morning.

Two girls had got off the bus at the wrong side of the famous Tottori sand dunes. They were from Kyoto, had rung in sick to their offices, and were taking a day off. We trudged over the dunes, me with bare feet and the girls in their heeled city shoes. The sand felt great between my toes.

The sandhills were covered with names written in the sand in huge characters, and as we got closer to the coast the wind picked up. I could see the crowds from a distance, and we were soon at the Sand Dune Centre and among the tour groups. Impeccably dressed groups were trooping through the sand, taking 500 yen rides on bored-looking camels, and trying to get sand out of their shoes. The Kyoto girls took photos with me. After all, I was much more interesting than the camels!

It was with much pleasure that I said goodbye to Route 9 as it turned inland on its route to Kyoto. I was happy to stick to the coast with its smaller roads and less traffic.

The coast was spectacular. At Uradome there were countless accommodation houses, and a big yellow bulldozer was rearranging the sand on the beach. Rocky outcrops hid sandy coves and there was little room between the coast, and the heavily forested mountains. The whole area had a sleepy feel about it, and I also relaxed, stepping down a pace or two into cruise mode.

It was sunny and hot. A group of surfers was making the most of the waves. One was taking a break.

"G'day. How's it going, mate?" he said in a distinctly Australian accent. For once, it was my turn to be startled.

"Yeh, I spent six months surfing on the Gold Coast. Worked at night, surfed during the day," he explained. "I'm from Kyoto, but when I came back I moved to Tottori for the surfing."

I asked him for some advice as to my route. He laughed.

"I don't want to go there by my foot! It's very steep." His English was almost perfect. Just the odd slip-up, and of course, that accent!

There were six little girls playing outside the Higashihama Primary School.

"Oh it's a foreigner!"

"No I'm Japanese," I contradicted them. This produced a lot of funny looks. One came closer.

"You're very tall! And you've got blonde hair on your legs! You must be a foreigner. But you speak Japanese!"

I left them there playing in the sand. The school was perched above the waves, and was covered with brightly-coloured flower boxes. A well-tended, attractive community asset. A few hundred metres on, I turned. The little girls were still waving at me and, I think, wondering if I really was Japanese.

Uncrowded beaches before the summer vacation!

According to a map at the tiny station, Higashihama has sixty-five minshuku. When I stopped for an ice cream, though, the woman in the shop told me that only about half were still in operation. There were only a few young people living in town, and as the owners got older, they closed their minshuku. The town was packed in the summer holidays, she said, but that was only for six weeks a year. It was impossible to make a year-round living relying on tourists. The town had an attractive white sandy beach and the waves were rolling in. I made a mental note to take my children there in the future, but not in the summer holidays.

Just after three I crossed into Hyogo Prefecture. The road was high above the coast, winding around tight corners and dropping, then re-climbing all too regularly.

A huddled fishing village along the San'in coast.

Igumi was the first fishing hamlet I came to in Hyogo. The harbour was full of squid boats, and an unshaven old man in a track suit was staring out to sea.

"I have a bad back," he said, "so I can't work. Usually we leave at 5 in the evening, fish for squid all night, and return at 7 or 8 in the morning. Then we sell at the market here. What's not sold locally is sent off to Kobe and Osaka."

The village had a population of 670, he said, and I could see the houses huddled close together so as to protect themselves from bad weather. There was an unmistakable smell of fish in the air, and squid were drying on racks beside the footpath.

"The weather forecast says rain," I said to him. "What do you think?"

"It won't rain today," he replied, and I felt that the wiry, silver-haired old fisherman was more likely to be correct than the TV weather forecaster.

"How far is it to Moroyose?" I asked, turning to leave.

"Ichi ri chotto," he said. A little over an hour walking. In the past, one "ri" was the equivalent of what a man could walk at normal pace in an hour. It was considered to be about four kilometres. I knew that my normal pace was five kilometres per hour, so I was about an hour away from my target. It intrigued me that in Japan, a land known for precision in time and measurement, I could still find someone who calculated distance in "ri".

Empty, broken crab shells lined the road on the way out of the village. Crash! What was that? Crash? I looked up.

"Caw! Caw!" Crows! Dropping crab shells out of the trees onto the hard road, trying to break them open to get at scraps of meat. Crash! Crab shells stolen from a huge pile at the fishing harbour. All the best meat taken by humans. Caw! Caw!

Moroyose had a small harbour, protected by fingers of land jutting out into the ocean and a huge concrete breakwater. I had made a reservation at the Youth Hostel and had to share a room with an American named John. Having been in Japan a total of three weeks he considered himself an expert on the country, and was single-handedly on a mission to correct the trade imbalance. He also had a big mouth and couldn't stop talking. I just sat and listened with a pot of sake admiring my ability not to get into an argument with him.

My 34th day on the road was a day of climbing and descending under a hot sun and bright blue sky. It was impossible for the road to stick to the rugged twisting coastline. It turned inland with a calf-hardening climb to a pass, followed by a knee-knocking drop down the other side into a fishing village back on the coast.

On one such descent, I ran into a young man who was pushing an old rusty bicycle up the hill. A duffel bag slung over his shoulder, he was wearing heel-less slippers and puffing badly. Our eyes met. We had something in common. Physical exhaustion! He was on his way to Shimonoseki. He just shook his head and laughed when I said that I was on my way to Hokkaido.

At Amarube, the road passed under a 48 metre high railway bridge that towered above the tiny fishing village. The road turned inland, but with the aid of the long trestle bridge, the railway could stay out by the coast.

And underneath was a statue. A memorial statue to the six people who had died when a train tumbled off during a winter storm in 1986.

"It was just lucky that there were so few people on it!" said the big-smiling lady shop-keeper with the silver eye-tooth.

"Why is it that gaijin who speak Japanese speak it so correctly? People around here speak so badly that it's hard for even me to understand sometimes!"

Her shop was dark inside, and I'd put my sunglasses on top of my cap when I'd entered, so I would't forget them. Of course when it came time to leave, I couldn't see them anywhere.

"What are you looking for?" she asked.

"My sunglasses! I'm sure I had them when I came in!" She was giggling uncontrollably.

"They're on top of your head!"

Route 178 turned inland at Satsu, leaving me with a magnificent, little-used toll road along the coast. Near Satsu Station was a spectacular field of purple and white irises between a couple of decrepit, weather-battered buildings.

"Do you sell them?" I asked an old man working in the field.

"No I grow them each year for people to come and look at," was his smiling reply. "People come from a long way away to see my irises!" he said proudly.

John Denver was crooning "Country Roads" over the loud-speaker system at a roadside drive-in above the coast. But there wasn't a sign of life. Overgrown undergrowth was trying hard to hide a bus that had been left to rust and rot between the trees.

No-one answered my call.

I was the only person in the shokudo at Takenohama, a bright little town on the coast. The proprietress made me an oversized portion of gyudon—shredded beef and onions on a bed of white rice, with red ginger thrown in to add a "bite."

"You should see this place in mid-summer!" she said. "Between July 20th and August 20th you can hardly move as there are so many people on the beach. And you can't get a carpark."

When I left, she gave me a ticket to the onsen, a new building overlooking the beach with a spectacular view. I relaxed in the sauna, listening to the piped enka, traditional Japanese music, and staring out to sea.

I set up my tent in the dark at the camping area on Bentenhama Beach just as it started to rain. Within a few minutes I was in my sleeping bag as it poured down outside. The rain stopped about midnight, and unable to sleep, I sat on the beach watching the bright lights of the squid boats far out to sea and listening to their radios. The crackle and talk carried over the still sea. I missed my family, wondering what my wife and sons were up to in Osaka, not really all that far away.

It was raining again when I got up and the wind had picked up. Waves were crashing over the breakwater, and I could see this sort of weather was not uncommon. The pine trees I had been camping under were bent over at extraordinary angles away from the sea.

People were putting out their garbage, and children were heading off to school under umbrellas as I trudged back through town and out onto the toll road around the magnificent rocky coastline. Every now and again I came across huddled hidden hamlets in reclusive coves. The wind and the rain tried to drive me off the road, but I stuck to it and finally reached Seto.

A good looking woman was selling frozen crabs to no-one. It was June, and winter is the season for crabs. She was reading a newspaper in her stall and we talked while I recovered with an ice cream. My map showed a potential shortcut, but neither she nor the other two people I asked in the village knew of it. I stuck to the road I was on!

An old woman on a motorbike that was hauling a home-made trailer cruised by with a big smile on her wrinkled face. She was delivering vegetables and I passed her several times on her round, only to be overtaken a few minutes later. After three such meetings she stopped for a chat. She must have been near 80, with gold in her teeth and a real sparkle in her eye. Her local dialect was taxing, but we battled through. She handed me three big red tomatoes.

"I grew them myself!" she said proudly. "Eat them when you get to the pass. You'll need them by then!"

She wasn't wrong.

I didn't think the climbing would ever end, but just as I entered Kyoto Prefecture in cloud and spitting rain, a sign marked the pass. The descent was much steeper and I virtually tumbled into Kumi-hama, at the southern tip of a lagoon-like bay of the same name.

The town seemed dead. As I was looking for a shokudo, an unshaven, scruffy guy with dull eyes came up and thrust his hand out for me to shake. He smiled revealing big black gaps. The teeth he had were tobacco-stained yellow. The stink of alcohol mixed with his breath nearly knocked me over.

"Where are you going?" he grunted.

I had a little debate with myself over the answer. I had found that if I answered "Hokkaido" to this question, I would inevitably be trapped for ages answering the next string of unbelieving questions. Whereas if I answered with the name of a town not too far down the road, I could avoid this hassle.

This looked like a situation worth avoiding. I plugged for the second option.

"Mineyama," I replied.

"Mineyama? Mineyama?" he questioned. "What will you do in Mineyama?"

Trapped. I suppose I could have said I had a friend in Mineyama, but being honest, I said, "Well actually, I'm walking to Hokkaido."

"Hokkaido? You're walking to Hokkaido! What are you doing in Kumihama?"

"Looking for a shokudo," I answered truthfully, eager to escape his company. Another local was staring at us. The gaijin and the town drunk. What a pair! "Is there a noodle shop in town?" I asked.

"A noodle shop?" He looked confused.

"You know, ramen, udon!" I encouraged him.

"Yes, yes, I know. Let's go together." So we wandered the backstreets of Kumihama until we arrived at a great little udon shop. Udon are thick white noodles, as compared with the thinner grey soba, and Chinese ramen noodles. He showed me the entrance, but looking sheepish said that he wasn't welcome.

"I am alcohol," he announced somewhat proudly in English. We had been speaking Japanese and his words took me by surprise.

"Yes, you are," I uttered, feeling sad for him.

The shop had a concrete floor and five small tables. My entrance caused quite a stir. Partly because my backpack almost knocked the sliding door off its rails, and partly because the dumpy woman owner who had huge arms uttered a loud "urghh" when she saw me. The four patrons just stared.

Once I had made my comment on the weather in Japanese, though, everyone went back to what they were doing. I sat next to a poster of Konishiki, the massive 260 kilogram Hawaiian Sumo wrestler, feeling a little less conspicuous. Boiled eggs were 50 yen, and while munching out, a local and I pored over my map, looking for the best route to Miyazu.

"I always wanted to bicycle the length of Japan," he said, "but I never got round to it. Now I have a wife and children..."

"Big One Pachinko" was doing a roaring trade as I turned inland onto Route 312. The click clack of machinery making silk cloth for kimono was with me much of the afternoon. Rather than in a big factory, the cloth was made in small sheds attached to individual houses, I had been told at the shokudo. It was a major source of income for the area.

Some of the old buildings housing the machinery looked so decrepit that I could push them over. I resisted the temptation.

"Liquors and Gift Nose" was written in English above a shop in one small village. I spent a full five minutes staring at it, wondering what they could possible have been trying to write. Actually the lack of interesting Japanese English, or Japlish as it is sometimes called had been a disappointment. Japlish has been providing gaijin with a few good laughs for years but recently with the influx of foreigners into Japan, most of the major boobs have been fixed.

In Omiya, where I stopped for dinner in a teishoku restaurant, I shared a table with a truck driver. He had a crewcut and was smoking while he was eating.

"You're looking for a place to stay? You don't need a place to stay! You have a tent, don't you? You can put it up anywhere. Nobody will complain. There's a temple a few kilometres on. On the right. Why don't you put your tent up at the temple?" He was gruff and had the direct Japanese that is common among truck drivers.

"Good luck," he grunted as I left.

I took his advice. It was dark by the time I found the turnoff to the temple, and the road was lined with rice paddies, filled it seemed, with croaking frogs. It wound up into the hills to a set of stone steps. As soon as I set foot on them, a safety light came on, illuminating the area, and after I had called out a couple of times at the entrance, an elderly priest shuffled out to greet me. He didn't even blink on spotting my gaijin face and was quite happy for me to pitch my tent beside the old wooden temple.

"Please be careful with fire," he said. "This temple is 80 years old. The previous one burned down!"

One of my better camping spots!

There had been a temple at that site since the year 1260, he said, and he had arrived there at the age of 4. His father's elder brother had been the priest, and when his father died, he was sent there.

"Life was hard when I was growing up. We had the task of rebuilding Japan after the war. Nowadays, youngsters have the time to play soccer and baseball. I'm envious. We were busy building roads. The youth of today are reaping the benefits of our hard work. But they don't seem to appreciate it!"

He had the typical priest's crew-cut but was in a casual shirt and trousers.

"I have to get changed," he said, looking at his watch. "We have parishioners coming. You are welcome here."

I pitched my tent beside the temple. The complex was rectangular with a large open area in the middle. The temple was at one end, with the priest's residences down the sides and the large entrance gate at the other end. I sat on the well-worn wooden steps, gazing at the stars in the dark cloudless sky. The wind whistled through the tall bamboo surrounding the temple.

The first wave of guests arrived, obviously perplexed by the purple one-man tent pitched in front of their temple.

"Don't worry! Don't worry!" the priest reassured them. "It is only a wandering foreigner." I waved, smiling my sweetest smile.

A few minutes later, someone started playing the piano. I knew I recognized the first few bars. What was that tune? And then it came to me. It was hardly what you would expect to hear at a Buddhist temple! "Glory, Glory Hallelujah!"

I had told the priest that I would be up and away early, but when I crawled out of my tent at 7:15 he was pottering away in the garden. And he had already been to the market in Miyazu to buy vegetables at 5:30!

"I've been to Tokyo," he said. "And to Osaka. But I could never live in a big city. I've been here my whole life, and I could never leave. I love it here!" He was a contented man.

As I strode back down to the main road, an old man was pushing a baby buggy full of farm tools to work. He was wearing a straw hat, a khaki sweatsuit and tabi (Tabi are Japanese style socks that have hard soles and look a bit like mittens. The big toe has its own compartment, while the other toes are bunched together.) He just stopped and stared, ignoring my hearty "Ohayo gozaimasu." Further down the road, I looked back. He was still staring.

Amanohashidate, the Floating Bridge of Heaven, is famed as one of the three classical sightseeing spots in Japan. It is also the place where legend says that Izanagi and Izanami, the Gods of Creation, formed the islands of Japan with the dribbles from their jewelled spear.

The bridge itself is a three-and-a-half kilometre long sandbar covered in pine trees, that separates the Aso Lagoon from the sea. I took advantage of the warm peaceful weekday to sit on the sand in bare feet and take what I thought was a well-deserved rest. An occasional group of well-dressed tourists wandered around the southern end of the bridge. Once again, I thanked my good luck for not having been there in the weekend.

I was feeling quite buoyant, and with good reason. After 36

days and 1,200 kilometres of walking, I was about to meet up with my wife and elder son Riki for a day of rest and recreation. Quite a prospect for a walker with sore feet.

I virtually flew around the coast to Miyazu, consuming curry with a deep-fried pork cutlet for lunch in a busy resturant. I am often astounded to find long-drop toilets in fairly modern buildings, but the one in that Miyazu shokudo really captured my attention. It even had a high-pressure water pistol-like attachment for washing away any debris! I wouldn't want to let my son loose in there.

I had just turned a corner in the rocky coastline and was faced with the long sandy beach of Yurahama when two cars, heading in opposite directions, stopped to offer me a ride. Out of a huge rust-coloured 4WD Landcruiser hopped a short tubby priest in his gowns. He must have just had a shave, as there wasn't a sign of hair on his head. His big black eyes were magnified by thick glasses.

"Where are you going?" That debate again.

"Hokkaido."

"You're going the wrong way! Hokkaido is back that way," he laughed, pointing back the way I'd come.

I laughed too. "No, no, Kyushu is that way. I've just walked from Kyushu. Hokkaido is this way," I replied indicating the direction I was going.

"You're wrong," he insisted. "I'm on my way to a temple in Tottori and it's this way."

"I'm sorry, but you're wrong. I've just come from Tottori."

"Look, we'll ask this man," the priest replied, his big eyes blinking away. A young man from the other car on the far side of the road came over.

"Haro, I help you," he said falteringly in English.

Oh no, I thought, what next. The priest grabbed the young guy by the arm.

"This gaijin is walking to Hokkaido. I was just telling him he's going the wrong way."

"He's walking to Hokkaido?" The young guy was confused.

"Yes, I'm walking to Hokkaido," I threw in to add to the confusion, "And I'm going the right way."

"You're walking to Hokkaido?" he repeated. "Well ah . . ."

"Are you from around here?" I asked him, a little frustrated.

"Yes I'm from Maizuru."

"Which way is Maizuru?" He pointed in the direction I was going.

"Which way is Miyazu?" He pointed in the direction I had come from.

"So which way is Hokkaido?" I felt like I was teaching a geography class. This one had him stumped.

"Well, it must be this way," he replied, pointing to the way I was going. The priest was a bit red-faced.

"So Tottori is that way," he said quietly. "Oh! . . .Why are you walking to Hokkaido?"

"I'm looking for the real Japan. I don't believe the Tokai is the real Japan. I'm looking for it." I knew this would produce a silence, and it did.

"Wait a minute," he said, scurrying off to his 4WD. He was back in a couple of minutes, thrusting a 10,000 yen note at me.

"No thank you, I have enough money."

"Please take it. It is my donation to your search. People give me lots of donations. You are doing a good thing," he insisted.

I looked at the young man in the black baseball cap. He nodded in agreement.

"Well thank you very much."

"I have to go. I'm very late," he said. "Please remember me." And he raced off, squealing a U-turn and headed off in the direction he had come from.

"Priests are very rich. Everyone gives them money and they don't pay any tax," the other driver commented enviously. "Will you teach me English?"

"I'm sorry but I have to meet my wife at Yurahama station in ten minutes," I lied.

"Would you like a ride?"

"Thanks anyway, but I'm only walking."

And ten minutes later I did meet my wife at Yurahama station quite by accident. She was two hours ahead of schedule and was leading our two year old out of the station. She looked more beautiful than I remembered.

We walked inland, into the hills to the Government lodge, and had a marvellous day off, swimming at the sandy white beach.

5. FROZEN BADGERS

The two-carriage train pulled out of the tiny station, and I waved to my wife and son until they disappeared far in the distance. I was alone again.

I crossed the Yura River mouth on a railway bridge. The walkway was beside the single track, and a yellow line marked how close it was safe to venture. The wind was whistling and wind-surfers ripped along below me. There wasn't much room and I was relieved to reach the other side without encountering a train. A surprised old lady working in her vegetable garden pointed me onto a minor road into the town of Maizuru. I could see a constant stream of cars on the main road on the far side of the river.

Maizuru is an industrial port and the scenery matched what anyone would expect. Huge oil tanks and cranes towered above me, and everything seemed rusted. I escaped the man-made may-hem, ducking into a yakiniku shop for lunch. Yakiniku is basically strips of meat, either chicken, pork or beef, that the customers cook themselves on a grill in the middle of the table. The meat is then dipped in a tangy sauce and eaten. The teishoku, or set menu, that I ordered included miso soup, pickles and tabehodai (eat as much as you like) rice.

On my entrance though, the waitress squealed and disappeared out the back. From what I saw of her she was quite cute, and I wasn't as impressed by the waiter who had obviously drawn the short straw and come out to serve me. He relaxed when I spoke in Japanese, and the waitress even reappeared. I devoured three bowls of rice to the surprise of the assembled staff, and the waitress presented me with a Kiss Mint candy when I left.

The port, often visited by foreign ships, was truly international. There was a ten-pin bowling complex, a KFC outlet, and even a red London double-decker bus outside McDonalds. The "Fresh No. 1" supermarket had a huge Statue of Liberty holding an over-sized banana as its logo. And to my surprise, three separate gaijin rode past on bicycles as I walked through town.

The road headed inland up a long valley, and the humidity rose rapidly until it was positively sticky. Nasty billowing black clouds were coming in from the sea, although it was relatively clear ahead. A woman walking her dog and carrying a pooper-scooper warned me that it would rain heavily for thirty minutes and then stop. It held off as long as it could, until the inevitable happened.

The skies opened and a torrential downpour pounded the ground around me. Fortunately, the eaves of a coffee shop beckoned, and although it was closed, I spent the next half hour sprawled out on the entrance mat with my shoes off. My wife had brought a second pair to our meeting, and they were well into their first day. I had learnt my lesson well and was busily attacking them with my pocket knife when the rain stopped as suddenly as it had started. The humidity had dropped sharply and it seemed like a different day. Only the huge puddles paid testimony to the ferocity of the precipital attack.

A dog hurtled out of a garage, teeth bared, and fortunately, like in a cartoon, reached the end of his chain only inches before reaching my leg. I swore and pretended to kick him, but then felt sheepish as I noticed his owner staring at me out a window. Dogs are a major hazard for walkers, and whilst I hadn't been bitten, on several occasions I had jumped nervously at attempted attacks.

The sun was out. Steam was rising off the road, and the stroll down to the coast from the pass was pleasant. But by the time I reached Shirahama, all the shokudo were closed. There was a barber shop called "Hair Box", but little else was open at 7 pm. After buying provisions at a supermarket, I wandered down to camp beside the beach.

Camping at Shirahama, Fukui Prefecture

The camping area was on sandy ground in a stand of pine trees next to the beach. I was the only camper. Waves broke on the beach only metres away.

Rustle! Rustle! It was after midnight. Rustle! Rustle! Something was going through my garbage bag. Had I left any tasty morsels? I poked my head out of the tent, and a large white animal bounded off into the bushes. I rubbed my eyes. What was it? It looked like a polar bear! But I doubt it!

Sunday morning, the 39th day of my walk produced 100 percent blue sky. Not a cloud in sight.

At 6:30 six autocampers from a bit further along the beach were hitting sand wedges at a bucket. They weren't too good and golf balls were flying in all directions with much hilarity. A family was already out picnicking as I enjoyed a swim in the cool clear water before setting out.

At Wada beach, the sand was being shoved around by a bulldozer, preparing for a busy day, while the odd cluster of girls in bathing suits caught my eye. Maybe summer had arrived! I hoped so!

The road followed the coast for much of the morning with the sea sparkling on my left, forested hills inland.

I had lunch at Obama in a fast-food noodle shop. The staff wore red and white striped uniforms, and the restaurant, part of a chain, was sparkling clean. The noodles tasted mass-made, without the character of the classic little old noodle shop. My feet were aching, and after eating, I sat on a rock in the parking lot lancing a huge blister on my left heel. My new shoes were taking their toll. A family in the noodle shop were watching me, but when I waved, the mother tried to attract her kids' attention. No way! The gaijin was much more interesting!

I decided to walk in thongs, which initially brought great relief. Once again the road turned inland, away from the twisting coast. Up yet another valley filled with rice paddies from the mountains on the left to those on the right. A sea of green. When I had left Kyushu in May, the paddies were mud, with only freshly-planted seedlings, but by that stage, in late June, on the Japan Sea Coast of Honshu, those seedlings had grown so that a vivid green covered the countryside. And they still had months to grow before harvesting in late September, early October.

I almost walked right past the Wakasa Onsen. It wasn't marked on my map and was in what looked like an office building. It was markedly different inside though. There was a TV in the sauna and I watched the end of a women's golf tournament with a man from Osaka who was dreading the drive home that evening.

"My wife is from around here. I bring her and the kids back to see her parents about once a month. We always drive back to Osaka on a Sunday afternoon!" he moaned. "The traffic is diabolical! I always prepare myself for the drive with a visit here. It's the only place I can relax."

I alternated between the sauna and the "mizuburo", the cold water pool, and felt totally refreshed.

I felt even better when, only a few kilometres later, Route 303 and much of the traffic headed off right to Kyoto and Osaka, leaving me to head back out to the coast over yet another pass and down another paddy-lined valley.

A small statue surrounded by pots of sake, cans of beer and instant noodle packets marked a spot where someone had died in a road accident. The presents were for the deceased. His favourite food and drinks. It was tempting on such a hot day.

"Don't do it!" said my conscience, sitting on my shoulder. I left the beer where it was.

Mikata looked promising on my map, but there wasn't much there. One open shokudo next to the sleepy station. Kindly, an elderly couple let me in the back door to their already closed shop to buy provisions. The old man filled my water bottle, saying:

"Gambatte, you're still young, so you can do it!"

It was dark and I was walking with my torch by the time I reached Mihama. Pachinko Dynamic was packed with avid pin-ballers and I could see all the smiling red faces in the restaurant next door through the window. A young man drew me a map to the camping ground where, of course, mine was the only tent. I had covered 52 kilometres for the day, and my feet felt like it. How had I got that far?

It was about 8 in the morning when I walked back through Mihama. Schoolchildren on bicycles raced by, and at a car repair shop, the staff were doing calisthenics to what I assumed was the company song. The manager was leading by example, exercising with great enthusiasm. There wasn't too much energy being exerted by his staff though. One of the women waved when she saw me watching.

The new Hatogayama tunnel, at 1,790 metres, was the longest so far. It took twenty minutes to get through, and I was relieved that it had a footpath. On emerging, the smoggy smokestacks of Tsuruga, another industrial port, beckoned, and it wasn't with much joy that I plodded towards them.

I had managed to walk right through the rubber on the bottom of my thongs when using them through especially painful periods. The sight of a large discount shoe shop brightened me up. Surely a shop of that size would have some thongs big enough. And they did! One pair of bright blue, high-heeled thongs with "Lightening Bolt" written in yellow over the strap. But my feet were so sore that I had to have them.

So I marched into Tsuruga in new sandals. The high heels forced me to use previously unused muscles in my legs which started complaining before too long. The soles of my feet felt as if they had been belted with a hammer for the last forty days, and my lower back started to ache. Things weren't going too well.

"What the heck am I doing this for?" I asked myself, for not the first time. And to help myself come up with a decent answer, I slipped into Mister Donut for a coffee and two chocolate donuts. The Beach Boys were singing "Surf City" almost thirty years after it was made and the sales girl told me to "Have a nice day" in English. I could see a ten-pin bowling alley over the road and I knew that Colonel Sanders and Ronald McDonald were bound to be lurking around the next corner. They were. Was this the "copy of America" I had been told about a few days before? Was this the real Japan? If not, what was it? Obviously Western culture had arrived in Tsuruga!

I jumped up and hobbled out. Out of Tsuruga as fast as my battered feet could carry me. Out onto horrible Route 8 with its roaring trucks spitting foul fumes, and its murky dark tunnels. I wasn't in a good mood! But what could I do except plod on and persevere. I could hardly pack it in and give up. So I kept going.

"Where are you going?" asked a young man in a suit. He was one of nine people waiting to fill twenty-litre plastic containers at a fresh water spring beside the road. There was a queue and each group had the maximum of five containers. The fresh water gushed out of a tap underneath a Buddhist statue. There was silence as the group waited for my answer.

"Well, today, I'm going to Yokohama," I replied. There was a village called Yokohama about six or seven kilometres further up the road according to my map, and it was my target for the day.

"Yokohama!" One old lady gasped incredulously. "How are you going? By bullet train?"

"I'm walking," I said, wondering what she was going on about. "It's not far, is it?"

"Eh! You're walking to Yokohama! You'll have to take the bullet train to get there today." Mine was not the only look of confusion. And then it dawned on me.

"I'm not going to the Yokohama that's near Tokyo! Isn't there a village called Yokohama just up the road?"

They all looked at each other. Nobody knew. So I pulled out my map, and yes, the village of Yokohama wasn't too far way.

"I'm from Tsuruga. I just come here to get fresh water," one man said, explaining his lack of local knowledge. It was generally agreed that I didn't have to queue since I only had a water bottle to fill and because I still had a way to go.

"He's walking to Hokkaido," one woman told her elderly mother.

"Ask him if he would like a ride to Yokohama," I heard her reply.

As it was, I didn't quite make it to Yokohama. I dropped into the Suizu Post Office to see if there was any reasonable accommodation nearby. Two middle-aged men sat at desks down the back, while a young man and giggling girl were up front to serve customers. There weren't any! Only me, and I was there to ask questions. I asked if they were busy and even the older guys laughed.

Yes, there were plenty of minshuku and ryokan in the seaside village, the young man said. Would I like him to call one and make a booking, he asked. He tried one.

"Hello. It's Tanaka from the Post Office. There's a gaijin here looking for accommodation. Do you have room?"

Silence.

"Yes that's right, a gaijin."

Silence.

"Oh! Well thank you anyway."

He tried another one. Same answer. He glanced back to one of the managers, who looked ready to take control. The older man was short and tubby, with a haircut that looked like a barcode on a billiard ball. He was wearing a grossly-bright silk tie that had me almost reaching for my sunglasses.

"I'll sort it out," he laughed at the younger man. The girl giggled.

He tried a number but with the same result. The girl giggled some more.

"Perhaps you'd better not say that I'm a gaijin," I said. This idea appealed to him. He tried it.

"Moshi Moshi. It's Sato from the Post Office. We have a guest here looking for a place to stay. Do you have room?"

He smiled at me, signalling OK. The girl giggled.

"He speaks Japanese very well. You shouldn't have any problems."

Silence.

"Oh, I'm sorry, didn't I tell you it was a gaijin!" He smiled at me. "You need time to prepare? OK! I'll bring him down at 5:30."

I had been the only customer for the half-hour or so I had been in the Post Office.

I left my gear, and using the directions I had been given, wandered off to fill in an hour at the shokudo.

"Oh I'm so glad you can speak Japanese!" sighed the owner and his elderly mother. "The last gaijin who were here couldn't speak a word! They were looking for a place to stay. Or at least, they made babies' sleep-sleep motions with their hands. So we rang the love hotel over the road. But we couldn't get them in until 11pm. The hotel was busy until then. So we had to entertain them for three hours! It was terrible! And we had to explain to them about staying at the love hotel. It was such hard work! I'm so glad you speak Japanese!"

I could see why gaijin are treated with such intrepidation!

Mr Sato walked me down to the minshuku. He must have been feeling bad for the owner, as he couldn't stop apologizing to her for all the trouble he was causing.

And there was no doubt that she looked as if she'd been cheated. Once we'd had a good chat though, everything was all right, and she became positively bright when I did my own washing. Her non-automatic washing machine was outdoors beside the road, its dirty water pipe dangling into the storm-water drain. The wringer was broken, and made a roaring sound louder than a truck. The sight of a gaijin doing his washing in Suizu was obviously unusual, and I attracted more than my fair share of attention.

I was the only guest, with two huge rooms to myself on the second floor.

"Weekends are busy," she said. "Fishermen come from Osaka and Nagoya, but weekdays are quiet." It was a Monday. "I wasn't expecting any guests tonight."

The TV weather-forecast wasn't very encouraging. A 100% chance of rain for the Fukui coast, with heavy rain warnings.

Swanee River blasted out all over Suizu at 6 am. The rain was pouring down outside. What is the point, I thought, of waking up everyone at 6 o'clock on a rainy day? I snuggled up in my futon.

The weather forecast hadn't improved. There were now flood warnings for Fukui. I watched the news on four different TV channels but all said the same. I thought about lying low for the day, but by then I was so used to getting up and walking that I couldn't. My washing was still wet and I cursed the fact that very few houses boast a clothes dryer. The owner must have been feeling sorry for me as she gave me a 500 yen discount and a packed lunch of rice balls to eat along the way.

So at 9 o'clock I was plodding through puddles and pouring rain. My friends at the Post Office laughed at the sight of me, the spotty girl giggling uncontrollably. After twenty minutes I was not in the best of moods.

I was completely soaked from head to toe by the pelting rain, despite my raincoat. Water oozed out of my shoes with each step, and I had given up avoiding puddles. My left arm was black from being squashed up against tunnel walls. And my legs were aching from the previous day's efforts in high-heeled thongs. I was not a happy chappy.

But then I met another walker and realised how lucky I was. I could see him ahead of me and, increasing my pace, caught up just before yet another tunnel. He was 49, he said, and he looked every bit of it. Unshaven and almost toothless, he was wearing a plastic bag on his head, a grubby whitish towel around his shoulders, and a cheap plastic raincoat. He was staring at the ground ahead and mumbling to himself.

He was, he said, a victim of the recession. Originally from Ono, some two days walk away, he had lived and worked as a labourer in Tokyo for the previous seventeen years without once returning to his hometown. The economic downturn had eliminated many construction jobs, and his had been one of them. With no employment and no savings, he was now forced to return, unable to cope with Tokyo's high living costs. His family were in Ono, and having used all his money for a train fare to Tsuruga, he was now stuck walking for three days. He had no luggage. Only a plastic shopping bag containing some dried squid.

He wasn't a fast walker, and my pace slowed so we could stick together and talk. We shared my rice balls, escaping the persistant rain in a bus shelter. What a pair! I certainly felt lucky. At least I was choosing to plod away through Japan. My new friend had no choice. He was in "survival mode".

We parted a few kilometres further on when the heavy rain drove me into a small restaurant for lunch. I gave him the rest of my obento and watched him slosh off into the distance.

Twelve construction workers were playing cards under an unfinished overbridge as I trudged into Takefu, their tools lying idle. The rain was pounding down. Only an idiot would be out walking!

"Are you French?" asked a gas station attendant. That was a new one!

A young policeman was talking on the phone to his girlfriend when I entered the Police Office outside Takefu Station. The sight of a miserable wet gaijin didn't faze him. He cupped the receiver, curtly asking me what I wanted.

I had been hoping to get an introduction to some cheap lodgings, but he just sent me out to try the three ryokan near the station. Raindrops were still bouncing off the pavement, and not surprisingly, all three of the ryokan became mysteriously full, despite the lack of shoes in the entrance halls. By the third refusal, my frustration was growing and showing. I managed to drip quite a puddle at the last place, to the annoyance of the owner.

I was running out of options. Back to the Police Station. The young policeman was off the phone and had been joined by two others, older and obviously superior in rank. All three sported crew-cuts and wore spotless grey uniforms. I hit it off with one of the older guys immediately.

"You're walked from Suizu?" he asked incredulously.

"Well actually, I've walked from Kagoshima."

"From Kagoshima!? There are flood warnings today, you know."

"Yes, I know," I answered, dripping all over the floor.

"Well we'd better find you a place to stay." He was on the phone for all of thirty seconds, before sending me off with a grin and a wave to a three-story accommodation house that catered mainly for visiting out-of-town workers on a long-term basis. I was happy to have a bath and just nap away the wet afternoon. The bear-like owner and her cock-eyed sidekick were watching cartoons on TV when I emerged for an evening stroll. They didn't endear themselves to me by laughingly saying that rain was forecast for the next four days!

It was pouring as I headed out on day 42. I was wearing my yellow raincoat with the hood up to keep the rain from trickling down my neck and soaking me completely. The only problem was that my peripheral vision was reduced to the point where I bashed my head on a "Beauty Salon" sign that was hanging too low. Not a good start.

The Hino River was a muddy brown raging torrent. As I crossed the long bridge, schoolkids riding bicycles, with extended umbrellas, greeted me. "Haro! Haro!"

I was heading straight into the mist-enshrouded mountains. My three-week march along the Japan Sea Coast was over, and turning inland, the mountains were to be my friends for the next three. My maps were to be of prime importance. On the coast, I didn't need to consult them too often, as rugged hills inland kept me close to the sea, heading in one general direction. The mountains were a whole different story. There were three different routes I could take to Ono, none of them direct. Maps needed to be carefully consulted and locals asked for advice.

The new problems I would be facing were brought to reality in a convenience store in Imadate. The three people in the shop all advised me to take different routes, and when finally they came to an agreement, another customer chipped in saying that the chosen road had been closed by a landslide in the previous day's rains! The prospect of an extra two hours walking for the day didn't appeal. Luckily the owner took pity on me and telephoned the local constabulary. Finding that the road was open, he told me the good news.

"That's great!" I said. "Will the weather clear?" They all laughed. Obviously it wasn't going to be my day.

The road I was on headed straight up the side of a river valley with forested mountains on both sides. The valley was filled with brilliant-green rice paddies with a hamlet of houses every kilometre or two. Village names were marked on the bus stop signs.

A bus crawled up the hill beside me at a snail's pace. The driver couldn't take his eyes off me, and neither, it seemed, could his contingent of elderly passengers. I smiled and waved, but they all just stared.

I stopped in a small shop where the lady owner and six locals were sitting on chairs sipping hot tea. There was a unified gasp at my entrance.

"Can you tell me how far it is to Ono?" I asked. There was a unified sigh of relief. According to my map, it was only 32 kilometres to Ono, but the last street sign had said 40. Such discrepancies don't matter when you are driving, but I can assure anyone, they get right up a walker's nose. My question caused a bit of consternation.

"It's about an hour," said an old man who was wearing a hat and sunglasses despite the rain. "You're wet!" he added.

"Well actually I'm walking." Another gasp. "Do you know how many kilometres it is?" I addressed the spokesman.

"You're walking! You're walking to Ono?" He confirmed my idiocy to the assembled gathering. "Well . . . it must be about 50 kilometres!"

This didn't make me feel any better. "According to my map, it can't be much more than 30," I said.

The crowd murmured. An elderly man gave up his chair and a cup of tea was put in my hand. My backpack was dripping on the floor. And then we had the battle over my map. It seemed fairly simple to me. Up that valley to the pass, turn left down the next valley, right up the next to another pass, and then drop down into Ono.

After ten minutes the owner was peeved at me. She insisted her advised route was much quicker, and it might have been by car, but to a walker, it looked nearly twice as far. She was more upset at the old guy in the sunglasses who had totally pooh-poohed her suggestion.

The rest of the throng debated the pros and cons of the other two possible roads, ending up in agreement with my proposed route.

"You're smart," an old lady told me. "You must be smart. We only let smart gaijin into Japan!"

The valley gradually narrowed, then started climbing steeply up to the pass. I was out of the paddies and into heavy forest, when I stopped for a chat with some roadworkers. They looked at me as if I were a bear that had come out of the woods.

"It's about 40 kilometres to Ono," one told me. By my estimate it was about 25! "Watch out for bears!" he added as I headed off. Not very encouraging.

I emerged from the tunnel at the pass into the Shimizu Valley. The characters for Shimizu stand for "clear water" and the valley was spectacular as it gradually widened. I walked the last kilometre or so into Nojiri with a bent-over old lady, who assured me that yes, three kilometres down the road there was a shokudo. Nojiri would best be described as an outpost. Its one store was the JA, the Japan Agriculture Co-operative shop, which catered for all sorts of needs. As well as being a bank and a Post Office, it also served as a shop for locals, selling food and farming equipment.

The old lady and I entered together, much to the wide-eyed amazement of the couple who ran the place. My wrinkled walking companion went off to do her shopping a couple of aisles away. It wasn't that I didn't trust her, but I wanted to confirm the existence of the shokudo before leaving. My map wasn't showing much ahead.

"Excuse me, the old lady tells me there is a shokudo a few kilometres down the road. How far away is it?" I didn't want the old woman to hear me questioning her information, but I could see that she was straining to listen.

"A shokudo? There's nothing between here and Ono!" the woman replied. Then for the old woman's benefit she added, "There used to be one, but it closed years ago! Nobody ever comes out here now."

"Yappari," I thought. "Yappari" is another of my favourite words.

Roughly translated, it means "just as I thought" or "as can be expected". If a Japanese saw a gaijin doing a particularly gaijin-like activity such as wandering out of the toilet still wearing the toilet slippers, he might say to his mate, "Yappari, only a gaijin could do that."

In this particular case, my "yappari" was based on the fact that the old woman, as I had suspected, probably hadn't been out of Nojiri for years, as she didn't know that the shokudo down the road had been closed. "Yappari, I was right."

I readdressed the lady behind the counter. "How far is it to Ono?"

"About twenty kilometres" was the reply. I was staring out the window at a road sign about one hundred metres down the road. Clearly marked on it was: Ono, 28km. This was starting to get frustrating.

The rain was pelting down outside. I bought some bread, cheese, and a grilled fish and sat eating on the bench in front of the banking counter. The lady who acted as the Postmistress, bank teller and shopkeeper brought me some green tea and interrogated me about my walk. It was lunchtime and during the next hour it seemed that the entire population of Nojiri plodded through the rain to the JA to perform their various chores. Each was given a full explanation of my existence, and of course, I was encouraged to "Gambare" along with receiving some strange looks. "Yappari. The gaijin is strange. What is he walking the length of Japan for?"

I was back on the road at one o'clock and was thoroughly soaked within a few minutes. An elderly lady who I had met at the JA cruised passed on a bicycle, an umbrella protecting her from the rain. She stopped a little further down the road, waiting for me outside a ramshackle building that turned out to be her house. As I drew up, she held out her brown spotted umbrella.

"I would like to contribute to your walk. But I have only this. Good luck!"

I had done a lot of planning before setting forth, but an umbrella had not made my list of things to take. The idea of walking through Japan under an umbrella hadn't even occurred to me, but I found the error of my planning. Spot, as I nicknamed him was to become a great friend as I battled through the longest rainy season in recent memory. I can heartily recommend to any long-distance walker— take a brolly!

Suddenly the rain became bearable. I romped down through the Ashibe River valley, turned right up a tributary valley and finally, after a seemingly endless climb, reached the tunnel at the top of the pass. I was feeling positively perky. I wrote my name and the date with my finger in the dirt on the tunnel wall, just in case I should run into a bear. At least my movements could be traced that far! I strode through the tunnel yelling loudy and listening to the echo.

The five roadworkers at the far end of the tunnel must have been wondering what was coming. "Yappari, a gaijin! A Japanese wouldn't make such a ruckus."

Ono emerged through the clouds far below me, and I tumbled out of the mountains into the old castle town. I was totally pooped by the time I got to the station. The police station was closed.

With the help of a kindly local I found a room in a small ryokan, a Japanese-style inn.

"If you didn't have a room, I was going to take him home to my place!" I heard him tell the owner. "My wife would have been surprised!"

I was even given a big room, as all the small ones were full. It had been a long 44 kilometre-day in tough conditions. I needed a bath.

The owner tried to get me to wear geta, wooden sandal-like clogs, when I went for an evening stroll, but my feet were so sore, I couldn't even get them on! On my return, he lectured me on the history of Ono and convinced me to explore the town the next morning.

Ono was worth exploring. After a breakfast of ham and eggs which I suspected were cooked specifically for me, I headed out along the route the owner had designed for me, leaving my gear at the ryokan to pick up later.

First was the Asaichi, the morning market, where from March to December, from 6 am each day, vegetables, fruits and trinkets are sold by venders who sit on the cobbled sidewalks. Most of the vendors seemed to be wrinkled old ladies with terrible teeth, some with their backs bent at amazing angles from too many years working in the fields.

Ono Castle sits atop a lone hill overlooking the countless temples below. The castle itself is now a museum and the surrounding grounds, an immaculate park. It seemed like a serene world, suspended above the town. But then I could hear electioneering vans below, racing about with their singular loud messages.

"I am Masuda Kazuhiro. Vote for me! Vote for me! Masuda Kazuhiro. Vote for me!" So often that it sounded like a tape recording. Didn't he have any policies?

Two old men were sitting on a bench admiring the view.

"Thanks for coming," said one. "Not so many people come here. If we had a bullet train, lots of people would come to see our beautiful castle! But the Government's not interested in Uranihon, the back of Japan. They just pour all the money into the Tokai and forget us!" He was quite bitter.

"Please tell people about the beautiful town of Ono!" said his mate as I left.

I visited Ono's famous fresh-water spring with its pure drinking-water and, on my way back to the ryokan, noticed my reflection in a shop window. It didn't look quite right. What was it? Then I realised. I was walking without a backpack!

The road out of Ono headed straight for a "V" in the mountains, the Kuzuryu River gorge. Before long I had left the plain, with its fields and paddies, and was into the steep sided gorge. Overhead signs encouraged safe driving, and the dents in the metal safety barriers along the road, showed that their existence had saved many vehicles from plummeting into the river far below. Scars in the road had been caused by tyre chains, and in places the road was covered by a steep roof to keep the snow off in the winter.

I was walking into the "yukiguni" or "snow country" quite happy it wasn't winter. The road shared the gorge with a single train track, and in the small village of Katobara, I took a break in the JA, the Japan Agriculture Co-operative shop. It was next to the station. A total of seven trains per day passed through the seventeen-house village, and surprisingly the lady running the JA had been to my hometown in New Zealand. She was a ski racer, recently retired, and spent the winters on the nearby skifield.

"The amount of snow gets less and less every year," she complained. "And the ski season gets shorter and shorter."

The gorge has several hydro-electric dams, and at one man-made lake, a fisherman in camouflaged gear gave me some riceballs wrapped in cabbage leaves. He had driven from Nagoya, leaving at 3 am, and was heading home without a catch, even though we could both see fish jumping out on the lake.

The gorge was narrow and steep and there was barely enough room for the road. The railway track had disappeared into a twenty kilometre tunnel far before.

I hadn't seen anybody for what seemed like hours when I

rounded a corner and found the Heisei no yu Onsen. It was a lovely wooden building with a rotenburo, an outside bath that looked out into the forest, and I spent an hour soaking in the hot water. It was run by a friendly family who were so concerned at the sight of my feet that they gave me all sorts of pads and medicines. I was having a lot of problems with the big toe on my right foot. The nail was in-growing, and the pain when I put my shoes on was excruciating.

Around a few more corners, scars on the side of the mountains marked my destination for the day, the Kuzuryu Skifield. Ski runs had been cut in the forest, and chairlift pylons were easily recognisable. My map marked a campground there, along with a resort village, catering for skiers in the winter, and mountain-lovers escaping the sticky hot east coast in the summer. There were accommodation and eating houses, and I dined at the "Restaurant Windy", chatting with the lady owner who had arrived by way of an introduced marriage from Hokkaido twelve years before.

"I haven't been back. It's just too hard to get to from here."

The "Pub Theatre Aurora" had certainly figured out how to make its profits. Its sign advertised its "eat all you can, drink all you can" evenings. "Tabehodai, nomihodai." Males were welcome for two hours for 6,000 yen, while women had to pay only half that amount.

The only other camper had come by car, and was so happy to see me that he broke open a 700 yen bottle of whisky which we consumed during the course of the evening.

"I've never seen a bottle of whiskey so cheap" he explained. "I just had to buy it to see what it tastes like!" It tasted cheap, but certainly kept out the mountain cold.

My auto-camping friend was well-equipped. He had a fold-out table and chairs set, a BBQ and all sorts of fancy lights and cooking appliances. A social welfare worker, he was on his way home from a conference.

"My wife's going to kill me! She's pregnant. Told me to come straight home . . . but I couldn't miss a chance to go camping."

We discussed social welfare, politics, and the state of the world until we weren't capable of discussing anything at all!

There was no doubt in my mind that it had been a cheap bottle of whisky. In fact there was very little in my mind when I crawled out of my tent. It wasn't only the sky that was cloudy. Fortunately, my friend was well-equipped for such an event. We shared strong coffee for breakfast, and by the time I set off at 9:30, he had decided to take it easy and visit the hot springs that I had been to the day before. He wanted to be in tip-top condition before facing the wrath of his pregnant wife who had expected him home the night before. He wasn't sure she'd believe his story about drinking with a gaijin!

I spent the morning on a curving road surrounded by forest heading deeper into the mountains. It followed the river, skirting its long narrow man-made lakes, frustrating me on more than one occasion, when I thought I had found a shokudo. I found only the boarded-up wrecks of old buildings.

Then, just after midday, and still suffering the effects of bad whisky, I stumbled upon on old, run-down wooden building that boasted a sign saying "shokudo". The equally old and run-down couple who ran the place had just come back from picking mountain vegetables, and welcomed me with all sorts of delicacies. The building, they said, was 111 years old, was all wooden, and had been built without using any nails at all! I believed them. It looked like it could come crashing down around us at any second!

The shokudo was undoubtedly the dustiest, most cluttered I had ever been in. It doubled as the local shop, although I had't seen another lived-in building for hours and doubted if there were any other "locals". Cans and jars were piled high along all four walls. Great slabs of keyaki, zelkova trees, served as tables, and there were few windows to let in any light, the reason being that winters were so cold, the old lady said. The walls were adorned with prints made of fish caught in the lake just outside. Instead of stuffing trophy fish, Japanese tend to make a print by dipping one side in ink and pressing it onto paper to preserve the exact memory of its size.

The collection of stuffed animals surveying the room was amazing. Various birds, a badger, a deer and a fox were all staring at me, while iwana, char, swam about in a huge fish tank, ready for human consumption. Even a mamushi, the pit viper snake I had been warned about, was coiled with its jaws sprung in the bottom of a huge jar containing home-made alcohol.

"It's good for my bad back," the old lady said, laughing like a hyena. . . .

Her grey, unkept long hair made me think of a witch, and her grin revealed only one front tooth. She had a pot belly to match any elderly beer guzzler, and she sported a fair bit of facial hair. A real character.

Most of the year, she said, fishermen drove out from the cities in the weekend. They would arrive at about 3 in the morning, fish all day, drink all night, then depart just before the next lot arrived. She didn't get any sleep, she said, thus explaining her haggard appearance. If they were too drunk she didn't let them drive, making them sleep in the next room.

"It's lucky you came on a Friday, or I wouldn't have had time to talk to you!"

She showed me pictures of winter. The building was virtually buried in snow. No one came, she said. Life was hard in winter. And then she revealed her eccentricity. I had asked her about wild life. Going to the freezer, she pulled out some frozen bears' claws. I wasn't too keen on the idea of wild bears, but I tried to look brave.

"Do you eat them?" I inquired curiously.

"I would if I knew how to cook them!" was her reply. She dug deeper in the freezer. I wasn't watching. My eyes were fixed on a bear's skull on a bookshelf!

When I decided that staring at the bear's skull wasn't doing my confidence much good, I looked back to find her cradling a furry object as if it were a baby. She was even petting it like a kitten. I looked a bit closer. It was a badger! But not a normal badger. It was a frozen badger! And it had come out of the freezer.

"I keep him to show my customers. They all want to see a badger." She had me worried. I wondered if she had a frozen gaijin in there!

I changed my lunch order to noodles! What could she possibly hide in a bowl of harmless noodles?

By the time I left, my education had been broadened.

The sign said specifically that only cars and trucks could use the new tunnel. Walkers, cyclists and motorcycles had to use the old road over the pass. I swore, wondering if I should pretend to be a hopeless gaijin who couldn't read Japanese street signs. But surely there was a reason.

So I walked the extra three or four kilometres in pouring rain and then began the long descent into the Nagara River valley. The road snaked down the mountain, past a snowless ski resort, past

A frozen badger!

huge construction for a new freeway linking Nagoya and Koyama, and finally into the town of Shirotori, population 12000, and hometown of some good friends of mine. "Spot", my umbrella, had kept me relatively dry, but my main discomfort was my toe, which was rebelling against the constant punishment.

It didn't take much to convince me that a day off was in order. With this in mind, it didn't take too much persuasion from my friend, a sports teacher, that I needed a minor operation on my toe.

"Not a problem!" he said. "Do it all the time!" he said. "Won't feel a thing!" he said. "Perhaps you'd better have some sake first," he added. So I polished off a bottle of sake.

Quite a contingent of teachers from the school had turned up to meet me. I'd had a friendly tussle with the judo coach who accidently caught an elbow in the nose. We were all quite merry, and even the surgeon looked wobbly.

And then operation time arrived. My toe was wrapped in ice for twenty minutes as I beefed up the anaesthetic. Surely I wouldn't feel a thing. But I didn't like the look of the needle that was being heated to be used to pop my bloated balloon of a toe and then slice the nail.

One teacher sat on each shoulder, one on each leg and the operation began. I couldn't see what was going on, but it didn't feel good. Suddenly, sharp excruciating pain. That's all I can remember!

6. HIGHLANDER

The road climbed steadily following the Nagara River out of Shirotori and into the mountains. The river was wide, shallow, and swift-flowing, mostly white-water, but every fifty metres or so there was a fisherman in a straw hat angling for ayu. The ayu is not caught with ordinary bait. It is a small fish, about 20 centimetres long, that defends its territory with great gusto, which leads to its downfall. The bait is a plastic ayu look-a-like with hooks sticking out which is cast into the river. The ayu, thinking its territory is being invaded, attacks the bait by knocking into it, thereby foul-hooking itself. It is considered a delicacy, which explained the uncountable numbers of hopeful anglers out on that warm, sunny Sunday.

Ski areas were appearing with regularity, and the resort of Hirugano Kogen boasted 68 accommodation houses of various levels. The noodles I had for lunch and the provisions I bought at the supermarket were outrageously expensive. I was preparing for a night on the road as, on my map, villages were few and far between. I wandered out of town, past the "White Pecker Pension" and the snowless ski slopes.

The road was all over the place. Twisting, climbing, descending, until finally I was on the road to Takayama. Unexpectedly, I came across a small shokudo in time for dinner.

"Ichiban subarashii kosu!" the young chef told me. "The best possible route!" He had come out of the kitchen to check out my map and give me some advice. "Urayamashii!" (I'm jealous) he whispered so that his mother, who ran the place, couldn't hear. "I would love to do what you are doing, but . . .". He was 24 and, being the chonan, the eldest son in his family, had traditional responsibilities to his parents that his mother seemed intent on enforcing. She was keeping a close eye on us, making sure I wasn't corrupting the one who would look after her in her old age.

"You are doing a great thing," he encouraged me, with obvious anguish. "I am stuck here!" He didn't make the final comment, but I could read his mind.

The climb to the pass seemed endless. I was surrounded by a newly-planted pine forest. About 400 metres from the tunnel at the pass, a black sports car roared by. It sped into the dark tunnel. Suddenly there was a squeal of tyres, a roaring engine, and I waited for the crash. Instead, the car shot out of the tunnel backwards and screeched to a halt about a metre from my sore toe. The dark tinted electric window buzzed down to reveal not the mafia-types I was expecting, but a pimply young couple about 18 years old. The blast of "heavy metal" just about knocked me over.

"Would you like a ride?" the girl asked shyly.

"Thanks anyway, but I'm only walking," I replied.

She smiled and was about to say something, but her boyfriend hit the accelerator. The car shot off like a bullet and was in the tunnel in two seconds flat, leaving me staring at black tyre marks on the road. I felt a little vulnerable.

It was already dark as I wandered into a tiny village of about fifteen houses, wondering where to spend the night. There was nowhere to pitch a tent, and the hamlet didn't boast a shop, let alone a place to stay. Frogs were croaking in the paddies.

I wouldn't have noticed the run-down house hidden in the darkness, or the man sitting in its shadows, had it not been for the cigarette the man was smoking.

"Where are you going?" he asked, breathing heavy alcohol fumes over me.

Since I wasn't in a hurry, I opted to tell him about my journey. I finished by asking him if there was a place where I could pitch my tent.

"Well there's the shrine . . ." he said. "It's going to rain, so you'd better be under cover. I'll just check next door at the Mayor's house." He raced off for a couple of minutes and, returning, led me up a side road to an old wooden shrine. It started spitting as we arrived, but there was plenty of room under the wooden roof to keep out of the rain.

"Please make sure you don't burn it down!" was his only request.

I laid out my sleeping bag out of the wind, using my backpack as a pillow, and stared out at the now pouring rain. A bolt of lightning lit up the valley and the shrine roof above my head. I was open to the elements, yet protected from wind and rain. It was a nice feeling.

Towering trees surrounded the little shrine. The rain hadn't let up, and it had turned cold overnight. I was wearing a jersey for almost the first time on the walk and lay snuggled up in my sleeping bag, not keen to get out of my warm cocoon.

Stone statues covered in lichen and moss stared at me through the heavy rain, and I could see steps leading up to a larger shrine building in the forest above. My breakfast as I lay there was of cold fried squid and chocolate rolls. Then at 7:15, depressed by the rain, I was back on the road, with Spot protecting me as best he could.

The rain continued through the morning, and after a couple of hours I was hobbling, thanks to my sore toe and ankle pain, the result of a break a few years before. I took rests in little bus shelters that had their owners' bright-colored personal cushions on the benches. Most had a dustpan and brush for keeping them tidy, and were spotless.

There were very few villages until Mikka, where I found 500 yen on the side of the road and used it to buy my lunch.

Takayama is a tourist town tucked in the mountains, often visited by gaijin. When I purposefully strode into town to complete my day, I didn't notice one head turn to stare at me. It made me feel reasonably normal again! The girl at the Visitors Centre at Takayama Station spoke robot-like English and didn't even come close to breaking into a smile. She gave me a map in English and sent me on my way, before I could ask any of those tricky questions that gaijin are notorious for.

Takayama, like Ono where I had been a week before, is famous for its Buddhist temples. It is known as "little Kyoto," and it was at one of those temples, the Tenshoji, that I spent my 47th night on the road. The temples are in a line, to the east of the station, on a hill overlooking the town. The Tenshoji moonlights as a Youth Hostel, and it was with great relief that I sank into a futon for a nap in the late afternoon. I knew I had a big night ahead of me!

My friend in Osaka, who had presented me with the beer coupons, had an uncle in Takayama who liked drinking. I had had to call Osaka to get the uncle's phone number, but everything was arranged for me to meet him at his restaurant. The only problem was that the priest insisted the temple door would be locked at 9:30!

"But I have an important meeting," I said, all to no avail.

I turned up at the appointed time, and the uncle, who treated me as if I were his nephew, produced the specialty of his restaurant, eel. I don't know how many ways there are to cook eel, but I tasted all of them that evening. And I ate every part of an eel that I imagine it is possible to eat. We knocked off a bottle of sake while eating.

"I should show Craig-san around Takayama!" the uncle said to his wife in a big loud voice. She was onto him though!

"Don't make him drink too much. He's got a long way to go!".

We left her in charge, wobbling out into the street. First stop was the pharmacy, which was just closing. His friend the chemist, a fellow Rotarian, took one look at my toe, produced all the necessary goodies and announced that I'd be fine in a week if I followed his advice.

Serious business completed, we ducked down a side alley into another world, the entertainment zone. The first bar we entered specialized in raw shellfish. The owner was an "old girlfriend," my new uncle admitted with a smile, and we were well looked after. She even rang the Tenshoji to announce that I would be late home, but only managed to get the priest to extend my curfew by half an hour!

Next stop was an "Akachochin" or "Red lantern". Small bars can be easily identified by lit red lanterns that hang outside their doors. The specialty of the house is usually written in kanji on them—"yakitori" or "soba". This particular one specialized in Chinese noodles, or ramen. My new uncle was obviously a regular. A town celebrity. It seemed that everyone knew him wherever we went. I ordered my favourite, chashumen, and received a steaming hot bowl of noodles in soup, capped off with thick slices of pork, bean sprouts and spring onion. A feast fit to finish the night.

My new friend returned with me to the Tenshoji in order to placate the priest, but even though it was well after 11 when we arrived, the doors were unlocked.

"Tell him you were with me," my new uncle said as he staggered back down the street. I wasn't sure if that was a good idea.

The theme tune of "Arthur" was the temple alarm-clock. I was feeling the result of the evening's excesses, and when I sat down to the standard Youth Hostel breakfast of rice and raw egg, I was surprised to find that my egg didn't break, no matter how hard I battered it. It had been hard-boiled!

"My egg's hard-boiled," I said to the priest's daughter who was watching me with intrepidation. After all, I was the gaijin who had broken his curfew!

"Yes, that's right" she agreed.

"Can I have an egg like him?" I said, pointing at a nice raw one a Japanese bloke at the end of the table was mixing into his rice, along with some soya sauce.

"But gaijin don't like raw eggs," she told me.

"I eat anything," I said, cursing those gaijin who had come before me and not eaten their raw egg. I suppose that it was nice of them to boil me an egg, but I was sick of being different. Couldn't I just be regarded as normal, and be given a raw egg like everyone else?

But then another gaijin came in. He sat down with a cup of tea.

"Your egg's been boiled!" I said.

"Oh thank God!" he exclaimed. "I'm Buddhist and I come here once a year. But I can't stand the food!" I felt like throttling him.

I stopped for some noodles at a drive-in in the mountains. Two youngish women wearing the blue apron and white hair-scarves of staff were stealing looks at me and giggling, their hands covering their mouths. I smiled my best smile back.

"What are you laughing at?" I enquired. They giggled.

"Ashi ga kirei—you've got beautiful legs!" one said. Not even my wife has told me that!

"You're very brown, and you've got such blonde hair!" The other said, reaching out and rubbing my arm. I looked at my arms, then my legs. Yes, they were brown, weathered by a month and a half of walking in shorts and short-sleeved shirts. I reached down and pulled my shorts a bit higher up my thigh, revealing the standard lily white skin of someone with my complexion.

One blushed. The other squealed and the manager came over to see what I was doing to his staff.

I was climbing a long river valley, and it felt good to put my map away, take my watch off, and wander on.

A businessman in a suit and tie stopped and tried to force me into his car. He was speaking halting English, and I could see he wanted a free lesson. He was so upset that I wanted to walk, refusing to accept his kind offer, that he eventually slammed the car door and roared away in a most agitated state.

Then the climb steepened. My calves were aching. The hairpin curves carried me higher and higher into the forested mountains. There was nobody around. Not a soul. And then I heard it.

"Fujii Takao, Fujii Takao. Vote for me. Vote for me. Thank

you very much. Fujii Takao, Fujii Takao . . ." over and over. Mindless political campaigning that would be banned as noise pollution in most countries. Sure enough, a campaign car finally appeared with three green-gloved doll-like beauties waving in unison along with a man who I assumed was Fujii Takao. They waved at me with great enthusiasm. I'm sure there hadn't been anyone to wave to for ages. Campaigning was really hotting up with the elections less than two weeks away.

The tunnel at the pass was two and a half kilometres long, and it took me half an hour to stride through it. When I finally reached the high point, it was after five, and I had been climbing constantly since 11 that morning! The drop into the hot springs resort of Hirayu was spectacular in that the road spiraled down on concrete legs. It clung to the side of the forested slope and passed a bare green ski area, until finally levelling out into the resort village.

My new uncle in Takayama had arranged my accommodation at his friend's minshuku, and through his introduction, I was warmly welcomed. I must have been a tad smelly after my 39 kilometre day as the owner's wife seemed keen for me to have a bath. I duly obliged and soaked in the hot murky water that came straight out of the ground.

I shared the bath with a 52-year-old grandfather from Kanazawa who proudly announced that he was staying with his mistress. His exact words are difficult to translate, but basically, his main complaint was that she did not "put out" enough. There he was, spending all this money, risking castration at the hands of his wife, and he wasn't getting as much as he wanted. So to speak.

Then he became inquisitive. There I was, wandering around Japan all on my lonesome. Was I "getting any?" He had heard that Japanese women were very "kind" to foreigners. He looked me up and down as I got out of the bath, saying that yes, he was sure Japanese women would be kind to me.

Dinner included raw horse meat, a delicacy in the central mountains, and a small trout that the owner had caught himself. I sat with a couple aged around 60, who marvelled at my perseverance.

"A Japanese would have given up by now and called a taxi" the husband said. "Or if a Japanese had the konjo (guts) to do what you're doing, he certainly wouldn't come into the mountains. He would stick to the coastline".

They had visited some caves earlier in the day which are well known for the calcium in the water. The husband, recently retired from a pharmaceutical company, forced me to drink three cupfuls from a flask they had filled in the caves. He then decided, as had my friends in Shirotori, that he should operate on my toe. His work background, coupled with his phenomenal sake consumption had convinced him that he had what it took to be more than a competent surgeon.

When I finally escaped and got to bed, I found that the owner's wife had laid out two futon, end on end, as she thought I was too long for one!

My new friend, the self-proclaimed toe surgeon, sat at the breakfast table and drank a full bottle of beer before he started eating. Since retirement, this was his body's daily morning requirement, he said, grinning at his frowning wife.

My eyes were glued on the weather forecast. It seemed there was a possibility that the recent rotten weather might clear and give me a decent shot at climbing Japan's fourth highest mountain, Yarigatake, or "Yari" as it is affectionately known. My excitement was building, as this was one of the major goals on my walk, and it looked like I could achieve it on my 50th day out.

"Don't worry," said the toe surgeon. "Even if it rains, you'll be OK. Yari is so high that you'll be above the clouds!"

So it was with bubbling enthusiasm that I said my sayonara, passed the Cafe Moustache and headed out of town. My initial goal for the day was the Abo Pass, at 1,780 metres above sea level, crossed by the highest national road in Japan.

The climb was steep, through beautiful forest. Birds were crying, and the sound of running water was constant. The serenity was only broken by the sound of my laboured breathing, and every now and then by a car that struggled past in low gear, spitting black fumes. The Grandfather and his mistress overtook me, waving their encouragement, followed by the "beer for breakfast" retiree.

At 10:45 after an energy-sapping climb, I was finally at the pass, crossing into Nagano Prefecture. The man running the one tiny shop sported a scraggly black moustache and beard, with hair dangling down below his shoulders. He was so impressed that I had walked from Hirayu that he presented me with a drink. But he flat out wouldn't believe that I had walked from Kagoshima. He spent the summers running his little shop high in the mountains. But as the road was closed much of the winter by heavy snow, he spent his off-season working in a factory in Tokyo. He left little doubt as to which he preferred.

Hirayu Onsen tucked high in the mountains
of Gifu Prefecture.

To make up for all the climbing I had done, the road snaked down what seemed like a near-vertical mountainside. With each hairpin curve, I could see the road below through the trees. On one such corner, I met a huge sightseeing bus, slowed to a crawl by the tight turns. The full complement of faces stared out at me, from barely a metre away.

By the time I had reached the turnoff to Kamikochi, it was lunch time, and I took a break at the cabin on the corner. It was real mountain country. I was in the heart of the Japan Alps.

"The only way into Kamikochi in the winter is to walk!" said the owner.

The sign above the entrance announced that, due to congestion, private cars were not allowed up the dead-end mountain road from the 10th of July until the 3rd of November. I was glad it was only the 7th of July. Surely it would not be busy!

I entered the dark tunnel opening wondering why there was a green traffic light. There didn't seem to be any traffic. Water was gushing out of the ceiling and the uphill gradient in that narrow hole in the rock seemed too much. Suddenly the world changed. Or at least, the light must have changed. The line of 23 vehicles that had built up at the red light at the other end of the tunnel poured by, pressing me up against the wet walls. The eighth car was my "beer for breakfast" buddy and he slid to a halt, wound down his window and thrust a hand out for me to shake.

"Incredible! Incredible! You've walked all this way!" His wife leaned over, handing me a can of cold tea, while the vehicles behind that had narrowly avoided a mid-tunnel tail to tail pile-up honked their horns.

By the time I reached the far end of the tunnel, another 18 cars were lined up at the red light. The sight of a wet gaijin emerging from that dank hole was too much for the couple in the first car. I got a good view of their jaws dropping, and the reaction wasn't much different from the next 17.

The road wound up the spectacular Azusa River Valley. The river looked pristine and inviting, while the mountains towered above on both sides. Huge rock scars marked spots where avalanches had rumbled down into the valley, carrying all vegetation before them. The sun warmed the valley, and by the time I had reached Kamikochi village at the end of the road, I had built up quite a sweat. The carpark was full, as was the visitors centre.

After my experiences at Daisen where the trail I had been advised was fine turned out to be a goat track, I thought it advisable to find out about my planned route over the mountains.

"No problems! Easy to follow! Popular track!" the man in the information centre said. It sounded familiar. The exact same words as the fellow at Daisen.

Rations for hikers were outrageously over-priced, but I had no choice. I bought three days' worth, which bulked up my backpack, waved goodbye to the fashionably-dressed tourists who were watching me, and set off at three o'clock. The trail for the first ten minutes or so was packed. But after I passed the famous Kappabashi Bridge where cameras clicked continuously, numbers reduced considerably, and I was soon on my own. I took the side track to look at the Myojin Lake, famous for its reflections, but was so disgusted at the prospect of having to pay 200 yen to look at a lake that I voiced my opinion to the startled official and stomped off. Back on the main trail, I stopped at a hut that was selling refreshments. Choosing an ice-cream that had 100 yen written on the wrapper, I took it up to the counter to pay, passing over the appropriate coin.

"That's 150 yen," the man said.

"But it's got 100 yen on it," I showed him.

"All ice creams are 150 yen," he insisted.

"You're joking! It says 100 yen!"

"It's 150 yen!" He was getting agitated.

"Keep it then you robber!" I said, slamming it on the counter. I reverted to English for this final comment. I was getting in a foul mood, and my stride lengthened as I left so-called civilisation behind.

The valley and the track gradually narrowed. Mt Hotaka loomed high to the left with patches of snow extending down low. It was great to be back in the mountains, but my body needed to adjust to a different type of walking. On the roads I could walk without lift-ing my knees, but on the rough mountain track, I needed to pass over tree roots and rocks. My ankles weren't enjoying themselves.

Then at 6:30 I stumbled upon a mountain lodge that was barely marked on my map. It was hard to believe that, come the summer holidays, thirty-two people would sleep in the room I was given. For the month from July 20 to August 20 the whole area would be teeming with vacationers, and once again I was happy with my timing. There was only a group of six bankers from Osaka, three men and three women. I didn't want to climb alone, and so I accepted their invitation to join them the following day. The only problem was that they planned to leave at five! We shared some plum wine, and anticipating a big day, I was in bed by 8:30.

"Be careful on this mountain!" I thought to myself before going to sleep.

Thursday the 8th of July was my 50th day out. It was also my earliest start. At 5:00 am we were taking a team photo outside the lodge, and barely ten minutes later, my sore right ankle was moaning about the infringement on its rest time. It wasn't any happier in the snow a bit further on either, and was becoming a worry.

Climbing to Yarigatake (3,180m) in the North Alps.

We passed the remains of a mountain hut that had been destroyed by an avalanche. Further testimony that I wasn't out on a Sunday stroll. Yarigatake shouldn't be taken lightly.

My banker friends weren't in peak physical condition. We were climbing in untracked snow, and my fifty days of walking was better preparation than their office hours. The valley was full of snow and the map said to follow it to the top. One of the girls went for a slide. She screamed as she slid 50 metres on her backside into rocks, but all was OK. It was taking too long to get anywhere, so I pressed on ahead.

The head guide at the hut just below the summit was a big guy with ears like cauliflowers. He had been a keen judo man.

"Do you have an ice pick and crampons?" he asked. "Because if you don't, you should probably give up on crossing the mountains to Nakabusa. The trail is still covered in snow in parts. If you go you'll be the first person to cross from the Yari end this season! You should have come a few weeks later," he said.

Oh no! An ice pick, or crampons, hadn't made my list of things to take. And the bloke at the Visitors Centre had told me that my intended route was in good condition!

"They never come up here!" said Big Ears. "Most of the people they talk to only walk as far as the Kappa bridge!"

To go back around the long way would add a couple of days walking. I explained my situation. Fortunately, he was sympathetic.

I left my backpack and set about the final push to the top, while he radioed ahead to see if anyone knew what the track to Nakabusa was like.

Yarigatake, at 3,180 metres has a spear-like peak. With steel ladders and chains embedded in the near-vertical rock over the last couple of hundred metres, the peak is accessible to those who have made it that far. I clambered up to find myself alone to celebrate my achievement. Of course, the view was spectacular, but my joy was tempered as I looked down on the trail to Nakabusa. It is known as "Ginza Juso" because the numbers crossing it in mid-summer are similar to those walking in the Ginza in Tokyo. But at that time, in early July, there wasn't a soul. I carefully picked my way back down to the hut. The whole area was potential broken-ankle territory, and I was well aware of the dangers of hiking alone.

My big-eared mate had been watching my descent. He was standing there with an ice-pick.

"You look pretty confident in the mountains. Take this," he said, handing the ice-pick to me. "Do you know how to use it?"

"Basically," I replied. He gave me a quick demonstration anyway.

"If you slide, dig it in and hold on!"

He hadn't been able to get through to anyone on the radio.

"Just drop it in when you get to Nakabusa Onsen," he said, giving me the address. "You should be OK. I'd go with you, but I have to work. I'll radio through to the Otenshou hut at 6 to make sure you've made it. If you haven't, we'll come looking tomorrow! Good luck!"

Very encouraging!

"Here, take some water," he said as I was leaving, giving me a litre of water that was for sale at 200 yen. Water was helicoptered in as rainwater was considered not safe to drink. It grated against my principles to pay for water, but it was certainly better than paying 300 yen for a can of drink that cost 110 yen at the bottom of the mountains.

He laughed at Spot, strapped on the side of my backpack.

"Everyone thinks I'm crazy, wandering around the mountains using an umbrella! But I see that you're crazy too!" We had something in common, and I could sense our mutual respect.

The track to Nishidake was along a narrow ridge line. Every now and then, the ridge was knife-edged and the trail had to drop off to one side or the other and skirt through areas of snow that still covered slopes of rock scree. Over these narrow areas of snow and ice there was nothing to hold on to, and most extended downwards for three or four hundred metres. A slip would mean a lengthy slide at speed into the rocks below. It was scary stuff and I knew that a slide would result in a night outside with some sort of injury.

The first two such crossings went well. I was on the left of the ridge, using the outside of my inner foot, and the inside of my outer foot, digging them into the snow. The ice-pick was in my outer hand, ready to dig in should I slide.

On the third crossing I did just that. I overbalanced into the slope and my feet slid out! Instinctively my left hand dug the ice-pick deep into the snow. It didn't hold! I was still sliding, but slowly, as the pick dragged my speed down. And then it dug in. I lay there panting. I dug in my knees, then my feet, and slowly headed back up the slope on an angle to where the track was marked at the far side of the snow.

"What the hell am I doing?" I asked myself. But I didn't have much choice. I wasn't going to go back. That left only one option. I kept going.

Once again, steel ladders and chains made the trail passable. The final climb to Nishidake was steep, and breathing heavily, I took frequent breaks. But Nishidake was only half way. It started to drizzle and I was walking in cloud. There was more snow to cross, and a couple of times I broke through up to my knee. Yarigatake appeared through the clouds far to my left, and it was hard to believe that I had been sitting on top of it barely four hours earlier.

I was completely exhausted. My ankle was ready to give up,

while my right knee, which still has some floating cartilage from an old rugby injury, was complaining bitterly. My right hand had a deep cut on the palm from poor use of the icepick on a slide, while some blistering was the least of my worries.

But then almost dead on 5 pm, the hut appeared out of nowhere. To say that the staff were surprised to see me is an understatement. I was their first guest for the year, and they couldn't believe I had come from the direction I had. At 6 on the dot, my mate from the Yari hut called on the radio to check I was OK, which was reassuring.

The staff and I spent the evening drinking whisky and discussing bears. One had appeared at the kitchen window the previous year, and another had cleverly broken into the supposedly bear-proof bins. And then came the stories of people missing in the mountains. Had the bears got them? Not my favorite topic.

Stories of midsummer hiking were almost as scary. In another couple of weeks, there would be 150 people each night ranging from 10 to 80 years old. Most would be in bed by seven and up and away by 5 the next morning.

"Asobi mo shigoto mitai," the boss told me. "Even when they're on holiday, it's like they're working! Japanese people don't know how to have fun."

My room didn't have curtains and I woke at 5:30. The weather forecast wasn't good. Thinking it best to get off the high mountains before it set in, I started early. The wind was whipping the clouds around and it was cold and drizzly. Spot threatened to blow away or at least turn inside out.

I was picking my way along a ridge line when a red figure appeared in the clouds before me. I was confident. I'd never heard of a red bear. It was a hiker in red weatherproof gear. Needless to say, a gaijin in shorts and a T-shirt wandering along under a brown spotted umbrella in the clouds was not what he expected to run into. Or so he told me. He was heading the same way, and had spent a sleepless night in his tent wondering if it would be blown away. Due to the weather, he was giving up on his intended hike. It was great to have someone to walk with. It took the pressure off. I could now quite safely break my ankle without worrying about survival!

As survival insurance he had a "kumayoke" tied to his backpack.

Best translated as a "bear repeller", it was a small bell that rang as he walked. The idea is that it is best to have a bear hear you coming, as he will run off. If you surprise him by turning a corner and running smack into him, the chances of becoming "bear breakfast" are much higher. I wished someone had explained that to me at the start of the trip. The best my wife had come up with was that I should "play dead" when confronting a bear! I had told my friends at the hut the previous night about my wife's advice. They had all laughed.

"I'd run like Hell," the "mountain man" manager had said.

High in the North Alps above Nakabusa Onsen

The trail down to Nakabusa is renowned as one of the three steepest hiking tracks in Japan. I was happy to be descending. We met the odd group who were climbing. Red faces, heavy breathing and panted questions of "how far to go?"

My knees were about ready to give up when we finally fell into the onsen village of Nakabusa. I dropped off the icepick, wrapping my last two beer coupons around the handle. He may never know what a big favour he did me, my big-eared mate. Responsibilites taken care of, we retired to the bath. The old ryokan was creaking with age, but out the back was a brand spanking new bath-house made of "hinoki" or Japanese Cypress. The walls and ceiling were natural timber, while the main bath, about the size of a squash court, was of stone. Natural hot water flowed from a spring at one end, and boulders and stone seats were strategically placed in the bath itself. It was the perfect spot for a tired, smelly hiker to rehabilitate. The steaming water soothed my aches and pains, and when I finally emerged, only my toe, which hadn't enjoyed the mountains, was bothering me.

It was thirteen kilometres out of the valley back to civilisation. The sky had cleared, the day was warm, and the cicadas were deafening. There was no traffic and we wandered down the middle of the road. It was downhill the whole way, mostly shaded under overhanging trees.

When we finally parted, my hiking partner headed off to catch the train. Before leaving, though, he hung his kumayoke on my backpack.

At 6:30 I arrived at my friend's house in Tokiwa for a well-earned rest. It started to rain a couple of hundred metres before I reached his front door. When he saw me he had a good laugh. My shirt had been on inside out since Nakabusa!

My wife and son arrived about half an hour later.

Early morning volunteer fire brigade practice in Tokiwa, Nagano Prefecture

7. THE GRINNING EEL

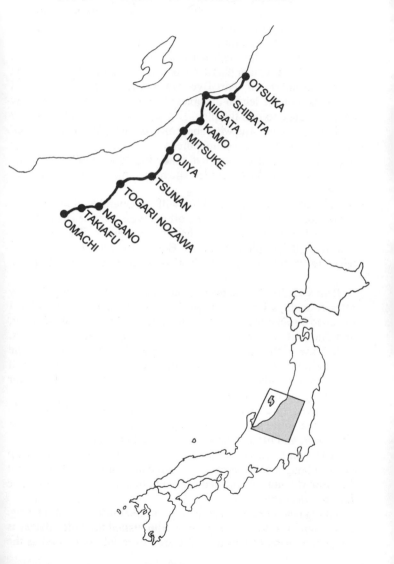

My break in Tokiwa was for longer than anticipated. One look at my big toe was enough for my friend to pack me off to the local hospital. The doctor looked keen to cut. But we decided that that would keep me out of action for too long. As it was, I was off my feet for four days. It was thought that I had lost too much weight, and my friend's charming wife did her best to fatten me up with large helpings of local delicacies and endless bottles of beer. This much-needed attention plus some tender loving care from my wife had me wondering if "Part Two" was really necessary. Couldn't I just walk half the length of Japan? Surely my toe was a halfway decent excuse to pull the plug. But what would my friends say? And my sponsors? And what about all those people who had helped me so far? The noodle shop ladies who had let me sleep in their restaurant? The priest who had made his "donation" to my trip? The mountain man who had lent me his ice-pick? What a decision!

I had to go on!

Monday, the 12th of July 1993 will be remembered for the huge earthquake near Okushiri Island, off the west coast of Hokkaido. A 36 metre high tidal wave swept through the island's village at 10 pm, and over 200 people were killed. Bodies were swept away, some never to be found. I decided not to sleep on any more beaches.

It was 12:30 and had been raining heavily all morning. Finally after four days I was back on the road. Under my umbrella, I marched through the town of Omachi, over the raging Takase River, and climbed up into the cloud-enshrouded, forested mountains. Below me in the valley, the road to Hakuba, site for part of the 1998 Winter Olympics, was closed due to the rain. It was a dull day, and head down, I trudged on past a deserted ski area, forever climbing and descending.

A rusted, tyre-less minivan, parked in a paddock of grass, was home to a white goat. He sat, looking out at me through its open side-door, and bleated, proud of his weather-proof housing.

A laughing old lady measured her height on my body in a shop where I bought an ice-cream. She came up to my belly-button. But I'm sure if I had straightened her bent back, she would have made it to my rib-cage.

At Ogawa, I checked out the supermarket just as it was closing. It was obvious that not too many gaijin visited the little village, as I was the target of unashamed stares from adults as well as the children. And then in the shokudo across the road, I was surprised to find that the waitress was the same woman who had just served me in the supermarket.

When I finally reached my target of Takafu, an old man was standing out in the rain waiting for me. My friend in Tokiwa had arranged a ryokan and, because of the weather, had been so worried that he kept calling the old man to see if I had arrived safely. I was bustled into the low wooden building, swiftly interrogated, then made to report my safety. The old couple treated me as a son, forcing me into a bath so I wouldn't catch cold, and filling me with hot tea. They pored over photos of my family.

"Our son moved to Tokyo with his family. He doesn't come home very often," the old lady said sadly.

My room virtually overhung the muddied flooding river and when I needed to urinate in the middle of the night, it was out the window and into the river instead of waking everyone in the creaky old wooden ryokan.

When I was planning my walk, a friend who is an airline pilot expressed interest in joining me for part of it. He often flew into Japan, he said, and could arrange a few days off. Perfect, I thought. He can join me in the high mountains where it's not too smart to hike alone, and he can walk in front in case we run into a bear. But our schedules got out of kilter. I arrived in Kamikochi ahead of plans, and his flight was cancelled.

We had managed to communicate through my wife, though, and alternative plans had been made. Sure enough, as I wandered up to Nagano Station on a warm sunny day, there was only one gaijin sitting outside, Andy. He was ready to walk.

Nagano was a hive of activity with major construction leading up to the Winter Olympics. Tokyo had received a major boost to its transportation system in time for the 1964 Olympics. Overhead expressways had been built on huge concrete pylons, relieving congestion on the streets below, and the city had been modernized in preparation for a watching world. Similar things were going on in Nagano nearly thirty years later. I had spent the morning dodging various road and bridge constructions that would link Nagano City with the resort areas chosen as sites for the different events. There was little doubt that Nagano was already buzzing in anticipation of its time in the spotlight.

Taking a break at Zenkoji Temple, Nagano City.

We walked the stone street to Zenkoji Temple, famous as a mecca for Buddhist pilgrims travelling from afar. The street was lined with souvenir shops selling every kind of "omiyage" imaginable from boxes of cookies, to wooden back-scratchers, to stuffed toys. One Japanese custom I am not overly fond of is that of "omiyage" or souvenirs. Basically, the custom states that if you're on holiday or are off having a good time, you should take something back for all those who are slaving away in your absence. And we're not just talking about one or two omiyage. You need something for just about everyone you know, including the pet dog. Honeymooners are the hardest hit. They need something for everyone who attended and contributed to the wedding. Buying a hundred gifts would not be unusual and honeymooners seem to worry so much about these obligations that it rather puts a damper on things.

The shops we passed were obviously prepared for hordes of visitors, but it was a Thursday, and there were only a few groups of pilgrims following their flag-bearing leaders.

We sipped the pure water using bamboo ladles, and watched the worshippers throw their coins and pray to Buddha. It was peaceful and relaxing.

Later we strolled through the northern suburbs before finding an old friend's house. It was a change to have someone to walk with. And to speak English.

The evening was spent at the local sento, having a soak, and admiring some colourful tattoos. Andy just about got out of the next day's walk by slipping as he sat on his stool, sending it careening into another bather a couple of spots away. Luckily it wasn't a tattooed mobster!

We headed off early on a beautiful warm sunny day only to find that it was rush hour. The option was the stopbank on the Chikuma River. It was high and gave a commanding view of the wide valley and the mountains on each side. This was apple country, and in true Japanese fashion, the apple trees looked white-leaved, the result of enthusiastic spraying.

Apples in Japan are thinned and individually bagged to produce bigger fruit of perfect appearance. I was used to seeing paper bags on trees, but to Andy it was a novel experience. As fruit are often used as gifts, appearance is of paramount importance, and fruit with skin blemishes cannot command high prices.

The valley narrowed, the road split, and we made the right decision to stay on the left of the river. Most of the traffic turned right. At a drink machine on the side of the road, Andy showed the enthusiasm of someone new to exploring in Japan. He wasn't prepared to settle for a Coke, but keen to try something unusual. There were quite a few options, including cans of "Grapefruit Tea" and "Black Lemon". I was grateful for Andy's presence. I wouldn't have noticed. Such little items of interest tend to escape my attention, as I am used to living and being in Japan. It was good to be with someone whose thoughts could take me back to my first visit to this fascinating country.

And at the noodle shop where we stopped for lunch, it was the "waribashi", the wooden throw-away chopsticks that caught his attention. My sources tell me that in 1992, 24 billion 520 million pairs of wooden throw-away chopsticks were used in Japan. The library of comics for customers also caught his eye. These comics are generally sexist, violent and about as thick as your average telephone book. Commuters pore over them on trains, and it's not unusual to see a suited salaryman staring at grossly pornographic comic sketches while sitting next to a uniformed schoolgirl.

It was a welcome break for lunch. Andy, unused to walking twenty kilometres before lunch, was blistering up, and my ankle was moaning again.

Asking for directions

The first person we met after lunch was a plastic policeman. He was standing to attention under a streetlight, so that he could be seen at night I suppose. I could only guess at the reason for his existence,—to stop speeding motorists who would rip around the corner, mistake him for the real thing, and hit the brakes. In any

Western country I'm sure he would have been spraypainted, had his head broken off, or been totally uprooted, but there in orderly Japan, he was immaculately dressed, if slightly weathered.

And then a few kilometres down the road, a real policeman waved at us from among the bushes on the side of the road. He was perched on a stool, a cigarette hanging out of his mouth, wearing headphones and fiddling with a gun-like instrument.

"I'm catching speedsters!" he replied when we inquired what he was up to. Sure enough, a couple of hundred metres down the road, there was a whole team of police hidden up a side street. They didn't look too enthusiastic though. Four, including two women, were playing cards around a table and there seemed to be a "picnic-in-the-sun" attitude. One bloke was talking on the radio.

"Gaijin! Walking! What would they be walking out here for?" He looked up, smiling, and gave us a big wave.

Suddenly Andy hobbled. From behind, he looked like a sprinter who had broken down with a torn hamstring. Only he was walking, and he hobbled. He doubled over in pain. Now we're in trouble I thought. I rushed up.

"Are you OK?" was the best I could come up with.

"Aaarghh!" he groaned. "Aaarghh."

It looked pretty serious. Will his new wife ever forgive me I wondered.

"Aaarghhh! It popped! It popped!"

"What popped?" Maybe it's his achilles tendon I thought.

"That bloody big blister on my foot," he moaned. He continued moaning. I laughed.

A tiny red 500 cc car pulled over.

"Can I help?" an exceptionally attractive young woman asked, smiling an exceptionally pretty smile. "Would you like a ride?"

I could see Andy melting. I almost melted myself. "What's she saying?" he gasped, grabbing my arm.

"She's asking where we come from," I lied.

"Liar!" he croaked. "She's offering us a ride, isn't she?" "Take it! Take it!" he said from a splayed position on the footpath. It was at this point I realised that Andy really wasn't a dedicated walker.

"Thanks anyway, but we're walking," I reluctantly replied to the girl who had the loveliest big black eyes. She was quite exquisite.

"Take it! Take it!" Andy groaned. "Take it you bastard!"

"Thank you very much for stopping, but we're only walking," I repeated myself. This was a tough one. Such a lovely temptress! "It's a nice day," I added lamely.

"You bastard!" Andy groaned in the background.

"Well good luck!" she said, winding up the window, revealing a generous cleavage while leaning over the empty passenger's seat. She drove off.

"Aaarghhh!" we both moaned.

"She was sent to tempt us!" I said. He almost hit me.

We staggered on to Togari Nozawa Onsen, the target for the day. The village was asleep and all the shokudo around the station were closed except for one. And there was no-one in that one either. We slumped at the nearest table. Andy still wasn't talking to me for resisting the temptress. I coughed loudly and let out a loud "Sumimasen!" Nothing.

It was after five and all the main sumo bouts for the day would be coming on TV. I switched it on loudly, and eventually an elderly lady emerged, rubbing her eyes.

"Did Wakanohana win?" she asked, unfazed at the sight of two unexpected gaijin slouched in her restaurant. "What do you want?"

"Tell her I want a beer. A beer!" Andy had been gabbling in English since she had appeared.

"We'd like two beers please—and some noodles."

"I'm sorry, we're closed," she said.

"You're closed!" I asked incredulously.

"We're closed," she replied.

"She says she's closed," I said to Andy.

"Shit!" he said in English. She looked at him. He didn't look good.

"What's the matter with your friend?" she asked.

I saw a glimmer of hope.

"He's torn his hamstring. We've walked from Nagano and he's not well." With perfect timing Andy coughed a throaty cough and looked like he was about to vomit.

"Well, I can give you some beer, but I haven't got any noodles. How about some curry?"

"We'll eat anything!" I said. "Well, almost anything," I added looking at Andy.

We stayed at a ryokan not far from the bottom of the skifield.

Winter was obviously the busy season, and the accommodation village was almost deserted. The chairlifts could be seen extending up over grassy slopes which were lined with forest. The new onsen was magnificent. I soaked away while Andy sat on the side. His feet were blistered raw and the water was too hot for them. He had walked 40 kilometres for the day on unprepared feet, which was quite an impressive effort.

Two young boys were practicing karate kicks on each other, with the occasional howl as a well-aimed kick struck an unprotected ribcage. Their grandfather watched, grinning from the bath.

"Water's too hot for him, is it?" he asked me, nodding in Andy's direction. It is a well-known "fact" about gaijin that they can't handle hot water, that Japanese baths turn them into lobster look-alikes.

"He's OK. He's torn his hamstring," I replied.

A night off his feet had done wonders for Andy's resolve. We were walking down to the station.

"It's a shame I've got to go. But duty calls. I'd have loved to have walked another day with you," he lied. There was a bad copy of an American Indian totem pole at the station. We took a picture with it and then his train left. I was alone again.

I am a terrible singer, but as I got back out onto the road, I couldn't help but break into a few lines of "On the road again". After all, singing was better than talking to myself.

The valley disappeared, becoming the Chikuma River gorge. The new road on the far side of the river had captured most of the traffic, and I was free to wander without my map, down the middle of the road. It was too good to last however, and eventually the roads joined up.

I knew I had found a good shokudo by the number of trucks that were parked outside. Truckies, affectionately known as "un-chan," know the best routes, the cheapest and fastest shokudo, and up-to-date road conditions better than they know their mothers. CB radios pass on all the good information. On other occasions, when hitch-hiking around Japan, I have even been passed from truck to truck by white-gloved un-chan in brightly-decorated trucks who have called ahead on their CBs and organized my next ride. I have a good deal of respect for Japan's truck drivers.

This particular shokudo was almost totally obscured by parked trucks. I found out why. It was air-conditioned. It had three TVs tuned to different channels, and a good-looking waitress who flirted with all the customers. It had a huge library of grubby comics. It had an endless supply of cold wheat tea. And best of all, it had delicious, yet reasonably priced food in big helpings. A truckie's dream come true. Mine too. It was hard to leave—especially when I could see that it had started raining.

A little after two I passed the prefectural boundary and entered Niigata. It was pouring rain again, and though Spot was doing his best, I was totally saturated. My map showed an onsen, and I decided to escape the onslaught of wind and rain.

The onsen was in a large, seemingly deserted ryokan. I paid my 300 yen, carefully placed my soaked gear in front of the fan in the changing room, and gleefully entered the steaming bathroom. One wall was a huge window overlooking the swollen, muddied Chiku-ma River. Along another wall stretched a long, metre-high fish tank full of black eels and small silver fish. It was perfect. I took a stool in the corner, shaved, and lathered my body with soap. The hot water was exhilarating. I felt clean and human again.

Then, just as I was washing my hair, I heard voices. Female voices I was sure. The door opened. The mirror in front of me was steamed up. I didn't have much choice, so I looked over my shoulder. In trooped five octogenarian ladies, wrinkled bodies, sagging breasts. I don't know who was more surprised, them or me. They must have had prior warning by my gear in the changing room, but they weren't prepared.

One stopped talking in mid-sentence. Silence. I could hear the second-hand on the clock ticking.

"Oh I couldn't have gone into the women's, could I?" I asked myself. I actually checked later, but no, I was in the men's. There wasn't much I could do. I carried on washing my hair.

Initially surprised, they weren't perturbed for too long. When I got up and entered the bath, they were all sitting around, chatting in an almost unintelligable local dialect. I smiled to the nearest. She smiled back. I usually get on very well with "obachan", elderly grandmothers, but in this case, striking up a conversation was somewhat difficult. There was no doubt about it. I would have to look them straight in the eye. It seemed easier to stare at the eel in the fish tank who had just managed to bite off half a fish's tail. Actually, it seemed to be laughing at me in my predicament.

"Heavy rain today, isn't it?" I made an effort. One old lady's back was like a banana. Another had breasts that hung to her navel.

"Yes, but it will stop soon," one replied. It was obviously rather difficult for her as well. I looked back at the fishtank. The eel was grinning at me.

"Too bad they didn't bring their twenty year old grand-daughters," I muttered to it. Just the thought of it was enough for me to feel relieved that they hadn't. Things might have become even more embarrassing.

It cleared up as the old lady had predicted. The humidity had gone with the rain, and after my long soak, it was a pleasant walk on to the town of Tsunan. My timing was impeccable and at five o'clock I was eating curry and rice with a thick, juicy, deep-fried pork cutlet (tonkatsu) and watching the sumo with the owner and another couple of patrons in a small shokudo. Akebono, the huge Hawaiian, was at it again, pummeling his smaller Japanese opponent, looking every bit the champion. One of the other patrons looked over at me as if to say "Bloody foreigners!"

Less than a hundred metres up the road, as the shokudo-owner had told me, was a small ryokan. It was a Saturday, and I didn't like my chances of getting a room.

"You're lucky it's a Saturday," the owner told me. "We're full during the week with workers who are building the new dam. They go home on Saturdays and come back Sundays. Saturday is the only night we have free rooms. I don't think Suzuki san will mind if you have his room tonight".

Mr Suzuki must have been a heavy smoker, as the room stank of cigarettes. Apart from that, though, everything was great. I soaked in the bath, did my washing, and watched baseball with the Grandfather. It was 7-6, bottom of the 9th inning, two out, bases loaded, and the TV time-slot ended. On came a soap opera. Outrageous! Even the Grandfather, used to this sort of thing, was visibly upset. And then in the next set of commercials, replays of the Grand Slam home run that we had missed! Yakult had come from behind and beaten the Giants, everybody's favourite team, on the last pitch of the game. And all of Japan, except those in the stadium, had missed it! But what can you do?

The 18th of July 1993 was the day of the General Elections. I had been passing election posters for weeks, and it was the day when all those faces that had been pasted all over the countryside would find out if they were to be successful politicians. The main benefit to me was that my eardrums wouldn't have to rattle to any more noisy amplified speeches. There wouldn't be any more campaign cars to avoid on corners, and there was a reasonable possibility that I wouldn't have to watch Prime Minister Miyazawa on TV anymore. All very encouraging.

The old couple in the ryokan weren't very interested. We ate breakfast together. They were so encouraged by my wolfing down my rice and raw egg, that the old man brought out some of his home-made pickles.

"No one else will eat them!" he explained. They weren't bad. He got so excited that he got his camera, which looked distinctly prewar. "Okashiina!" (That's strange!) he grunted when he couldn't make it work. "I haven't used it for years, but it was working".

The old lady had dusted off a globe that had been hiding in the corner. She was inspecting Iceland.

"Where's New Zealand?" she asked politely.

I spun the globe through 180 degrees and pointed down, almost to the bottom of the big ball.

"It's about the same size as Japan," I explained. "It takes about ten hours to fly there".

"But Japan looks so small!" she said turning the globe back to Iceland. "We're such a small island country!"

I strode out into the rain packed with supplies. The old lady had made me rice balls, and presented me with a carton of milk, as well as a towel with the ryokan's name on it. The old man had proudly made up a small packet of his pickles. They waved furiously, and I seriously considered returning to escape the downpour.

Roadside drains weren't handling it at all. Huge puddles were unavoidable, and since my boots were soon soaked, I just trudged on through. Trucks threw up sheets of water that soaked me from head to toe. My only respite was when I reached Tokamachi and could walk under the long roofed shopping area that lined Route 117.

A mother had accosted her teenage son, who was playing video games outside a bookshop.

"Why didn't you come home for lunch? What are you doing

wasting your money on video games?" she scolded him. I couldn't help a grin, but my timing was bad. She saw me and gave me a look that sent me packing.

"It's the same all over the world," I murmured to myself as I fled her glare.

At a small restaurant where I cunningly sat on the tatami (so I could take off my boots) the owner explained the origin of the town's name.

"'Toka' means the 10th day, while 'machi' means town. This is the 10th day town. Traditionally, we have a market day here on the 10th of each month. Muikamachi is about 15 kilometres away. 'Muika' means the 6th day, and the market day there was always on the 6th of each month. It doesn't really happen any more though," he said sadly.

"You should wear a hat when it rains!" a lady at a small roadside shop told me. "We have acid rain that blows over from Russia. If you don't, all your hair will fall out!"

"I don't have much to lose anyway," I laughed, taking off my cap. I had been sitting on my backpack eating an ice cream when she had brought out a deck-chair for me. Gratefully accepting her kindness, I stretched out, resting my feet on my pack. Within a couple of minutes she was back out with a foot-stool. We had quite a yarn.

"I've heard that Niigata rice and sake is the tastiest in Japan," I said.

"Yes that's right. We have such pure water."

"But you just said there was an acid rain problem!"

"Yes that's right." She smiled, and escaped my next question by going inside to get me another ice cream.

"We're full," the lady at the ryokan in Yusawa told me. I gazed around. There were no shoes in the entrance hall. "We're full with construction workers. They've gone home for the weekend but will arrive back this evening," she explained. "There's a ryokan about four kilometres away in Shiodono."

I decided I didn't like construction workers! It was going to be tight if I was going to make it to Shiodono in time to see the final bouts of the final day of the Sumo tournament. Forget the election results. All the locals seemed to have. Focus was definitely on whether Takanohana could beat Akebono and force a playoff.

I strode up the road in overdrive swirling Spot in my right hand like a bowler-hatted English businessman. On a day of on-and-off rain, Spot spent most of the time unsheathed, ready to beat off any attack by unexpected precipitation, and I had become quite expert at decapitating weeds just above ground level with a flick of the wrist. When I had a break, Spot was sheathed with straps on the right side of my backpack. He was easily drawn however. All I had to do was reach over my right shoulder, grasp the handle, and whip him out, just as Musashi had drawn his long sword. It was quite good fun actually, although I was careful there was no-one around when I would rip into action, drawing Spot in a flash, and slicing a large leaf in two.

Shiodono didn't produce the expected ryokan, and I was swearing vehemently for the following two kilometres until I found both it and a shokudo. It was 5:45 and I could hear a roar as I strode up to the latter. The crowd had eyes glued to the TV, and no one blinked as I rushed in. Excitement was obvious, and all Japan must have been celebrating Takanohana's win and the upcoming three-way playoff.

I had a few minutes, so I rushed next door to the ryokan.

"We're full," the young man said.

"That's right, we're full," his mother said, appearing behind him. It wasn't very convincing. When I had entered I had heard someone whisper "Tell him we're full," and once again, there were no shoes.

I stomped back to the shokudo.

"They said that they're full," I said to the waitress, who was sympathetic.

"They haven't got any other customers. Can't be bothered opening for just one person. They're not very friendly to anybody," she confided in me. "You'll have to go to Ojiya. It's about 5 kilometres".

It wasn't my day. I was feeling thoroughly brassed off. But then, Akebono, the gaijin monster, came out and crushed Waka, then Takanohana to take the Sumo title, and I felt better.

The lights of Ojiya sparkled ahead of me, around a bend in the Shinano River. It was dark and I was wondering what to do. My tent seemed the only option. Or possibly a shrine or a temple on the outskirts of town. Something was bound to turn up. That was half the excitement of what I was doing.

A priest was conducting a ceremony in a house beside the road.

Through the window I could see him in his long brown robes, bald and bespectacled, surrounded by candles. Before him sat a large group of people sitting on the floor. Perhaps they could pray for a place for me to stay. Hardly likely.

But then my prayers were answered. I rounded a corner, and there, smack in front of me, was a lit-up sign outside a ryokan. And not only that, I ventured inside and came face to face with the white-faced beauty of Ojiya. She was quite stunning. My jaw must have dropped in the same manner that most ryokan owner's jaws dropped at the sight of me.

"Aah . . . excuse me," I stammered, "do you have a room for this evening?"

"Yasui ho ga ii desho?" She had summed me up in a glance. "A cheap one would be better?" she was asking me. I suppose I was looking a bit rough. I had been trudging through puddles most of the day. It was dark and cool out, yet I was in shorts and a not-so-white T-shirt. Yet she hadn't even blinked when I'd entered.

"Yes, that would be fine," I answered. She had high cheekbones and the perfect white skin associated in Japan with women of the "snow country". Her enormous eyes were as raven-black as her long hair which hung well down her back.

Quite a sight for an exhausted walker. I felt weak at the knees. She showed me to a room on the second floor overlooking the garden, pointing out the bathroom on the way. I took the hint.

When I returned from a leisurely soak, a maid was laying out my futon. She had placed a bowl of melon and lychees on the table.

"Compliments of the owner's wife," she said. "Her English is very good, isn't it?"

"Her English? She speaks English?"

"She's been studying for years."

I committed a basic mistake the next morning. I was enjoying a morning bath when I realised the voices coming from the bath next door were not female, but male.

"Oh oh!" I thought, "surely they couldn't have switched the baths overnight." But they had. All they had to do was switch the curtains marked male and female. They had. But fortunately I escaped before any ladies turned up to bathe.

"An American!" The white-faced beauty's mother-in-law

jumped when she saw me. The tiny old lady jumped so high that she almost got up to my chest level. "What's an American doing here?"

"He's not an American, and he speaks Japanese," the white-faced beauty said. The old lady turned to face me.

"Excuse me, please. Excuse my rudeness. I'm sorry about the poor quality of your accommodation and our food. Thank you for coming. Thank you".

"On the contrary, your ryokan is very fine. The food was delicious," I said. "And your daughter-in-law speaks excellent English," I added quickly. The white-faced beauty beamed a captivating smile, as did her mother-in-law. I knew I had made their day.

Route 17 north from Ojiya was major stuff. Vehicles roared by, and I had to spit out the bad taste in my mouth from the fumes. By mid-morning I needed a break. I stumbled upon a shokudo just opening for the day.

"They keep widening the road," the old lady with the mouthful of gold teeth complained. "This used to be a quiet, peaceful place. People stopped for a break, but now they just fly by. If it doesn't change then . . ." She placed both hands around her neck and coughed.

She had brought me a beer mug of wheat tea and some rice crackers and had sat down for a chat while her assistant made my meal.

"Try some of my miso soup. It's tasty," she said, getting me a bowl. "Twenty or thirty years ago, students who had no money would walk past here. Some stopped, and if it was in the evening, I'd let them sleep in the restaurant. Now, nobody walks. Nobody stops, either," she said thoughtfully. "I've never met a gaijin who can speak Japanese like you. You must be about . . . ah 25," she grinned. Was this old lady, who must be well past 70, flirting with me?

"Actually I'm 31," I replied.

"Well I was close," she said. "It's impossible to tell with gaijin. Some people say that you all look the same, but you look different".

"That's because I've got no hair! Actually most gaijin think that all Japanese look the same." She laughed and laughed.

"How many people live in Takiya?" I asked.

"I don't know. I'm too old and my head is terrible with numbers," she replied. We spent the next half hour pouring over photos of her trip to Kyoto, and when I finally returned to the rigours of Route 17, I was relaxed and ready for the onslaught of filthy fumes.

I sighed with relief. Fifty or so uniformed schoolkids got on their bus just as I was approaching the bus stop! In a tyre shop there was an extraordinarily cute woman tyre-fitter wearing pink overalls, and then just as I was entering Nagaoka, I passed the fashion hotel "New Dream Pal". Actually it looked like the sort of place one might take an "old dream pal". A "new dream pal" might accuse one of cheapness!

Nagaoka is a major stop on the Shinkansen line between Niigata and Tokyo, with several smaller train lines branching away from its station. I had no problem finding the station. There seemed to be about half a million bicycles parked outside the huge modern building, and about a half million people wandering around it. I actually found walking quite difficult. I was used to walking at a fast pace, but there were so many people around, I was slowed down to the pace of those around me. When I finally reached the station, I made a conscious decision to be a "real gaijin" for an hour. I bought an English-language newspaper, a hamburger and an ice cold beer and sat down beside a fountain, taking my boots off to relax.

Election results were still incomplete, but all indications were that for the first time in thirty-seven years, the Liberal Democrat Party might not be in power. They still held the most seats of any single party, but a multi-party coalition to oust them looked to be a definite possibility. Actually, nobody I had talked to seemed overly interested. There had been so many political scandals in recent years that a general distrust of politicians was evident. In Niigata, one of Japan's poorest prefectures, Tokyo and its seat of power seemed a long way away.

It was spitting as I crossed over Route 8, under the Shinkansen track, over the local train track, and through the green green paddies to Mitsuke. Three little boys were using their plastic umbrellas as machine guns. They stopped playing to stare at me from a distance. I whipped out Spot and stood on guard, grinning. They weren't impressed.

Mitsuke's hair salon sported a "menu" of services, along with a "price rist" in its front window.

I put on my best smile, but the ryokan in the main street was full. I decided to put myself in the hands of the local constabulary at the koban at the next corner. The lone policeman was talking on the phone. He looked up.

"Aah, I've got to go. A gaijin just walked in!"

Silence. "Yes, a gaijin! Call me back in five minutes," he hung up.

"What can I do for you," he said, looking at his hands.

"I'm looking for a place to stay. Are there any ryokan or minshuku near here?"

"There's one just down the road" he replied.

"I've already been there. They're full".

"They're full?" he asked, sounding surprised.

"Well, they said they were full."

"Oh!" He was catching on. This wasn't going to be quite the easy mission he'd anticipated. "I'll try another one." He looked up a number, picked up the phone and dialed.

"Hello. This is Tanaka from the Police. I have a gaijin here who's looking for a room".

Silence.

"Yes that's right, a gaijin. He speaks good Japanese".

Silence.

"Well, he's very tall. He's wearing shorts, and is carrying a huge backpack".

Silence. He cupped the receiver.

"Do you know about Japanese customs?"

"Yes, I've lived in Tokyo for ages. My wife's Japanese. I've walked from Kagoshima." As soon as I said it, I knew I shouldn't have.

"You've what?" he gasped.

"I've walked from Kagoshima."

"He says he's walked from Kagoshima," he said into the phone. Silence.

"From Kagoshima. His wife's Japanese, so you should be OK." Silence.

"Yes, I'm speaking to him in Japanese now." Silence.

"OK, I'll send him down. Thank you so much. I'm sorry to bother you with such a troublesome matter." He put down the phone.

"I'm sorry, but we don't get gaijin in Mitsuke. There's no reason for a gaijin to come here. There are some in Nagaoka, but none here." He gave me directions to the ryokan.

The phone rang. He answered it.

"No, he's still here. Call back in another five minutes."

Silence.

"No I can't. He's speaking Japanese!" He looked back at me.

"Would you mind showing me your wallet?"

"My wallet?"

"Yes, I need to check if you have money to pay at the ryokan. I am responsible," he said apologetically. I felt sorry for putting him on the spot.

There is no doubt that in the last few years or so the reputation of gaijin in Japan has gone downhill. An influx of unskilled labourers willing to do work that most Japanese would turn their noses up at has produced mini "gaijin ghettos" in major cities. Crimes committed by these people have been blown out of all proportion by the Japanese media, so that in rural areas such as where I was, a gaijin was treated with suspicion. I had felt that suspicion continually, throughout my walk. At one point, I had gone into a Post Office to send a letter. One of the older male customers had eyed me up and down before saying to the teller, "I'll wait until after he leaves." And the teller had looked relieved!

From the outside, the ryokan looked like an old tin shed, but when I slid open the front doors, I was greeted with classic Japanese decor. At street level, there was a concrete area which was as far as street-shoes were worn. Then one step up to a wooden landing, lined along the front with heel-less slippers for guests to scuff along in. It doesn't take long to get used to them. The main trick is not to lift your knees when walking. Novices should take care when they get to the stairs. The landing extended along into a corridor in both directions, but before me was a room with paper screens or "shoji" facing the street.

They had heard the front door open. One of the screens slid sideways and a middle-aged woman with curly hair and glasses stood staring at me. Behind her, seated at a kotatsu, was a tiny old lady, blinking through big thick glasses. A kotatsu is a low table, usually used in a tatami room, at which one sits cross-legged. They are great in winter, as they have an electric heater built into the bottom of the table. A blanket covers the table and the legs of those sitting there, warming up the body considerably. The only problem for gaijin is a sore back for those not used to sitting on the floor for long periods! In summer, the blanket is removed, and the kotatsu is a simple table.

"Hello. Tanaka-san from the Police Station sent me. I understand you have a room for me." I thought I'd better break the ice.

"We don't have a bed," she stammered.

"Not a problem," I replied assuringly. "I sleep on the floor every day. I have a futon at home!"

"We don't have any knives and forks!"

"That's OK, I use chopsticks every day." I bent down and started to take my boots off.

"Our slippers will be too small!"

"I've got small feet."

"We only have Japanese food."

"I like natto!" This stunned her.

"But . . . We've never had a gaijin before. Gaijin never came to Mitsuke!"

"That's alright. My wife is Japanese. I've been in Japan for ages. I speak Japanese. We've been speaking Japanese since I came in," I reminded her.

"Well, yes." She thought about it.

"How long have you been open?" I asked.

"My grandfather started this ryokan sixty-four years ago," she replied proudly.

"And you've never had a gaijin?"

"You're the first!"

I explored Mitsuke and chose a small restaurant down a back street for dinner. Monday nights were obviously not the busiest, and for the hour I was there, I was the only customer. When I arrived back at the ryokan, only the Grandmother was seated at the kotatsu. As in any country, Japanese grandmas love baby photos, so I produced mine for prolonged inspection. She ooohed and aaahed over them as my own mother had, before bringing out her family album.

She was 74, she said, and had never been out of Mitsuke in her life. When she was young, she remembered deep snow covering Mitsuke in the winter, but in recent years very little fell. Life had become much easier, she said. Then, as I departed for an early night, she paid me a great compliment.

"It's just like having a Japanese to stay!"

Every morning, the first five minutes on my feet seemed like an hour of excruciating pain. I would hobble around waiting for my feet to get used to having weight on them again, and sometimes my right ankle would jam up completely, almost dropping me to the ground in pain. Getting up in the morning wasn't much fun.

It was nearing the end of July, and it was exciting to hear everyone, including the weather forecasters, predicting the end of the rainy season in a few days. Whilst I had been in "official" rainy season for almost the entire sixty days I had been walking, only the last twenty had soaked me to the skin. Of the previous twenty nights, only two had been spent outside, and Spot had come in for heavy usage.

But summer was on its way. Summer vacations were due to start the day I left Mitsuke, and I was looking forward to meeting the hordes of students who would be let loose on the country-side over the next month. Campgrounds were bound to be full of people, unlike those I'd stayed at so far, and the beaches bound to be crowded with excited holiday-makers. The carnival atmosphere of summer in Japan was about to start, but could the weather be counted on?

A gasoline station was about to have its opening ceremony as I walked by. Huge banners proclaimed "Open" in English, but potential customers would have had trouble getting to the pumps. Between them was a small stage, complete with a miniature shrine, podium, microphones and balloons hanging from the roof. There was even a red ribbon to be cut. And in the forecourt were five neat rows of chairs for the guests who would no doubt be arriving shortly. Five or six men in ill-fitting suits were racing around checking everything. One gave me a big wave, but not an invitation.

The Niigata Plain seemed huge from where I was at its southeastern boundary, at the foot of the mountains. It extended to my left, from far behind me, to far in front, and all the way out to the sea. It is fertile agricultural land, irrigated by the Shinano River—Japan's longest, but I was surprised to see industrial encroachment on the farming land. Small industrial towns followed one another, and green paddies mixed in with factory buildings was the norm.

"How far is it to Sanjo?" I asked an old women.

"Not far for you," she cackled. "You'll be there is no time! You've got such long legs!"

Sanjo was my lunch destination. A vibrant town, it had more than its fair share of clothing boutiques and chic shops, a benefit, I imagine, of having its own Shinkansen Station. But I wasn't looking for fashionable clothes as I left the noodle shop I'd had lunch in. I was looking for crutches! My ankle had jammed up completely, and every time I put my right foot down, a shooting pain hit me harder than a sledgehammer. I could only put the minimum of weight on my right foot, virtually hopping along on one leg.

For the first time on the trip, I thought that I might not make it. It hadn't really occurred to me that I might have to give up because of injury. I was mentally prepared to beat off any psychological reasons for giving up that might hinder me along the way, but the thought of injury hadn't entered my head. As one young lady had told me years before, I was the most persistent person she'd ever met, and I had the most perseverance. But there I was, possibly to be cheated out of my big adventure by a broken ankle that hadn't healed properly. No way!

I slumped on the ground outside a convenience store, had two chocolate ice creams in quick succession, and tried again. Still sore. I took off my boot and massaged my whole ankle and foot. I tried again. Better, but not great. Then after a few hundred metres, the ankle warmed up and I could hobble along at a reasonable pace. After a couple of kilometres, it was back to its normal self.

"Oh no," I thought, "not just five minutes of pain each morning, but two kilometres! Please, no!"

But I managed to get to Kamo and find my friend's family's liquor shop. What great timing. I couldn't think of a better anaesthetic for a sore ankle.

My friend's grandfather was a sound believer in the "Hayane hayaoki" principle. Early to bed, early to rise. Family legend had it that the old man got up at four each morning, did his exercises, pottered around, and opened the shop, which sold groceries as well as liquor, at 5:00am.

"Are there any customers at that hour?" I couldn't help asking.

"Not a soul," the old man said. "I get the odd customer around seven. They buy cigarettes on the way to work".

"Why don't you open at seven then?" It seemed logical to me.

"I can't. We've been open at five for so many years that everyone knows we're open then. What if someone came at five and we weren't open? That would be a disaster!"

"What do you do?"

"I watch the news, read the newspaper, have breakfast with my grandchildren at 6:30. The "kotsusenso" starts about seven." It was the first time I had heard rush hour called the "traffic war" but he explained by saying that the street outside was so narrow that there was at least one accident a week. "Then we're open right through to eight at night. We're busiest in the evening with deliveries. Japanese are becoming lazy. You don't have to go out to get anything now. Just use the telephone and get it delivered. Not much fun for us, but we have to do it too. To stay competitive."

We had been drinking delicious chilled sake all evening. A local brew. The Niigata sake I had been told about. I got up to go with the grandchildren to the river to let off fireworks. But as had happened earlier in the day, I almost fell over when I tried to walk. I'm not so sure, however, that I can blame my ankle entirely for the stagger!

It was a brilliant, sunny day as I set out from Kamo. I had spent the morning signing autographs for the grandchildren and as many of their friends as they could drag off the streets on their way to school. My washing hadn't dried overnight. My kind hosts offered to dry it and send it on, but since I didn't know where I was going, it was a bit impractical. Consequently, I was back looking like a rag man with socks and shirts hanging off my backpack. Still, I was feeling perky. "Had summer arrived?" was the big question.

In Kamo's main shopping street an old man in tattered clothing was checking all the drink machines for uncollected change. A woman was carrying a baby on her back in a way common in Japan. The baby is virtually wrapped on in a shawl, and peeks over one or the other shoulder. I was in for a surprise, though, as I got a bit closer. It wasn't a baby, but a small white dog!

I escaped from the main road as soon as possible, and moved over to the road along the stop bank of the Shinano River. There was a pleasant breeze blowing up the river which was now wide and deep, most of its tributaries having entered, as we got close to the sea.

Then with Niigata about seven or eight kilometres away by my estimation, the river took a wide sweep to the left, and I decided to head over through the paddies to where a huge construction project was well under way. Fully ten metres above the ground a wide road was being built. Huge amounts of earth had been shifted to build up a platform, and a constant stream of dump trucks were bringing even more. The raised platform extended as far as I could see, both behind me into the mountains, and before me into the prefectural capital, Niigata City. I followed a dirt road at the base of the platform.

"It's the new freeway from Niigata to Fukushima" a "guardman" told me. "Guardman" is a good bit of Japlish to describe a security guard, though he didn't have much to do, as construction wasn't going on in his area. I stopped for a yarn. His uniform was immaculate. The Buckingham Palace Guards would have been proud. From the ubiquitous white hardhat, to his shiny gold belt-buckle, to his polished black boots, he looked quite the part. The only problem was that he was unshaven and had a fag hanging out of his mouth.

"How far to the Prefectural Administration Building?" I asked. He looked thoughtful.

"If you're walking . . . well, about 40 kilometres" was his reply. I knew it couldn't be more than 6 or 7.

"What if I was in a car?" I couldn't help asking.

"Well, in a car . . . about 40 kilometres." He looked at me sideways.

"Which way is it?"

"It's that big building over there," he said, pointing to a tall building that dominated the Niigata horizon.

"Is it OK if I walk through here?" I asked, indicating the construction area ahead.

"Well . . . watch out for trucks" was his reply. I couldn't help wondering what he was there for! As soon as I was out of his sight, I climbed up the side of the raised platform to check out the view and see if I could follow it all the way in to Niigata. It wasn't sealed yet, and steam-rollers were doing their bit. I hadn't been up there for two minutes before a car with two hard-hatted, hard-nosed men pulled up.

"What do you think you're doing? How did you get up here?" one barked. I used the natural defense.

"I'm sorry, I don't speak Japanese," I said slowly and clearly. In English, of course.

They looked at each other and visibly moaned. One tried again.

"This is a dangerous construction area. You'll have to get off!" indicating savagely with his thumb.

"Pardon?" I replied, looking in the direction his thumb was pointing. He was getting exasperated. I looked over the side.

"Down! Down!" he said again, pointing over the edge. "Down!"

"Oh, you'd like me to go down. OK! OK!" I said climbing over the rail. He understood "OK". "Have a nice day," I said smiling at him. But the two of them were just shaking their heads.

One of them moaned the equivalent of "bloody foreigners".

Niigata, with a population of nearly half a million people, is a big city—the twenty-third largest in Japan according to the Japan Almanac. An industrial city with a major port, it was flattened by bombing during World War II. Niigata was, however, rather lucky that the weather was clear over Hiroshima on August 6th, 1945, as it was one of the alternate targets for the first atom bomb.

At the Visitor's Centre at the station, the middle-aged male attendant politely asked in English if I had come by bullet train from Tokyo.

"Well actually, I've walked from Kagoshima," I replied in my native English.

"Aah, you've hitch-hiked!" he said thoughtfully.

"No, I've walked." He turned to the female attendant beside him.

"This gaijin says he's hitch-hiked from Kagoshima," he said, in Japanese, laughing disbelievingly.

"No, I said I've walked from Kagoshima. And I have!" I said in Japanese. He looked as if I'd struck him with a sword. The lady just laughed and took over.

"I'm looking for somewhere cheap to stay. Is there anywhere for about 3,000 yen?"

"Gaijin usually stay at big hotels." She looked in her files. "We've never sent a gaijin to this place, but . . ."

"Anywhere is OK," I replied. And I spent the night at the Niigata Port Workers Welfare Centre.

The pachinko parlour down the road was full. The bright lights

and clanging of machines enticed me in, and I spent a full hour
trying to figure out if there was any skill attached to what seemed
like a mindless game. The guy next to me jammed his machine
with a coin so that it kept operating while he went off to relieve
himself, and while he was away he won more balls than he'd started
with. Maybe that was the best technique. It was certainly better
than mine.

Clint Eastwood, as Dirty Harry, was growling at baddies in
Japanese on TV when I got back. Only his Magnum sounded the
same. When I woke up the next morning, the TV was still on.

It was a brilliant day when I set out at about eight. In fact, it was
so bright that I had my sunglasses on from the start. Traffic was
pouring into Niigata. I wandered out past the airport before heading
inland towards the day's target, Shibata. I had to cross a couple of
major highways, but eventually found a minor road that paralleled
them and had little traffic. The only problem was that it had little
of everything else as well.

A flattened turtle was frying in the hot sun, a victim of the "traffic
war". And just down the road was a duck farm. Thousands of ducks
were quacking and waddling around a fenced-in pond, oblivious
to their cordon bleu fate. I quacked a few times and received a
thunderous reply.

There were only two other customers in the shokudo I found for
lunch, and they were drinking beer out of litre-size glass mugs
while watching TV. The news was still mainly election results—
various experts discussing possible coalitions and probabilities.
But Japan had heard it all before, and in an unheard-of move, one
of the customers turned the TV off! I had never seen this done in a
shokudo before! In fact, I'm sure a blaring TV is as essential as a
stack of comics for a successful shokudo. I must have been seen as
an interesting alternative as I was peppered with questions from
the two customers, from the middle-aged waitress, and from her
husband, the cook, who came out of the kitchen for a beer and a
smoke.

"Yes, but what's the point? What's the point of walking to
Hokkaido? It doesn't mean anything!" one of the customers
harangued me. He had a "bar code" haircut.

"I want to see what Japan is all about. I've lived in Tokyo. My
wife is from Osaka. But Tokyo and Osaka aren't the 'real Japan'.
I want to see the 'real Japan'," I answered.

"Why don't you go by car?" he asked. "It wouldn't take as long."

"If I went by car, I wouldn't be able to talk to everybody. Cars are fast. Because I'm walking, I talk to everyone along the way. To farmers, shopkeepers, construction workers. To everyone I meet," I replied. "And . . . I'm looking for a bit of adventure in life," I added.

"His daughter said the same thing," the other bloke chipped in, grinning. Mr Bar Code scowled.

"I'll never forgive her. She just up and left!" he growled.

"Where did she go?"

"To Hokkaido. One day she just hopped on her motorbike and said she was going to Hokkaido! I'll never forgive her. I forbade her to go, but she went anyway." He wasn't happy. Adventurers weren't in his good books. No wonder he'd been giving me a hard time.

"When did she go?" the mama san asked quietly.

"Last Friday! I'll never forgive her."

"Did she say when she's coming back?" She poured him another beer.

"Next Tuesday!" he scowled. I couldn't help laughing.

"Ten days! What are you worrying about? She's coming back next week!" I said. From the look on his face you would have thought she'd eloped with a Martian to Hokkaido. Or worse, with a gaijin!

"But what's the point of going? She's got everything she needs right here in Sasaki! I forbade her to go and she just went!" Good on her, I thought. "Think of all the money she's spending," he complained.

"Well you're already on your second 800 yen beer for lunch. I'll bet she's not spending money like you are!" I said, regretting it immediately. The silence was deafening. He wasn't happy, the narrow-minded twit! But the mama san came to the rescue.

"How do you do your washing?" she asked me.

My friends live not too far from the Shibata Cultural Centre. An attractive new building surrounded by gardens and trees, it was obviously a great source of community pride. The only "cultural" event being advertised, however, was a visit by the same troupe of pro wrestlers whose faces I had seen plastered all over walls and lamp-posts the length of Japan. The "Headhunters", faces painted to look particularly evil, stared at me out of the posters. I had, however, seen them too many times to be horrified.

It certainly looked as if summer had arrived to stay. Day 65 was warm and sunny. I started out with a hangover, thanks to one too many cups of sake with a good friend I hadn't seen in ages. His wife tut-tutted as we over-ate and over-drank, but as he explained to her, not too many gaijin friends come to visit in Shibata. We had such a good time that I was a tad worried about prospects for the next evening. Hirayama san had arranged for me to stay at his parents' place, about 35 kilometres away and right on my course. His father, he said, made sake and a stunning variety of fruit alcohols. He and his wife would follow in the car, after he finished work for the day.

I was coming to the northern corner of the Niigata Plain. The mountains on the right were growing steadily closer, and I could see the point where they dropped into the sea, not so far ahead.

I was wandering along, not really concentrating on what was going on around me, when a white car stopped on the other side of the road. The driver got out and crossed the road with a map book in his hand. Here we go, I thought, getting ready to decline a ride.

"Do you know this area?" he asked me, squinting. He was fiftyish and bald, wearing an open-neck shirt.

"Well I've got a map," I replied. "Where are you going?"

"I'm trying to find Tomioka. It's not on my map." I pulled mine out and he gazed at it for a few minutes before giving up. I had a quick look.

"Look, here it is." I recognized the kanji instantly. "Just go straight down this road for another three or four kilometres." He was staring at me with a strange look on his face.

"I thought you were Japanese! You're just like a Japanese. You read Tomioka in Kanji! Unbelievable! Thank you, thank you very much!" He backed out onto the road still staring at me, narrowly missing being bowled over by a speeding car. He jumped, bowed to me three or four times, and scurried off to his car.

I passed a sign in English for "skunk cabbage 5km" just before crossing the Ara River. It was a tough decision, but I decided probably not worth going 5 kilometres out of my way to find out what "skunk cabbage" was. I let my imagination play with it for a while.

A watermelon vender on the side of the road called me over. He had a large tent and a couple of hundred melons in his refrigerated truck.

"Eat as much as you like! I always give melon to walkers. Yesterday a girl came through on a bicycle. She was cycling to Kagoshima. She ate half a watermelon in 15 minutes! I'll bet you can eat more than that! Go ahead. Eat as much as you like."

The melon was cool and sweet, and by the time I waddled back out onto the street half and hour later, I was glad I'd been competitive with the cyclist.

The Hirayamas live in a tiny village of 15 houses that is like an island surrounded by green paddies for about a kilometre in each direction. From Iwafune Station, I had only a couple of kilometres to go.

"Where are you going?" asked a man weeding the garden outside his shop. I thought I'd surprise him.

"To Otsuka."

"To Otsuka! To Otsuka! Who do you know in Otsuka?"

"Hirayama-san." He laughed.

"They're all called Hirayama in Otsuka! Which one?"

"Hirayama-san, the judo teacher." My friend had warned me that morning. "Make sure you ask for Hirayama-san, the judo teacher. There are fifteen families in Otsuka, and thirteen are called Hirayama!"

"Well good luck." He shook his head, laughing. "A gaijin going to Otsuka!" he murmured to himself.

I turned off the main road and headed for Otsuka, a small village in a sea of green paddies. Hirayama Island. Four little boys were trying to catch tadpoles in a paddy by the unsealed road. They wore the unmistakable yellow caps of elementary school kids and were on their way home. One spotted me and all stopped to stare. I thought I'd break the ice.

"Hirayama-san, what are you doing?"

Eh! Not only was this giant gaijin going to Otsuka, but it knew their names. It was too much for one little guy. He squealed and ran off home. The other three gave me an escort, and by the time we had reached the small cluster of houses, another four kids were waiting for us. It was a triumphant arrival, and I was positively beating off questions until we got to Hirayama-san, the judo teacher's house.

"How old are you?" One kid guessed 120!

"How tall are you?" Another said 230cm!

"Can you dunk a basketball?"

"Of course," I lied, "but I've got sore feet, so I don't want to right now".

The Hirayamas had an old wooden house of classic Japanese design. Summers are hot and winters are cold, especially along the Japan Sea coast. Consequently the open plan is ideal for summer. Breezes can blow through an open house with screens opening it to the elements. In winter, shoji, paper screen doors, or fusuma, thicker sliding doors, are fitted to divide the living area up into small, easily heated rooms. A case study in efficiency, only those rooms required for living are heated.

The main living area opened on to a beautiful garden of maples and moss. Except for the modern conveniences, it felt as if it were part of the 18th century.

And the Hirayamas themselves were wonderful.

"You're the first gaijin ever to come to Otsuka," said one young boy.

"He's not. He's not. My parents said that a few years ago two gaijin came on bicycles selling books!" insisted another.

"That's right, Jehovah's Witnesses," confirmed Mr H.

8. BEACH PARTIES

AKITA

HONJO

FUKUURA

SAKATA
YUNOHAMA
TSURUOKA

NAKAHAMA

MURAKAMI
OTSUKA

My day off in Otsuka was marvelous. I managed to catch up on all those things I had been meaning to do for ages, such as write postcards, mend my shoes, and cut my hair. Hirayama Island was like a relaxing resort.

"Shall I fix your shorts?" asked Mrs Hirayama, holding up my tattered trousers and barely suppressing a giggle. Half the crotch had worn away, but they were much more comfortable for walking. I just had to be careful of the way I sat.

"No thanks, they're easier to walk in like that!" Mr Hirayama laughed aloud, and I'm sure all of Otsuka will remember me for my breezy shorts. She had done my washing and had me all prepared for the push up the coast.

Mentally, I wasn't quite as ready. I had a steady throbbing in my head, thanks to Mr Hirayama's various brews. A master of the tea ceremony, he was definitely not a master of brewing. His mixture of shochu and ginger had been palatable, I'll give him that. But his kiwifruit concoction had boasted unpeeled, wizened-up fruit that looked like the sort of things I find in my son's diapers, floating in a big jar of yellowly liquid. It took quite an effort to empty my glass. No sooner had I done so than an earthquake rattled the house.

"Don't look at me. I didn't do anything!" I joked, but nobody got it.

The village kids had followed my every move, and I had even caught two watching me have a bath. A pair of brothers arrived for my departure, bringing a mamori to keep me safe on my travels. It joined the others on my backpack. They had drawn rather flattering pictures of me in my walking gear. Incredibly long legs, a mop of yellow hair and a big nose. It was tough to leave, but when I finally tore myself away from all the care and attention, as on the first day, I had an escort through the paddies. The kids didn't know whether to wave or cry, and even Mrs Hirayama had a tear in her eye. I did too.

The paddies around Otsuka were huge—at least the size of a football field. A credit to Mr Hirayama's foresight, they could easily be worked by machinery, unlike the countless small, irregular shaped paddies that had been there for centuries. A couple of years before, he had taken the plunge and invested in converting his small labour-intensive paddies into a few machine-manageable larger ones that were competitive and more productive. He could now produce more with less effort.

His other wise move was to encourage his son not to be a farmer, he said. He foresaw that it would be difficult for a family to live by farming alone. Another income would be necessary. And so his son, my friend, had become a schoolteacher. With the new, big paddies, it was easy to supplement a teacher's salary with the production of rice without spending too much time on farming.

A man in a green baseball cap was trimming his hedge.

"Watch out, there's a typhoon coming," he warned.

"Don't sleep near the sea tonight. Stay in a train station." And he ran inside to get me a coke and some cookies.

It was so hot and sticky that I knew something was on the way. I dropped into an air-conditioned convenience store in Murakami for an ice block. It was difficult to leave.

But then I was on Route 346, the Sasegawa Coastline road, and beside the sea for the first time in a month. "Trucks Prohibited," read a large sign at the turn off. It brought a smile to my face. Trucks usually have confident, professional drivers. Some were too confident, though, passing within a whisker of my shoulder if I didn't jump back in time. Trucks in tunnels were especially hairy, and as my map showed plenty of tunnels in the next 30 kilometres, the sign meant that I could relax a little. I only had to worry about cars with their wild drivers!

The road and the train line followed each other around the coast, which was a succession of rocky outcrops, sandy beaches, and pine trees reaching down to the sea. A train-spotter with powerful binoculars on a tripod was just below the road, about one hundred metres from the tracks, and twice that from a sandy beach packed with summer revellers. He was staring through the binoculars with great concentration. I couldn't see any trains though. Only a bunch of girls on the beach in swimsuits!

Every now and then I came across a cluster of shabby, weather-worn minshuku huddled together.

"They only have one month in the summer to make any money," a beach parking-lot attendant told me. She looked like Darth Vader from Star Wars, bundled up in a mixture of hats, scarves and handkerchiefs, so that I could see only her eyes. The idea was to keep the sun off. She wore long trousers, a long sleeve shirt and gloves despite the mid-day heat and, from a distance, looked as if she was in armour.

The classic Japanese beauty has always had very white skin. White symbolized purity, and white skin was also seen as the sign of an upper-class woman, who would not have been working in the fields. I had noticed throughout my walk that women working outside tend to go to extraordinary lengths to cover themselves up and protect their skin. Make-up is also traditionally white, and is caked on when traditional clothing such as kimono are worn. The first time I met my mother-in-law, she was so pale that I thought she must be sick. (I can write this, as she doesn't understand English!) And whenever we visit, one of the first things she does is to insist my wife put on white make-up.

Darth Vader was collecting parking money at the designated bathing beach. Her carpark was nearly full.

"After August the 20th I go back to working in the fields," she explained. "We need to make as much money as possible over the summer."

600 yen for cars and 500 yen per person to go out on the beach seemed pretty steep. The beach didn't boast any facilities except things holiday-makers could pay for, such as showers, shade-roofs, and mats. The only thing free was the public toilets. I used those and soaked my cap in the handbasin. It was dry within 15 minutes.

And during that quarter of an hour I had passed another couple

Everything a summer holiday-maker could need!

of beaches—not designated bathing beaches but beaches neverthe-less. They were free, yet only a few vacationers were having fun in the sun.

An elderly lady in a wetsuit, pushing a wheelbarrow of seaweed came up a track from the beach. She nodded a greeting and was still staring when I turned around a couple of hundred metres down the road.

The roadside stall at Hayakawa sold every kind of beach equip-ment imaginable. The owner brought me out a deck chair and a mug of iced tea. I sat next to a huge blow-up banana float, took off my boots, and consumed the rice-ball lunch Mrs Hirayama had made me while chatting with the owner and her gaijin-fever-struck son. As it turned out, Niigata was having the only decent weather in Japan, while Kyushu and Western Japan were taking a pounding from the typhoon. The forecast wasn't too encouraging though.

At the next beach, a generator was sitting on the footpath next to a huge 4WD, whirring away, providing electricity to a family underneath an open-sided tent. The ultimate in luxury. An electric fan at the beach.

It's amazing how fast the best laid plans can go awry. At 6:00 pm Route 345 met Route 7, a kilometre before the place where a camping area was marked on my map.

"There are two or three shokudo there," Mr Hirayama had told me. "You can eat and then camp at the campground." He obviously hadn't been there in a while.

"No, there's no shokudo here," said the lady at the gas station at the intersection. "There's a drive-in about a kilometre past the turn-off to the campground, though."

"It's bound to be open on a Sunday evening," I thought. I resisted the temptation to leave my back-pack at the campground turn-off, in case the drive-in was closed. Just as well. Because, of course, it was. It was getting dark when I sat swearing outside the shokudo door. I had no supplies and little choice but to go on.

Four high school students on their way home from the beach escorted me into Fuya. The fourth and last shokudo was the only one still open and it was about to close as we arrived. But thank-fully, the husband and wife team saw me as an interesting diversion for a Sunday evening. I ordered noodles with a pork cutlet on top, "Katsuramen", and while the husband was cooking, the wife served me miso soup, pickles, rice and a delicious mussel soup as "service". The husband had collected the huge mussels that day, and that was their evening meal.

"Katsuramen isn't enough for you," the wife scolded me. "If you're going to make it to Hokkaido, you need to eat twice as much as that. You're so big!"

And as I got ready to leave, the husband gave me a pack of rice balls, some pickled plums, and a can of beer. "For breakfast" he said.

"You can camp on any of these beaches," he said. "People camp anywhere they like in the summer. No one will bother you. Good luck."

His wife showed me back out to Route 7. It was after nine and dark, like inside a cow. I was happy the typhoon had stayed away.

My map showed a camping area at Nakahama, which the husband had told me was next to a pachinko parlour, just past the chicken factory. It was hard to miss. The chickens were making a racket, and on the side of the road were three vending machines selling eggs. Three eggs for 50 yen. The pachinko parlour was packed, and its bright neon lights lit up the whole area. I followed a track down to the beach, which was brilliantly lit up by a big bonfire. An old bus and a truck were parked not too far from seven tents, and a group of men were having a raucous party around a smaller fire and barbeque.

"Look, it's a gaijin! What's he up to? Oi! Oi! What are you up to? Come and join us!" I had been spotted by a guy relieving himself beside the truck. He was having trouble rearranging himself, fumbling with his fly. "Oi! Oi!" Red, sweaty, excited faces turned, and within seconds I was seated at the smaller fire fighting off a barrage of questions in a local dialect, eating pigs innards off the BBQ, and guzzling beer. Without exception, the nine guys were completely sozzled, which made it even harder to understand their questions. Most were big, solid guys in T-shirts and shorts, towels wrapped around their foreheads, bellowing deep, hearty laughs. Fortunately one of them was sober enough to speak standard Japanese and interpret when I was in trouble.

"We're from Yonezawa, in Yamagata. We bring our families out here each year for a holiday at the beach. The wives and kids go to bed early. We don't!" He laughed, opening another can of beer for me. I was only half way through my first.

"Japanese woman! You like? You like?" sputtered a red-capped, red-faced whisky-breathing bloke in English, a couple of inches from my face.

"Ecchi Katsumi speaks English!" one shouted. Ecchi Katsumi received congratulations all round. He shook hands with everyone and tried again, this time from even closer.

"Japanese woman! Japanese woman! You like?" He spat in my eye, while cupping his hand at chest level.

"Yes, yes, my wife's Japanese!" I replied.

"Ecchi Katsumi love Japanese woman!" he continued. "I love your wife! I love his wife!" He laughed, sticking his foot into the red charcoals and letting out a squeal. "Ecchi" is another one of those hard to translate words. The best I can come up with is "pervert". "Me Ecchi Katsumi!" he stated proudly while inspecting his foot.

"He's ecchi alright," laughed a big bloke with huge arms. "He's been after my wife for years!"

The talk turned to gaijin women, and all proved that they should be in the "ecchi" category. Gaijin breasts were certainly a source of intrigue, and I found myself fending off all sorts of "ecchi" questions.

"I don't know, my wife's Japanese!" was a good excuse not to answer, but that just changed the topic slightly.

"We all come from the same part of town. All our kids are in the same class," my relatively sober mate explained. "Those four are road workers," he said, indicating Mr Big Arms, whose wife had to contend with Ecchi Katsumi, and three others. "I'm a teacher. Ecchi Katsumi has a shoe shop. He likes woman's legs. He's an electrician, and he works at the Post Office." He pointed at one guy who was trying in vain to open a bottle of whisky, and another who was frying more pig entrails. Another two had already disappeared. As it turned out, one had stumbled into and completely flattened Ecchi Katsumi's family's tent. His wife appeared, scolded everyone, including me, and led her perverted hubby off by the ear, much to everyone's enjoyment.

The party only broke up when the supply of alcohol and pig's entrails ran out. The fire gradually burned down, and I have no idea what time I finally crawled into my sleeping bag.

It was spitting at 6:30 when I was woken by loud music to find

Coastal camp-mates!

the whole group doing exercises on the beach, not ten metres from my tent. Wives and kids, overcome by holiday excitement, were yelling and screaming, while the husbands, having somehow found an alternate source of alcohol, were exercising while guzzling on cans of beer! As soon as I gingerly emerged from my tent, a beer was forced into my hand.

"It'll cure the hangover," Ecchi Katsumi encouraged me. He was already well under way. I went for a swim instead. The water was cool and clear, unlike my head.

Mr Big Arms' wife was particularly attractive, and I could see why Ecchi Katsumi had been chasing after her. She nabbed me at breakfast, making me sit with all the kids and teach them some English while we ate curried rice. Actually, I was glad to be at the kids' table, as the fathers were washing their curry down with beer, and there was already an open bottle of whiskey on their table. Most of the children had mastered "My name is . . ." by the time I was ready to leave.

It was an emotional farewell. Ecchi Katsumi made me sign his cap "in case you become famous," and as we parted he made a lewd comment about Mrs Big Arms' buttocks.

Within a quarter of an hour I was in Yamagata Prefecture, having a much-needed break at a drive-in. It was a chance to clean my teeth, which felt as though they were wearing socks, and to get all the sand out of my underpants!

Route 7 continued to hug the coastline and in some places was outside it, over the sea. The mountains were so close on the right, that instead of turning in with each little bay, the road would take a shortcut over the water to connect up with the next bit of land. It felt strange to see fishing villages and boats on my right while the sea was on my left. The boats were launched on huge concrete slipways and would have to travel under the highway on their way to the open sea.

At Atsumi, I took the inland route through the town. An old man on a bicycle with no hair and no teeth rode by. He had a full case of beer on his carrier rack. "Thanks for taking the trouble!" he grunted.

At Yura, the main road turned inland to the town of Tsuruoka, leaving me with a minor road on the coast. Yura itself was a busy little port with more than its fair share of squid boats and concrete breakwaters. It boasted a campground on a narrow strip of land right next to the road and a Government Lodging House on a hill overlooking the beach.

"We're full," said the receptionist. "But you're welcome to use the bath." So I spent an hour soaking away the pain in my feet and staring through dirty windows out over the bay.

The young guy with the backpack on the other side of the road was staring at me. There was something about him I couldn't put my finger on. His legs, arms and face were almost black with sunburn. Something was familiar. He nodded a greeting across the road.

"You're walking to Hokkaido, aren't you?" he said.

"Yes," I replied. "You're walking to Kagoshima?"

Unbelievable! Two guys walking the length of Japan, and we should happen to spot each other on the same deserted piece of road. He was a 23-year-old from Tokyo who had taken time off from his company.

"I wish I could take my time and enjoy it like you," he complained. "My boss gave me seventy days off, and if I'm not finished by then, I have to go back to work. I'll have to take a train back to

Tokyo, even if I've only got a few days to go! I start walking at 6 each morning and walk till it's dark. I've been walking seventy kilometres some days!"

He just put his sleeping bag down anywhere, as soon as it got dark, he said, and got up when it got light to start walking again. With only one change of clothes, no tent and no camera, he was on a light-weight mission. His map had very little detail, as he planned to stick to the Japan Sea coast through the full length of Honshu. To cap it all off, he was walking in sneakers!

After we headed off in our appropriate directions, I felt a real sense of purpose. There was I, averaging 35 kilometres a day, hoping to finish in 100 days and complaining about sore feet! He was averaging over 50 per day and had to finish in seventy days! Suddenly my feet didn't hurt as much, and I positively raced the final six kilometres to Yunohama.

Yunohama is an onsen resort town with the added bonus of a long sandy beach.

"Sleep on the beach," a souvenir shop owner told me. "The hotels and ryokan in this town charge a ridiculous amount. Heaps of people sleep on the beach in summer. Go have a bath and a meal and come back for tea afterwards." He sent me off to the "locals' onsen" which was under the bus station and cost only 50 yen. The tiles were falling off the walls, probably because the water was so hot.

"Sleep in the bus shelter," an old man in the bath said. "Accommodation is too expensive in this town!"

There was no doubt that Yunohama was a real tourist town. Groups, families and couples were wandering the streets in yukata, light cotton summer kimono, and geta, wooden clogs, checking out the souvenir shops and buying omiyage.

At the noodle shop an elderly man and his young mistress were the only other customers. He was obviously enraptured by her youth and beauty, behaving as if he was forty years younger, like a love-struck teenager.

"Shhh. Maybe he understands Japanese," she warned him. He didn't notice that she spent more time looking at the gaijin who was more her age. I did.

I sipped tea with the souvenir shop owner, seated on fold-up chairs, outside his shop. Two drunks in yukata and geta wobbled up.

"There isn't any asobi in this town," one complained to my new friend. "Why don't you get a pachinko parlour, some hostess bars or something?"

"Some women!" the other added. Although early in the season, the shop owner had obviously had enough of that kind of visitor. He was forthright in his answer.

"Why don't you do something great instead of getting drunk and womanizing? Why don't you walk to Hokkaido?—like this gaijin!"

Instead of the beach or the bus shelter, I opted to climb inland to the Yunohama Shrine to spend the night. I still had memories of TV shots of the wreckage from the 36 metre high tidal wave at Okushiri after the big earthquake. The beach didn't seem too attractive a proposition. And the bus shelter was brightly lit in the middle of town.

"Nobody goes up there at night," the shop owner said, giving me directions and a melon for breakfast. "It looks like rain, so that's the best option".

It was almost 10 by the time I had climbed up past the last houses to the shrine, which was surrounded by trees and had a commanding view of the town and beach. Skyrockets lit up the sky, and I could hear revellers down on the beach. Murphy's Law though. My torch had been turned on in my pack and the batteries were dead!

I climbed the steps and settled down in my sleeping bag under the bell-like gong that worshippers ring when praying. The shrine's eaves extended far out, giving me ample protection should the forecasted rain arrive, and I had a beautiful view out to sea. The wind rustled in the trees, and the shrine roof cut a fine angle above my head. I was soon off to sleep.

Crick! Crick! Crickl! The unmistakable sound of wooden geta on concrete. Oh no! Just my luck. Midnight worshippers! Crick! Crick! Getting closer. A male and female voice in whispered conversation. It's amazing how fast you can adjust from sleep to total alertness. Crick! Crick! Louder and Louder. I could see them by the moonlight, getting closer. Oh no! They were bound to ring the gong, pulling the long, decorated rope that was just above my head. Time for a quick decision.

"Excuse me, but . . . " was all I could get out.

"Iiiyaaaa!" A piercing scream of fright and the girl crick cricked her way out so fast that all I could see was a blurr! Her boyfriend wasn't far behind, any romantic notions well forgotten. Within ten seconds all was quiet again.

Oh no! I thought, here comes trouble. And sure enough, five minutes later I spotted a couple of shadows moving quietly towards the shrine. I tried again.

"Excuse me, but I'm sleeping here. Is it OK?" The shadows stopped. I had caught them by surprise. There was a whispered conversation.

"It's OK. Just be careful not to burn it down" was the eventual reply. I could hear retreating footsteps, but stayed alert for the next ten minutes or so. Then just as I was drifting off to sleep . . .

"Oyasumi Nasai" came out of the trees below. "Good night."

I woke with the sunrise at 4:30, and by five I could see people swimming and playing on the beach, far below. The Sea of Japan was as flat as a pancake and there wasn't a cloud in the sky.

A man walking an Alsatian pupppy greeted me as I came out of the shrine gate.

"Good morning. It's a beautiful day!" I couldn't help but agree with him.

The "locals' onsen" was packed by six. Yunohama survives on tourism, and hotels need staff on deck by 6:30 to cater for the visitors. There must have been twenty men in there who all knew each other. Two or three sported impressive tattoos, and without exception, they were surprised to see me.

"What's he doing here?"

"Where do you think he stayed?" I could hear the whispers. The water was clear and hot, and I soaked for ages as wave after wave of locals came through.

"We're busy from 6:00 to 7:30 in the mornings, and then again after 8 pm," the wizened old money collector told me. He was unshaven and had no front teeth. Then as I hoisted up my backpack, he said "Thank you" in English.

The road stayed a couple of kilometres inland from the coast, running straight as an arrow through farming country. No paddies, but vegetables and melons were being grown in the sandy soil. Every now and then a gun blast would resound across the fields, scaring off any birds that had come to eat their fill.

Tall green pines grew at an angle, away from the coast, attributable to steady onshore winds. But the day was warm and calm.

The road ducked into a tunnel to go under the Shonai Airport runway, and then, a few kilometres short of the town of Sakata, a love hotel and driving range stood proudly next to each other. Talk about convenience. All the requirements for a busy young executive making sales calls!

By 10:30 I had already walked twenty kilometres and was taking a break in a bright, white fast-food centre in a department store next to Sakata Station, eating fried noodles and writing postcards.

The Shonai Plain, like the bigger Niigata Plain where I had been three or four days earlier, is a rich fertile river plain, surrounded by mountains in all directions except to the west, where it borders the Sea of Japan. Its base is the Mogami River, which flows westwards from high in the Yamagata mountains and hits the coast at Sakata. The plain extends along the coast for forty kilometres, and it took me a full day to walk its length, from Yunohama in the south to Nishihama in the north. I left Sakata, in the middle of the plain, and headed north at mid-day.

The old lady in the melon stall held up a rock melon and indicated for me to cross the road. The sky had clouded over and it was spitting. Time for a break.

She was seventyish with gold front teeth and thinning hair.

"You're walking! That's great! We get plenty of cyclists like them!" she said, pointing at a couple of students riding by with backpacks and saddlebags. Cyclists always gave me plenty of encouragement, raising their fists and yelling "gambatte", or "fight", if they were brave enough to try their English. "But walkers? We don't get any walkers anymore!" she continued. "Walking is the only way to see Japan. They've built bullet trains and freeways, but that's not the way to travel. I wish I was your age and had your long legs!"

She wielded her chopping knife expertly and within seconds presented me with a ready to eat rock melon. The rain had stopped and the sun was out. I could feel the heat oozing out of the rich sandy soil.

"Nobody's buying melons this year," she complained. "They say the bubble has burst, but I don't understand it. All I know is that nobody's buying melons. What have bubbles got to do with it!"

In a tiny shop at Nishihama, I surprised a child of about eight who was serving.

"Excuse me, but . . . " was all I could get out.

"Grandma! Grandma!" the little boy yelled, disappearing out the back. After a few seconds Grandma appeared to find out what all the noise was about.

"Excuse me, but . . ."

"Chikako! Chikako!" she yelled, waving her hand in front of her face as if it were a fan.

"What's all the fuss about?" came Chikako's voice.

"A gaijin! A gaijin!" the small boy kept repeating.

I tried again. "Excuse me . . ." A lady who I assumed to be Chikako appeared. "Which way is it to Nishihama Onsen?"

"It's about two hundred metres down the road," she replied in perfect English. Grandma and the kid were looking a bit sheepish. They had understood my question after all.

Dominating the horizon ahead was Mt Chokai, a 2,237 metre high volcano that sits on the border of Yamagata and Akita. It is known as Dewa no Fuji, Dewa being the old name for those two prefectures.

The slopes of the mountain reach down to the sea, and from Nishihama, I was faced with a rugged rocky coastline.

"There are plenty of shokudo and places to stay," an old man with blackened, grimy teeth told me. "You've walked from Kagoshima! Ha! Ha! Ha!" he chortled away. I was getting sick of non-believers.

I was refreshed from a long stint in the cold-water bath. On my emerging from the onsen, the sun had almost broken through, and within a couple of kilometres Route 7 was out on the coast, pinched between pounding waves and the great volcano. The wind whipped in off the sea, and my skin felt cool and dry.

It was up and down stuff. One minute I was down beside the surf, ten minutes later climbing high above the coast. I turned a corner at one high point, and there on my right, amongst the trees on the far side of the road, was a raucous party. Youngsters were jumping in a pool, yelling and screaming; others were seated around picnic tables under sun umbrellas; and smoke was rising off the BBQ. A long house was almost hidden among the trees in the background. I was about fifty metres away when I was spotted.

"Look—a gaijin walking with a backpack!"

Everyone stopped dead and stared at me. Something wasn't quite right. I had been the centre of a fair bit of attention over the previous 69 days, but not quite to this unbridled extent.

"Come! Come and join us!" shouted one of the adults, a beer can in his hand. Tempting stuff. I crossed the road, trudged through some scrub, and came out at the swimming pool. There was rather a hushed silence. Slightly embarrassed, I headed for the man with the beer can, and the prime example of a bijin standing next him.

"Sit down! Sit down! Join us! Have a beer!" He was a jovial sort, and the bijin had a lovely smile. A beer was pressed into my hand the moment I lugged off my pack.

"Thanks. What a nice place for a party. Are you on holiday?"

"Every now and then we bring the kids out for a break," he replied.

And for the first time, I looked around at all the faces that were staring at me. The adults, the children's parents I assumed, were seated at the picnic tables, doing their own thing, drinking and laughing. The stares I felt so strongly were from the kids. Then I understood why something hadn't felt quite right. Unmistakably, all were mentally handicapped.

"We're from a handicapped school in Akita. We drove down today for a summer break and go back tomorrow. It's a good chance for the children to meet a gaijin. I doubt if any of them ever have. I hope you don't mind," my host said. "Michiko and I are teachers. She speaks English," he continued, indicating the bijin.

"No, no, I can't," she countered shyly.

"Yes she can. By the way, she's still single." He winked. Michiko squirmed with embarrassment.

Fireworks came out after dark, much to the kids' excitement. Rockets wizzed up into the sky, each producing a mass of bright stars and roars of approval from the assembled children. Showers of colour took the attention away from me, for which I was grateful. Then out came the sparklers, sticks of crackling white light which the kids held in their hands and waved around with uncontrolled enjoyment. It was a magnificent occasion. The wide-eyed expressions of joy on the children's faces were captured time and time again by happy mothers as cameras flashed and videos filmed.

I was invited to stay the night.

"We only have two large rooms. The girls have one side. We have the other," the teacher explained. "Is that OK? It is a great chance for the kids to meet you. Also for the mothers. Some of them have to be with their children 24 hours a day. They never get a chance to do anything interesting. This is an opportunity for them all to get together and release tensions and pressure. I hope it will be a good experience for you too."

It was the most sobering experience of my life.

Suddenly the house was full of screaming. High-pitched screams of excitement. The mothers, the male teacher, and I were seated around a large table in the kitchen, drinking whisky. The boys were with us, all except Hiro, whom I had seen sneaking out the door on all fours. At fourteen, he was almost as tall as I, but thin as a rake.

Michiko had taken the girls into the bath. It didn't take two guesses as to where Hiro had gone.

"Oh no!" cried Hiro's mother, who was having the first five minutes peace she'd had since I met her. She was out of the kitchen so fast that I'd have nominated her to be an Olympic sprinter. "Hiro! Hiro!" she cried.

Two naked girls came flying into the kitchen. They were yelling too. "Hiro! Hiro!"

It was quite a scene. I didn't know what to do. But all the mothers were laughing.

"The ability to laugh is very important," the teacher said to me. "Otherwise the pressure would get to everyone." I laughed too.

The curtains were thin, and the children were up as soon as it was light. At 5:15, one of the boys was constantly opening and closing the curtains, another was turning the light switch on and off, and one was busily playing with himself. I had a hangover!

I sat beside Hiro's mother at the breakfast table. The previous night's whisky bottles had been replaced by bowls of rice and miso soup and plates of yakizakana, grilled fish. One or two of the mothers looked a bit worse for wear. The kids were totally hyperactive, and I didn't envy the mothers who were in for another day of hard, hard work.

"It's a pity more of the fathers couldn't come," I said to Hiro's mother. Only one had made it.

"My husband doesn't want to know. He was a great baseball player. He wanted a son who could play baseball. He doesn't want anything to do with Hiro." I could see the strain on her face. She changed the subject.

"I've never talked to a gaijin before. I've seen plenty walking in the street in Akita, but you're the first I've talked to. I thought gaijin were loud and aggressive. But you're very kind. You're kind to the children. And also to us. Thank you for coming."

I didn't know what to say. After all, I had been walking by, wondering what to do the previous night. I had been invited in and given food, drink, a place to stay. I had been shown great kindness, and yet I was the one being thanked!

"It is I who should thank you," I replied. She smiled.

I never found out if Michiko, the bijin, could really speak English.

Within a kilometre I passed into Akita, the fifteenth prefecture of my walk. It was Day 70. The weather didn't have any respect for milestones, however, and the rain was hosing down. I trudged on and on, past the village of Kisakata, until finally I reached Kanoura, where an onsen was marked on my map. It was too good to pass up.

The rain was getting me down. It was July 28th. Where the hell was summer? Walking on a bright sunny day was easy, but plodding through pouring rain was brain-numbing. Spot did his job, but I would be soaked to the waist, the wind blowing the rain sideways, under my trusty umbrella. And when it was raining, there was no one to chat with. Only an idiot would be out walking in a downpour. Or a stupid gaijin walking the length of Japan!

"This onsen is natural hot water pumped from hundreds of metres below the ground. It is 53 degrees. Please be careful," read the sign on the wall over the onsen. Actually, it said exactly how deep it was pumped from, but the paint on the sign was peeling, making it unreadable. I stuck in a wrinkled big toe. It had spent the morning in wet boots and resembled a white prune. Its pain threshold must have been deadened, as I had to put the whole foot in before wincing in pain and jerking it out. The water felt as if it was near boiling point!

It took me a good ten minutes to submerge my body, which felt like it was cooking. Once in up to my neck, I dared not move. It wasn't bad, as long as I didn't move.

An old man with silver hair and a sunken chest came in. He nodded a greeting and read the sign. "This will be interesting," I thought to myself. I was right. "If a gaijin can get in, it can't be all that hot," he was thinking to himself. In good form, he dipped a tub in the bath, throwing the water over his feet, in order to wash off any dirt before getting in.

But he couldn't suppress a whimper of pain. He looked at me as if to say, "How the hell did you get in there!?", but then swallowed his pride.

"Do you mind if I put some cold water in?" he asked.

"No, go right ahead" was my reply, trying not to move a muscle. But inwardly I was smiling. Another gaijin stereotype bites the dust!

It was only midday, but I was considering flagging the day away at Kanoura. As I sat watching the news after my bath, wondering if I would ever recover, the rain stopped. I'll bet the people in Kyushu wished it would stop raining. The main news was of a massive typhoon plundering the southern island, causing flooding, landslides, death and destruction. From the film on the TV, I could see why coastal towns needed all those concrete breakwaters! Nature was busy proving a few points. The end of the news wasn't very encouraging either.

"The typhoon should swing up the Japan Sea Coast, reaching Niigata and Akita tomorrow afternoon. Please be prepared," said the announcer. If ever I needed encouragement to get out the door and walk when it wasn't raining, that was it.

It wasn't raining, but it was a grey, dull day. The traffic on route 7 was getting up my nose, but there were few options. I got off it where I could, wandering through the little town of Nikaho, which the main road had by-passed when it turned inland temporarily. Motorists benefited from such by-passes, but the towns didn't look like they had. Run-down and with few facilities, they looked like they had been left twenty years behind. And of course, a kilometre or so past the town was Route 7, rearing its ugly head, and coming back to meet the coast.

Honjo was my target for the day, and I arrived at rush hour.

There are plenty of ryokan near the Police Station, I had been told, and without any fuss at all, the first one I tried was happy to have me. Maybe that was because they had a room with a bed! I was so exhausted that I just accepted what they gave me. Two 5:30 mornings in a row had really taken it out of me. I spent the evening in my room sipping sake and watching the flood warnings being repeated on TV.

The morning news wasn't any better. Heavy rain and flood warnings for the Japan Sea Coast of Tohoku, north-eastern Honshu. But it wasn't raining. Just dull and overcast. Would the gods protect me? I could only hope for the impossible.

But within ten minutes, my hopes were dashed. Torrential rain pelted down out of the heavens, positively bouncing off the footpath around me. It was too much for Spot. He wilted under the deluge, and I was forced to seek cover under the eaves of the nearest building, a new car showroom. For the next fifteen minutes I was an unexpected distraction for the three women in the office, who smiled, waved and giggled until finally one came to the door and asked me if I'd like a coffee. It was tempting, but just at that moment the fierceness went out of the rain, and I grabbed the opportunity to hit the road.

The respite didn't last for long though. Route 7 hit the coast again. There was a huge swell, and the cloud level was below the hills to my right. It was going to be a long trudge to Akita! My map said it was 36 kilometres from Honjo. The ryokan owner had said it was 60. But at the pace I was going it felt like a hundred. I would walk without looking at my watch for what felt like an hour, only to take a quick glance and find it had only been twenty minutes.

Trucks tossed up walls of water, drenching every square centimetre of me. I needed a leak, but I had come across a heavy construction area. "I'll have to wait until I'm through," I thought to myself. At the far end, a stop/go man in a raincoat was training a new stop/go man. The reason I could tell which was which was that the experienced guy had a brown, weather-beaten rough face, while the new man still had pale, softish skin. I waited till I was about 100 metres past them, then with great relief urinated in the bushes on the side of the road. The only problem was that the new stop/go man had stuck out his red flag. The traffic had built up quickly and by the time I had finished and rearranged myself, there was a huge, long line of cars backed up well past me. I turned

around to face the staring drivers and passengers, slightly embarrassed. What could I do? I took a bow and kept going!

The roadside drive-in at Michikawa was one of the rough, concrete-floor variety. There was a stuffed badger wearing sunglasses
to greet customers just inside the door, and prints of huge fish lined
the walls. I ordered the curry.

"You're lucky," said the daughter, her hair pulled back in a
white scarf. "That's the last of the curry".

I sat down to eat, watching the news of flooding all over Akita.
Somewhere inland, the deluge had even caused a landslide which
had derailed a train. "Don't go out unless you have to," the announcer warned.

"You're a bloody idiot!" I murmured to myself.

Four labourers came in to lunch. They were wearing black tabi,
sock-type shoes with the big toe separate from the rest, that work-
men wear.

"Four plates of curry," one grunted. They were already sitting
at the table next to me, pouring over comics.

"Sorry, we're out of curry," the daughter called out from the
kitchen. "The pork cutlets are good!"

In unison, they turned to look at me eating my curry. I put on
my best "Sorry about that guys" expression and went back to
watching the news.

"Four pork cutlets!" the leader scowled.

"Are you taking the ferry to Hokkaido?" the daughter, who was
paying me a fair bit of attention, asked.

"Yes, from Oma to Hakodate."

"We've got a discount ticket out the back. A travelling salesman
left it here a while back. We'll never go to Hokkaido. Would you
like it?"

"That would be great. Thank you!" She disappeared into the
kitchen. The labourers at the next table scowled. Not only did I get
the last curry, but I was getting the undivided attention of the rather
attractive waitress. The boys weren't happy.

She reappeared with a faded, tatty 10% discount ticket. I turned
it over. The date stamp said Showa 59, the 59th year of the reign of
the Showa Emperor, Hirohito. 1984. "I'll bet I have some fun
presenting this at the ferry terminal," I thought to myself.

Akita is famous for its bijin. A modern industrial city with 300,000 inhabitants, and the prefectural capital, it is a natural congregating point for the young women who leave their small hometowns, but don't make it as far as Tokyo. I was impressed. In fact, I was so impressed that I had a sore neck.

The typhoon hadn't let up, and if I said that the trudge up the coast had been fun, I'd be lying. But I had made it, and I was looking forward to a big night. Not only is Akita famous for its beautiful women, it is also well-known for producing excellent rugby players, and from my playing days, I had a couple of friends there.

"Not a problem. Not a problem," grinned Hiro. "We've arranged a room for you at the Sky Hotel! We'll go and check in and head out for a few drinks!" It sounded dangerous. It was.

Hiro, Shin and I started the evening off quietly with a few quiet beers at a restaurant on the 9th floor of the hotel.

"While you're here you should see some of the Akita night life. We have beautiful women here."

"I've noticed" was all I could say, rubbing my neck.

We wound through a myriad of tiny streets, all sporting various drinking establishments until we found the building Hiro was looking for.

"This building is great! There are five floors with three karaoke bars on each floor."

"How are you at singing?" Shin said, grinning.

Things started to get hazy after the first bar. At the third or the fourth, I'm not sure which, Hiro introduced me as an All Black and kept putting the bar hostess' hand on my knee. She had dyed brown curly hair, a low cut dress, a deep cleavage and didn't know what an All Black was. She liked gaijin, though, and was quite happy to keep her hand on my knee.

The bar had, like all good karaoke bars, a laser disc karaoke machine. This machine, however, had something extra. The singer would croon his or her chosen song, lights would flash, bells would ring, and somehow, the machine would come up with a score out of 100.

"We have a special prize for top score for the night," the hostess said coyly.

"It's not you, is it?" I murmured. Luckily she didn't hear me. I should point out that I was not dressed like a standard karaoke bar customer. I didn't have a tie or jacket. I had, however, changed my wet shorts and sports shirts for dry shorts and a dry sports shirt. Long trousers, I thought, were a luxury I didn't want to lug around. I think this was one of the reasons she wouldn't leave my leg alone.

"You have such hairy blonde legs," she whispered, sneaking her hand higher than my knee. But I was saved by Shin.

"It's your turn," he grinned, passing me the songbook.

I should also point out that I am an awful singer. And the more I drink, the worse I get. And I know I must have been pretty bad as, to this day I can't remember what I sang.

But as I finished wailing and handed the mike back to the Mama san, who had a somewhat forced smile on her face, the lights flashed, the bells rang, and the machine gave me a score of 84.

"Top score! Top score!" the knee-grabber cried excitedly. "You win! You win!" The next highest score was Shin with 70. He was actually pretty good. His rendition of "Love me Tender" would have made Elvis cringe, but I thought he wasn't bad. Not as bad as me anyway.

"It was fixed," I said to him laughing.

"I know. You were awful!" was his reply.

I woke up fully clothed, lying on my bed, in a room on the 5th floor of the Sky Hotel at 3:15 am. I needed a glass of water. Badly.

9. WHAT HAPPENED TO SUMMER?

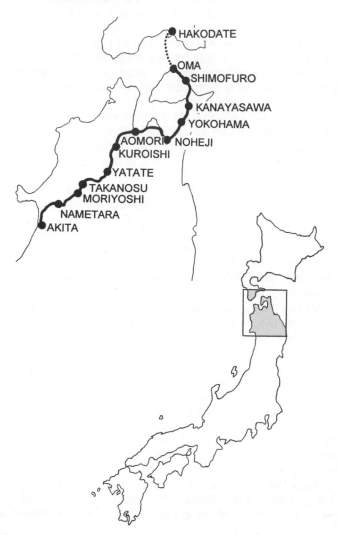

It was 10:30 before I had got my act together and recovered enough, to make a start. Hiro had come in for breakfast and from the 9th floor restaurant, we drank coffee and stared out at Mt Chokai, far in the distance. He didn't look well. He had staggered back to his office after midnight to find that half his workmates were still slaving away, and then taken advantage of a new service available in Akita. Instead of taking a taxi home, and forgetting where he parked his car, the average drunk can call a "hire-a-driver" company. A sober driver is duly delivered to the client's car, and after safely driving him home, he is whisked back into town by his company to do the same for the next wrecked individual. What service!

"If I bring the car home, it's a lot easier to convince my wife that I was just working late!" Hiro laughed. To keep me in his wife's good books I gave him the towel set I had won at the karaoke bar. "You were awful!" he said. I felt awful.

"Your friends have already paid your bill," said the sweet-smiling bijin of a receptionist. "Just sign here" she added in English.

I was out the door of the hotel at 10:30 and back fifteen minutes later. I'd forgotten Spot! But there he was, scruffy and brown, amongst all the sharp black business brollys in the rack. How could I forget such a friend? My plan was to hang him on the sign marking Cape Soya, which didn't seem so far away. If things went according to plan, I would be there within a month.

It was a warm, windy day, but the forecast was terrible. Ding Ding! Ding Ding! I was wandering down the middle of the footpath, still trying to get out of the sprawling city. Ding Ding! Ding Ding! I looked over my shoulder. An old lady on a bicycle was trying to get past. I had been aggressively ding dinged all over Japan, but this lady was exceptionally keen. She shooed me over to one side, waving her hand emphatically, and let me know what she thought with a big "harumph" as she pedalled by.

Just after lunch I happily said good-bye to Route 7, heading inland away from the coast. To my left the mountains of the Oga Peninsula were clearly visible, with a huge expanse of flat farmland between us.

"Lake Hachirogata used to be the second-biggest lake in Japan. It wasn't very deep." Shin had explained. "After the war, there was a real shortage of rice in Japan. The land was reclaimed and divided into ten-hectare farms that could easily be worked by machinery. It was a big effort to produce rice as quickly as possible, and it worked!" he added with strong parochial pride.

"Do you know teacher Andy?" I was being escorted by two eight year old girls. "He's an American too!" I tried to explain for the umpteenth time on tour, either out of a sense of national pride, or in an attempt to broaden their education, that I wasn't an American.

"Are you going to walk back to New Zealand after you get to Hokkaido?"

The wind was blowing a zephyr and the sky behind me was a deep purple with an orange tinge. The typhoon was on its way! Thunder rumbled up the coast. It was getting darker and more and more humid.

At Gojome, the road turned right towards the heart of the mountains, and I was winding up an ever-narrowing valley towards my target, Nametara Onsen. Only short people must walk in that valley, as I kept breaking cobwebs over the footpath with my head.

I checked directions at a tiny, cluttered shop on the side of the road. There was no room to move, and I managed to knock all sorts of goodies off the shelf. I was beginning to get that "big clumsy gaijin" feeling, a bit like Gulliver in Lilliput, but not that bad!

I was walking fast. Would I get to Nametara before the rain? I heaved a sigh of relief.

"Sorry, we're full," said the not-very-helpful owner. The skies opened with a thunderous roar, hailstones bouncing out in the carpark.

"Not a problem," said the extremely helpful restaurant manager. "Come and have some noodles and a bath, and then you can come back and stay at my place!" He was stocky and fortyish, with tight curly hair and a bushy black moustache.

So for the first time on my trip, apart from my hospital visit in Omachi, I hopped in a car. It was either that or be beaten to death by hailstones while trying to put up my tent for an extremely un-pleasant night.

"Don't worry," assured my new friend. "I open up again early tomorrow morning. I'll bring you back so you can start from the same place you finished tonight!" So we drove back down the valley with the broken cobwebs to Gojome, shared a few beers, and got scolded by his wife.

"I used to own a bar here," he explained. "But most young people leave Gojome for Akita, or even Tokyo. Economically, the town has gone downhill. Customers were only coming on Fridays and Saturdays, and then they stopped coming altogether. I had to close. Maybe things will get better in the future." He didn't look very hopeful though.

We were back at Nametara at 9:30 the next morning. The rain was piddling down. It was the last day of July.

"Temperatures today will be 7 degrees lower than normal. It seems that the rainy season is still with us. There will be heavy rain throughout Akita with flood warnings for the following areas . . ." the TV had said.

I had groaned. So had my new friend.

"It's Saturday, but nobody will come out today. Not with flood warnings. We're in for a slow day!"

"So am I," I thought. Just as I was about to set out he handed me a bit of paper.

"It's the phone number of an old girlfriend of mine in Hakodate," he said winking. "Give her a call. She'll look after you! She's a Hakodate bijin!"

Spot wasn't much use. He was slung over my shoulder to protect the back of my head from the driving wind and rain. My pack covered my back, but I had a cold, wet backside. It was a long, long trudge.

A truck driver stopped in the middle of the road, handing out a tomato juice.

"Gambatte!" Keep going!

And then I spotted my first bear! I didn't need my "kumayoke", though, as he wasn't going anywhere. He was in a cage that was so small it would have had a cockatoo complaining. According to the sign, he had been in there since 1979, taking three paces in one direction, turning, then taking three paces the other way. "Danger, don't put your hands in the cage," the sign read. The bear looked so bored, he would probably rip you to pieces just for something to do.

Finally, at 3:30 I made it to Moriyoshi, after a quick descent from a mountain pass. A gaijin was obviously a rarity. I pulled in to the Police Station for some advice. There was a poster of a gorgeous female in police uniform to encourage me, but sure enough, it was a man who came to the counter.

And I was after the cop in the middle!

"Where's she?" I asked pointing at the poster.

"You'll have to put up with me," he laughed. By the time I left fifteen minutes later, he had arranged me a ryokan in Takanosu about 15 kilometres down the road, drawn me a map, and reassured the owner three times that I was just like a Japanese and wouldn't be a problem.

"We're not going to have a summer this year. It's going to rain all August too!" he said pessimistically. "Good luck!" I wandered back out into the drizzly mist.

"You're Japanese is so pretty!" said the old woman selling barbecued corn outside Yonaisawa Station. "It's just like the Japanese on TV!"

I was slightly confused by the name of the place. My map marked it as Yonaisawa, whereas a sign outside the station read Komeuchisawa in Roman characters. Technically, both were correct, both being possible readings of the same Kanji characters. Only a local would be able to tell which was correct, which was the real name of the village.

"It's Yonaisawa!" said the old lady. "Whoever wrote Komeuchisawa was wrong!"

An old man was practising gateball by himself in the fading

light, and for about the tenth time that day, I woefully turned down an offer of a ride.

A flashing light signalled a police car, but when I finally got to it, it was a fake! It was elevated a couple of feet above the road, painted up like the real thing, but slightly rusted and with flat tyres. Still, I'm sure it was enough to make a speeding driver's heart jump. If he didn't know it was there!

The street-lights were on when I arrived at the bustling little town of Takanosu, soaked to the skin. The ryokan was having a major function downstairs, and black-suited dignitaries were arriving as I strode up out of the mist. I had walked 43 kilometres for the day, mostly in driving rain, but as the old couple were expecting me, they barely blinked. The dignitaries, however, unprepared, didn't show such self-control.

"Eh! A gaijin!"

"He's all wet!"

"What's he doing here?"

But I didn't care. All I wanted was to take a hot bath and to get off my battered feet. The old man handed me a business card.

"Please call Mr Nozaki. He left his card. Did you really walk from Moriyoshi? Mr Nozaki said you wouldn't get in his car! That's amazing!"

"Actually, I've walked from Kagoshima."

"Ha! Ha! Ha!" he chortled.

Mr Nozaki arrived on a bicycle after I'd had a relaxing soak in the tub and scared off a few more dignitaries.

"I didn't want to have to drive home," he explained. "They're very strict on drinking and driving here." He, like most Japanese, was an expert at riding a bicycle while using an umbrella.

On foot, we wandered down towards the station, to a street stacked with tiny bars. He picked one, and we entered to a warm welcome from everyone in the place.

"I went to university in Tokyo, then lived for three years in Osaka before coming back to Takanosu six months ago," he explained. "My family owns two kimono shops in town. I am 'chonan', the eldest son. It is my responsibility to take over my father's business and to look after my parents when he retires. Life here is not as exciting as in Osaka, but it is a good, honest life."

It looked pretty good to me. We were up to our second huge

handle of beer, and were tucking into the raw horsemeat and squid that the barman was testing me with. He oohed and aahed at each plate I polished off, reporting progress to some other patrons down the bar, and was particularly impressed when I ate the head of a shishamo, a small grilled fish.

"Half my Japanese customers won't eat that," he marvelled. "You're just like a Japanese!"

Mr Nozaki was very pleased with me. We eventually staggered out into the street and walked smack into a gaijin girl.

"Look, a gaijin!" he said to me, forgetting that I was one too. "I wonder what she's doing here?"

From the ryokan door I watched him head home, wobbling and weaving down the road on his bicycle, not bothering about his umbrella.

I was back on Route 7, which had turned inland and was following the Yoneshiro River Valley to the timber town of Odate. It was a drizzly Sunday morning, and cars were lined up outside the Asahi (morning sun) Pachinko Parlour, even before it opened at 9:30.

"I've been running this restaurant since before you were born" the man said smiling. His drive-in was called Karafuto, the Japanese name for southern Sakhalin, before it was taken by the Russians at the end of World War II. He took off his apron and sat down for a coffee.

"I was born on Karafuto. My two elder brothers died there," he said. "I remember it as my home. Fortunately, my parents brought us back to the mainland before the Russians came. We were lucky. My aunt," he continued, indicating his elderly helper, "had to hide in the mountains until everything calmed down. She has some terrible memories."

At this point she came over and joined us.

"The Japanese on Karafuto were sacrificed," she said. "Just like those on Okinawa. The Emperor didn't dare go to Okinawa until a few years ago, because they still remember. I remember too!" I sat riveted to my seat. "We should have been repatriated well before the surrender. The Russians interned our men until well into the 1950s, and when they did come back, they weren't men any more."

"Do you want to go back?" I asked quietly.

"I want to do ohakamairi; visit the graves of my two brothers," said the man who seemed to have aged as we talked.

It had stopped raining when I finally dragged myself away.

Odate is the home of the Akita dog, the most famous of whom was the legendary Hachiko. Hachiko was the pet dog of a university professor in Tokyo, who every morning would see his master off to work at Shibuya station. He would wait all day until his master returned. But one day the professor died at work and Hachiko waited outside Shibuya station for his return for the next ten years, surviving on scraps from passers-by. His story was known nation-wide, and contributions were sent from all over Japan to erect a statue to "Chuken Hachiko", faithful Hachiko. Today, his statue is a famous meeting place, and there are few Japanese who don't know of him.

The people of Odate were proud. "Welcome to Hachiko's Home-town," read signs as I came into the town which seemed like a hole in the cloudy mountains.

The woman at the Visitors Centre by the station tried to escape when she saw me enter. But she was trapped by another traveller. She giggled nervously when it was my turn, but somehow she managed to book me a room at an onsen ryokan about three hours walk away.

"He'll be there in about half an hour," she said into the phone. I'd already told her I was walking! Before she could hang up, I said, "Three hours. I'm walking! Tell them I'll be there in three hours." She cupped the mouth piece.

"But you can't. It's going to rain, and the train will take you right there!"

"He'll be there in half an hour!" she said into the phone and hung up, smiling at her victory.

I just shook my head and walked out. There was no point in arguing.

She was right about one thing though. It rained. And it rained hard. The valley was narrowing into the dark cloudy mountains, and it rained so hard that I gave up with Spot. I just resheathed him and trudged on, totally soaked.

In front of me stopped a van with the name of the ryokan I was booked at printed on its side!

The door was flung open.

"Quick—get in! Quick!" an old bloke yelled.

"Sorry, I can't. I'm walking."

"What? Quick get in!" he repeated.

"Thanks anyway, but I prefer to walk."

He shook his head.

"You're going to Yatate Onsen, aren't you?"

"Yes, I'll be there in a couple of hours."

He shook his head again.

"We'll be waiting." He drove off. I shook my head. What the heck was I doing?

The rain eased slightly. I was climbing steadily, surrounded by forest. Another Yatate van stopped, with a different driver. He didn't even test me.

"Keep going! It's not far to go! Good luck!" He sped off. I was expected.

I got there dead on 6 o'clock, and the whole staff came out to greet me. There were eight of them, including the kitchen staff, and the youngest would have been pushing seventy. The driver from the first van was still shaking his head. Two old ladies were trying to pick up my pack while I took my boots off, and when I wrung the water out of my socks, another whisked my dirty washing off to the laundry.

"You should have a bath," one said. I agreed with her. "Yatate Onsen is famous for being good for the internal organs. People come from Tokyo to bathe in our onsen," she said proudly. I didn't need any convincing.

The water was a rusty brown colour, and something resembling a calcium build-up was growing around the bath.

"You should drink it," said a wrinkly old fellow. "It's good for the organs." He tapped his scrawny rib-cage. It tasted terrible.

Dinner was exceptional. The only problem was that I invited a young cycle-tourer to join me and the meal that had been prepared for me proved to be much better than the one prepared for him. Embarrassment all round. I was certainly being well looked after.

He had cycled from Tokyo and was rather put out, being overshadowed by the gaijin walker.

"Your legs are so long that I bet you get to Kuroishi faster than the student on the bike!" cackled the old lady. She nudged her friend, who chortled away revealing a mouthful of gold. We were eating breakfast together.

"Do you come here often?"

"We're both 82! Been coming here since we were kids. Now we're old inakababa!" They laughed away, thoroughly enjoying themselves, calling themselves "old country women". To call someone an "inakamono", "a country person", is sometimes considered a disparaging remark, along the lines of calling somebody a "country bumpkin". Country people are often embarrassed in front of their supposedly-sophisticated city cousins, most of whom are only one or two generations away from being inakamono themselves.

"And you're only walking? You never take the train or hitchhike?" the other asked me.

"Never," broke in the van driver who was clearing away our dishes. "I tried to give him a ride when it was pouring yesterday. But he wouldn't get in. Said he preferred to walk! I thought he was crazy. But it's great! Great! He had an umbrella, but he wasn't even using it!"

This seemed to impress the assembled crowd of oldies.

"Your wife and children must be worried about you! Please hurry home to them!" the old woman said as I prepared to hit the road.

As with my arrival, the whole staff came out to see me off. They insisted on taking photos. Once again, my washing hadn't dried overnight, and when I hung it out on my pack, the whole group just about died laughing. One even tried to give me clothespegs! And they had made me an obento, a packed lunch.

"Please come again," they said as I made the round shaking hands. They had enjoyed having me just as much as I had enjoyed staying there.

Within ten minutes, at the top of the pass, I crossed into Aomori Prefecture, and by lunchtime had trudged down the narrow Hira River valley to Owani, a small onsen town with ski slopes cut into the forested mountains behind.

The valley widened into the Tsugaru Plain about 30 kilometres wide, the same in length, and surrounded by mountains. To my left was Mt Iwaki, Tsugaru no Fuji, its summit hidden by fluffy white cumulus clouds.

The western half of Aomori is known by the name of its feudal lords, the Tsugaru, whose base and main castle was in Hirosaki, clearly visible between Mt Iwaki and myself. I had escaped Route 7, and the road I was on skirted the foothills of the Hakkoda

Mountains, on the right of the plain. It was lined with apple orchards, the trees looking as if they were covered with icing sugar, the insecticide was so thick. It's no wonder Japanese always peel apples before eating them!

I had found an onsen. It had been a relaxing time alternating between watching TV in the sauna and gingerly entering the cold plunge pool. I was putting on my boots.

"Oi gaijin da!" "Look! A foreigner!" shouted middle-aged bloke with cheeks as red as cherries. He'd obviously been drinking, and was barely five paces away.

"Don't many gaijin come here?" I asked him. But he wasn't listening. He was preparing.

"H. . . H. . . How your name?" he stuttered in English. His wife, embarrassed, had him by the arm.

"Come on otosan (Father), we should be going. Atsuko's waiting!"

He stumbled. "How your name? How your name?" he shouted at me. He was having trouble with his shoes and they were slip-ons!

"Is everything all right here?" asked the woman attendant, coming out to the entrance hall.

"How your name?"

"No problems," I answered. "How far is it to Kuroishi?"

"How your name?" he muttered again.

"I'm so sorry," repeated the wife, leading her husband out into the carpark.

Sometimes it's not fun to be different.

In the main street of Kuroishi they were setting up for the Neputa festival. Two men were testing the microphone, in front of a make-shift grandstand.

"Tesuto, Tesuto!" one kept repeating, tapping the mike with increasing power. It sounded OK to me.

Although the more famous Nebuta festivals are in Aomori and Hirosaki cities, I knew the chances of finding a room were minimal. The big cities might have more glitz and money, but there is no doubt they are more tourist orientated. The Kuroishi "neputa" is more of a "locals'" festival. The kind of place that "festival fanatics" head for. However, the festival runs every night for a week, so I had a chance. And I could always pitch my tent in the park!

"Excuse me, are there any ryokan around here?" I asked the man who wasn't beating up the microphone.

"Eh! A ryokan? I doubt it. They're all full."

"Do you think anyone would mind if I camped in the park?" He looked thoughtful, then called over one of his assistants.

"Taka, see if you can find this gaijin a room." Taka was a tubby young man who looked happy to be away from carrying chairs. He had a new mission. His brother's souvenir shop was next door. His brother who could have been a twin except that he was as bald as a pool ball, got on the phone.

"Don't tell them it's a gaijin!" I suggested. He grinned at the idea and tried it. It worked, but I could see he felt a bit bad.

"Taka, can you run around to the ryokan with him? See you at the festival!" he said, waving.

Taka led the way. The ryokan had weathered grey wooden walls and dirty windows. He slid the door open.

"Excuse me! Excuse me! I've brought your guest!" The woman's jaw dropped when she saw me. "He speaks Japanese. I've been talking to him for ages. He's here to see the festival!" Taka turned and disappeared with alarming speed.

The Neputa Festival is a family affair.

Colourful neputa and taiko drums

"Shigeko, why don't you take the nice gaijin down to where the festival starts?" the owner said to her buck-toothed twenty-year-old daughter. She had taken an instant liking to me once we had managed to pick up her jaw, and I had told her she looked much too young to have a daughter Shigeko's age. Shigeko was on to me though.

"Sorry Mother, I have to study," she said, despite the fact that it was the summer holidays.

"Not a problem," I said, "I can find it. All I have to do is follow the crowd."

"Come and join us," said the old man with silvery, spiky hair, who was wearing a blue "happi" coat with his group's name on it. We were almost to the park. It was 5:30 and the festival was due to start at 6:30. I could hear the taiko drums from blocks away. Eight drummers in purple jackets, black pants, and black headbands were beating the taiko in unison. It was dusk and still warm. Sweat was flying. The crowd was watching with great enthusiasm, preparing for the excitement once dark approached.

The park was packed! Nebuta, or "neputa" as they are known in Kuroishi, are huge fan-shaped floats made of paper and wood,

spectacularly painted with dragons, warriors and female beauties.
Generators on wheels were being cranked up, illuminating the massive floats from the inside, and teams were already practicing their
chanting, the leaders perched high on top of the floats.

"Ari ari ari yah!"
"Ari ari ari yah!"

My team-mates don't look too enthused by my presence!

Each team was wearing distinctive happis. My spiky-haired mate
had introduced me to his group, and we had been tossing back
beers and drinking the atmosphere like there was no tomorrow. I
had ceremoniously been given a blue happi with "town" splashed
on it in red. We were the group from central Kuroishi. Our team
wasn't too intent on practicing though. Beers and the BBQ seemed
to be top of the list.

I went for a wander. There was hardly room to move. There
were seventy-four gaily coloured floats, each with its team that
included children to pull the float, drummers to beat the taiko drums,
and the flautists who came last. Each team had over one hundred
members all decked out in their team "happi." The splash of colour
was unbelievable. Excitement was building.

At 6:30 it was getting dark, and with a roar of excitement the first float pulled out. Kids and mothers pulled on long ropes, the callers on top of the floats shouted into megaphones, and the taiko started a steady deep beat. It took them a good five minutes just to get out the gate!

We changed from beer to cold sake, waiting for our turn. The sun had gone down, but it was warmer! Our team was out to win, to impress the judges. A hachimaki (headband) was tied around my head, and I was ordered to lead the kids. One little girl squealed with fear at having to be next to me and disappeared into her mothers arms to roars of laughter. Maybe the presence of the giant gaijin would be enough for the judges to award first place.

"Ari ari yah! Ari ari yah! Ari ari yah!" We were away seventh. Ruddy faces glowed with excitement. Sweat flew. Into it. As we pulled out of the gate, a gaijin cameraman jumped out.

"International Press," he yelled, blinding me with a huge flash. He was the only gaijin I saw the whole night.

The roads were lined with spectators, most joining the chanting.

"Ari ari yah! Ari ari yah!" The callers bellowed into their megaphones. We all cried in unison.

"Look! A gaijin! A gaijin!" I could hear the yells. People pointing.

The callers were taking turns on top of the floats. One calling, the other two using long poles to push away telephone lines, and wires over the roads. It had all been carefully figured out, and the huge floats barely missed the shop awnings. At intersections where there was a bit of space, we'd stop, still chanting, and the huge fan-shaped float would do a 360 degree turn to roars of approval from the crowd. Our nebuta sported a fiery-red fierce warrior with horns above his ears and a scraggly black beard. His fingers were like claws, and he had a terrible scowl on his face.

"Ari ari yah! Ari ari yah! Ari ari yah!"

Another cup of sake was pressed into my hand, then another. I tossed them back. We were almost to the judges. I could see the team in front stop and do two 360 degree turns as the crowd went wild, yelling and screaming.

"Ari ari yah! Ari ari yah!"

The following intersection was packed. Revellers flowed off the sidewalk. Families with picnics were sprawled over the footpaths. A clear, full moon sat high above us, watching the excitement. Chanting, I tried to spot the rabbit. According to the Japanese, it's not a man in the moon, but a rabbit. Even in my happy state I couldn't see him though!

"Ari ari yah! Ari ari yah!"

We had pulled the float over three kilometres when the crowds thinned down to nothing and we headed into a gas station to pack up.

"Thank you. Thank for joining us," everybody said, as we ate fried noodles and polished off even more beer. Once again I couldn't help wondering who should be thanking who. It had been a marvellous experience.

I went back to watch the rest of the floats, and by ten, when the last one passed the judges' stand, I was completely exhausted and could barely talk. Bright purples, oranges, yellows flashed before my eyes, and my throat was hoarse from all the ari ari yahs! What a night! It ended in a ramen shop.

"I saw you pulling the Neputa!" said the owner. "Please have this as a souvenir." He handed me a plastic fan advertising the festival.

Day 76 started out cloudless and breezy. My head felt cloudy, though. Especially after I disintegrated a low-hung barber shop sign, within five minutes of starting out.

I was heading north, through the old part of the town, when I came across a group of people crowded around a window on the footpath. A sumo "stable" was having a training camp inside, and posters invited the public to watch. Aomori has a proud record of producing excellent sumo wrestlers, and the assembled crowd was obviously knowledgeable. I took off my shoes and humped my pack inside for a break.

The training was hard. One muscle-bound monster was busily throwing around his younger, less experienced attackers, who were sent in to fight him in turns. He stomped around, threw back his head, slapped his thighs, and demolished ten opponents in a row. He was the "sempai" the senior student, and his authority showed. He earned his break, which came when the "sensei" or teacher grunted.

A tall, flabby "kohai" or junior was up next. He was huge, but had shown in his two meetings with the sempai that he lacked aggression. I didn't like his chances. He was covered in dirt and sweat from rolling on the "dohyo", the ring.

His first two smaller opponents shoved him around, and at a grunt from the sensei, the sempai jumped in with a handful of salt, rubbing it in the flabby kohai's mouth. He grimaced in pain, slapped his flanks and then his thighs and readied himself. He didn't make it though, and the next opponent rubbed his face in the dirt. There was no holding back, and he had to stay in the middle for another six opponents. His face was expressionless, except when he got the salt treatment, and at the end he could barely move. I am a keen student of karate and have seen some tough training, but that was brutal. It wasn't so much the physical work, but it was mentally demoralising. I left with great respect for those who had made it, but feeling sorry for those like the "kohai" who never would.

I met up with Route 7 again for the trek over the hills into Aomori city. I didn't have any choice.

"Are you from Misawa?" the old lady in the cluttered roadside shop asked me. Misawa, a small town on Aomori's Pacific coast is the site of a huge American Air Force base that at the peak of the Viet Nam War hosted 10,000 Americans. It's no wonder that any foreigner in Aomori prefecture is assumed to be an American.

"You're not an American?" she asked bewildered. "No, you can't be! You speak Japanese!" The American forces are not reknowned for their efforts to learn local customs, or the language. We chatted for a while. In came a truck driver, a regular.

"What's an American doing here?" he asked.

"He's not an American. Don't be rude to him. He speaks Japanese. He even understands our dialect!" she replied proudly.

"Hi," I chipped in.

"He's walked from Kagoshima!" the lady added.

"Walked from Yokohama? Why didn't he take the train?" he asked her.

"From Kagoshima, actually," I said, still not managing to get him to talk to me.

"How long did it take him to walk from Yokohama?" he quizzed her. She looked confused too.

"What's the point?" I thought to myself.

"Thanks for the ice cream," I said, making my escape.

"An American who speaks Japanese?" he was muttering, shaking his head.

"The Tsugaru dialect is the hardest to understand in Japan," the woman in the diner said. "I've been here for over twenty years and I still can't understand my mother-in-law sometimes!" she com-plained. For the second time on my walk I was considered so interesting that the TV in a shokudo had been turned off. The ultimate compliment.

"I'm from Hokkaido," she explained. "We speak standard Japanese there." Hokkaido is still considered the "frontier" in Japan. In America, pioneers went west. In Japan, they went north, mainly after the Meiji Restoration in the 1860's. Second sons, released criminals, and de-sworded samurai went north in search of land and new opportunities. They went from all over Japan, and if they had spoken their local dialects, communication would have been nearly impossible. Standard Japanese became a requirement, and I have heard it said that people in Hokkaido speak it better than those in Tokyo.

"When I go home for a visit, my mother complains that I speak Tsugaru-ben. Here, they laugh, because they say that I can't!"

"We get the occasional American from Misawa. Lately, lots of Russians have come here to buy scrap cars from my husband. He collects scraps for parts, but the Russians will buy anything. My husband doesn't even want to sell his cars, but the Russians offer him good money!" She shook her head.

Before the 53 kilometre Seikan Tunnel linking Honshu and Hokkaido was completed in 1988, all major transportation networks ended in Aomori. Ferries made the link to Hokkaido. Aomori was the city at the end of the line, and as I rolled down out of the hills, I had a great view of Aomori Bay with the Shimokita Peninsula far in the distance.

I had arranged to meet Kuma-san at the ferry terminal at the western end of town. But I had a couple of hours to wait, and the sun was shining. My legs and feet were aching, anticipating a day off. The grass outside the terminal was so inviting that I had a nap using my pack as a pillow. When I woke, the terminal was all action, preparing for the next sailing to Hokkaido. Cyclists, cars and motorbikes were pouring in, all heading north to the summer playground. I went for a stroll. On a narrow strip of land near the terminal there were at least a hundred tents crammed together, along with a crowd of holidaying revellers.

"Why's everybody camped here?" I asked a man who had just finished urinating in some bushes.

"Nebuta!" he replied. "We're here for the Nebuta Festival! When it's finished we're all going to Hokkaido!"

Kuma san and I spent the evening at the festival.

"Aomori gets so crowded," he said, "that they sail cruise ships up from Tokyo to act as floating hotels. Tourists come from all over. Lots of Americans come from Misawa. It's truly an international festival!"

It was. There were tens of thousands of people, but somehow it lacked that small town enthusiasm of the Kuroishi "neputa". The floats were bigger and infinitely brighter, but they all sported their sponsors' names. Instead of groups from all parts of town, there was the Asahi sponsored float, the Sony float, and the Suntory float. Commercialism had attacked the festival at its roots. The nebuta is a big attraction for Aomori, and no expense was being spared to see that visitors went home satisfied, telling their family and friends what a great festival it was.

I'm not saying that I didn't have a great time. I did. The famed Aomori bijin were in ample evidence, and with the aid of a few cans of sake, it didn't take much coercion to have me chanting and dancing along with everbody else.

One of the last floats was the biggest taiko drum I have ever seen. It was so big that it lay on its side, with three drummers pounding away at each end. The mystical booms enchanted the crowds to a fever-pitched high, and the chanting and dancing took on a new excitement as it proceeded through the wide streets of Aomori city.

It was a Wednesday evening and the onsen was packed. The woman collecting the money wasn't so busy that she couldn't stare at me as I got changed. I grinned at her as I took off my trousers, but she just grinned back. I could hear whispers in the onsen. The words "Amerikajin" and "Misawa" were easy to pick out. I felt like standing up and making a speech to announce that I was not an American from Misawa but it wasn't really appropriate.

An old bloke with curly grey hair and faded tattoos interrogated me in the sauna. His face was beetroot red and he stank of sake. But I plugged away, telling him of my walk, about my family, about New Zealand.

"But what is it like in America?" was his final question. I went out for a dip in the plunge pool. As the sauna door was closing behind me, I heard him say, "Yappari (Just as I thought!), an American from Misawa!"

As I strolled back to Kuma san's, I passed a sign in English for "live beer". Hopefully, it was as close as I would get to a "live bear". I went inside to investigate.

Another perfect day in Aomori City.

The dogs of Aomori were getting to me. Less intelligent ones would bark and growl from the moment they saw me, until I was out of sight. The sneaky, cunning ones were the ones to beware of. They would hide in their garages, crouching, waiting till I was level with them, then fly out with a frightening yelp until they reached the ends of their chains, barely missing my leg. Teeth would slam shut alarmingly close, and I would just about jump out of my skin.

As I walked out of Aomori with the sea on my left, Mt Hakkoda and its accompanying volcanic peaks loomed high on my right, covered in forest. The foothills came down to join with the coast ahead of me and I knew I would soon be climbing.

A group of about twenty-five students pedalled by on bicycles.

"Gambatte!" they cried, raising their fists in the air.

"Fight! Fight!" Some tried the best English equivalent they could come up with, encouraging me to keep going. But there was no way I was going to give up!

The road climbed over a hump of land before descending back down to the coast at Noheji Bay, and I found myself walking in a southerly direction with the sea on my left. It was a strange sensation. The Shimokita Peninsula is the shape of an axe, and I could see the handle that I would be walking up the next day, far across the bay. The wind was strong, and white-capped waves were whipping in, crashing on the rocks.

The fishing villages were depressingly grey with few signs of life. In a shop at Karibasawa the woman in charge was asleep in a tatami room adjoining the shop. I had to wake her up to pay for my ice cream. She didn't even bother getting up, but just rolled over and held her hand out for the money. She just looked at me dully when I asked her how far it was to Noheji.

"About five minutes," she grunted.

Stalls were selling hotategai (scallops) on the side of the road. "Frozen Delivery," the signs read. "Can be delivered anywhere in Japan."

Just as I left Route 4 with great glee, I noticed a lonely figure perched on a concrete breakwater staring out to sea. He was about 60. Our eyes met for an instant, but his darted back to the sea. As I walked by, I could see that the back of his shoes had been cut off to make outdoor slippers, easy to get in and out of. He was scruffily dressed, and epitomized the dreariness of the area.

At the Noheji Police Station, two policemen were attending the counter. One was a lot sharper than the other. When he saw me come in, he quickly picked up his phone and started dialing. When the other noticed me, he looked at his partner, who of course, indicated that he was busy. The one on the phone grinned as the other hauled himself out of his chair.

He arranged me a room at an old weather-beaten ryokan near the centre of town. It had been built in 1901 and the warped wooden floors had been worn shiny by generations of guests.

"You're lucky," said the old lady with incredibly thick glasses. "This is our last room. We're so busy at the moment!" I looked around. There wasn't a soul there, and there hadn't been any shoes at the entrance.

"Where are the other guests?"

"They've all gone to Aomori for the Nebuta festival. It's on every night for a week. It's our busiest time of the year. They run out of rooms in Aomori, so lots of people come here. It's only 40 kilometres away."

It had been a long hard 40 kilometres for me.

My room had only sliding paper shoji screens between it and the main corridor. The couple in the room next door watched TV until about 2 am, and the screens let in the morning light at 5:30 so I didn't get much sleep. I was feeling grumpy even before bashing my head on a door frame. I was sure it was the most solid bit of wood in the whole building.

But the old lady had made me an obento, and invited me in for coffee before I left.

"Aren't you cold?" she asked, looking at my sports shirt and shorts, and shivering. "We're not going to have a summer this year by the look of it."

It was the 6th of August, though it felt like the middle of October. Fool that I was, I had sent my fleecy sweatshirt home in an effort to lighten my pack, under the impression that, as in any normal year, I would be walking in high summer temperatures. I had been worrying about heat exhaustion, when I should have been worrying about freezing to death.

"You know, this is the first time in fifty years that they say they can't identify the end of rainy season. If it doesn't get hot soon, all the rice crops will fail."

It was windy, cold and cloudy outside. Within five minutes of starting, I put on an extra shirt and my cap for warmth!

A group was doing calisthenics in track suits down on the beach below the road. Where were all those Aomori bijin in their bathing suits? Tucked up next to their heaters! And where was the stupid gaijin who was walking the length of Japan? Out in the cold of course.

Unravelled cassette tapes lined the road for what seemed like kilometres. Drivers must have hung on to the tape while tossing the case out the window, until they had totally unravelled the works of their most disliked musicians.

It was another depressing day. It was Hiroshima Day, exactly 48 years since the world's first atom bomb was dropped on Hiroshima. The morning news had shown those same harrowing pictures that can only depress, and as I trudged up that cold coastline, it was hard to get them out of my mind. But then I came across a deserted kitten and spent the next twenty minutes swearing away at whoever could do such a thing to an innocent animal. It was hardly on the same level, but just as depressing.

The road stuck to the coast, with low green hills covered with cloud on my right. There was green pasture, and a couple of times I noticed that unmistakable smell of "cow", though none were to be seen.

A solitary student cyclist wearing an All Black cap stopped and walked with me for a few kilometres. He was from Nagoya and would spend the next couple of weeks cycling around the peninsula. He wasn't interested in Hiroshima Day though. August the 6th was also the day that Mr Hosokawa would become Prime Minister.

"It's great! It's about time we had a new party in power. I hope he can clean up the corruption in politics," he said, echoing the thoughts of just about everyone I spoke to. Little were we to know that within nine months Hosokawa himself would resign over a scandal involving money. I find Japanese politics depressing also, but on that day, there was reason for a new hope, and my new friend was expressing his. "I'll probably see you further up the peninsula," he said as he pedalled into the distance.

The town of Yokohama was deserted, apart from the bloke in the liquor shop who was watching pro wrestling on TV. It was clear from the first look he gave me that he thought I was the equal of Giant Baba.

"I hope it gets hot soon," he said. "Nobody's buying any beer. I brought heaps in for the summer, but I've still got most of it!" We shared some rice crackers. "I've got nothing to do during the day," he complained. "Nobody's bothering to go out in the cold. They all telephone their orders in the evening, and I'm stuck doing deliveries until late!"

The bells were chiming 5 o'clock when I got to Nakanozawa. The only shokudo was closed, and the two guys in the Post Office weren't helpful when I quizzed them about places to stay. And then there was no one in the police station, despite my pounding on the door. I was getting really upset with Friday, August the 6th. So I trudged on.

"There's a minshuku at Kanayazawa," said an old lady who was working in her garden, despite the cold. "I've got nothing else to do," she explained.

And so right on six I cleared a hill and came across a lovely family minshuku that even had a shop attached.

"I'm sorry we can't serve you dinner," the wife apologized, "we have a function upstairs. You can have the last room though." She had an enchanting smile.

The relief when I took off my shoes was orgasmic. 45 kilometres for the day had left my soles aching, despite the fact that in the early afternoon I had attacked my sleeping mat with my pocket-knife scissors, cut out an image of my foot, and slid it into my boot for some padding. It had been pounded flat during the afternoon, but I was encouraged enough to cut out another pair for the next day. At this rate, I wouldn't have much of a sleeping mat left on arrival at Cape Soya!

My "hell day" was almost over. The news was of more typhoons, flooding and carnage in Kagoshima, and the weather forecast was for more rain. I went to sleep early!

Cows were mooing as I had a shower the next morning. I opened the window to find the barn right next door. It was far more pleasant than the roar of a truck engine.

The twelve-year-old daughter wanted to learn some English, so she sat with me as I had breakfast. I was feeling pessimistic.

"It will rain today," I said, telling her to repeat.

"It will rain today." She was pretty good.

"It will rain today!" she exclaimed to her mother who came in carrying a big obento.

"I make them every morning for the construction workers who stay here. I made an extra one today!" she said smiling. "Please have it."

"It will rain today," the daughter yelled. "It will rain today!" She was like a cracked record.

"Good luck," said the mother. "Please don't forget us."

"It will rain today!" in my ear. I was regretting my English teaching effort.

The axe-head of the Shimokita Peninsula was formed by eruptions and lava flows from Mt Osore, at its centre. The dormant volcano's name means "mountain of dread", and it is believed to be one of only three places in Japan where spirits come to earth to catch up with what is going on. It was barely twenty kilometres away as the crow flies as I started out on my 80th day. A layer of thick cloud sliced it off not far above sea level, but I had seen enough the day before to know it was an impressive mountain.

It was cold again, but the rain was holding off. Maybe my little English student was wrong!

I stopped to watch a tatami-maker toiling away in his shop in Mutsu. He motioned for me to come in. His task for the day was to do the finishing touches, to put the reed cover on the packed straw board, and to sew on the ribbon edging. His hands were calloused and strong.

"It's easy now," he said. "We use machines for everything. I can churn out 25 or 30 mats per day, compared to the 5 or 6 we could make in a day thirty years ago."

"That's great!" I said.

"Not really," he countered. "Tatami-making used to be an art. A tatami-maker needed skill, and he could have pride in the quality of his work. Now, anybody can make a tatami. The emphasis is on making as many as possible, as fast as possible. We've lost a skill," he said sadly. "I couldn't compete if I tried to make tatami by hand anymore."

"Thanks for listening," he said as I left, handing me a packet of dried squid.

A gas station on the outskirts of Mutsu was providing excellent service. A car pulled up and the lady driver was swamped before she could get out.

One man did the pumping, and another checked her oil and water, while a young girl checked the air pressure in her tyres. All wore distinctive red and white striped uniforms. The fourth was obviously a raw recruit. He was in charge of the hose and looked like he intended to wash the car down for her. He waited until his team was finished at their chores and then made the ultimate mistake. He forgot to tell the lady to wind her window up.

She positively squealed at the soaking. I couldn't help grinning, but it was almost fatal. A low-hung sign off a telephone pole knocked my cap off as I walked underneath.

I soaked in the murky brown onsen water for about an hour, looking north, out over the cloud-covered hills and the green fields and down to the pounding surf. It was the first time I had seen the Pacific Ocean since leaving Cape Sata.

I was alone in the large bath, the only other bather having re-treated to the sauna on my arrival.

All of a sudden I felt wobbly, as if not in control of my balance. The horizon didn't seem level. It wasn't.

"Jishin!" someone shouted. "Earthquake!"

The building was shuddering. "And me in my birthday suit!" I thought. "It'll be just my luck if we have to run outside." I sheltered under the doorframe, naked. It stopped.

"Another earthquake off Hokkaido's western coast, near Okushiri Island," the TV announcer said excitedly. "Not so strong as the one in July, but felt as far away as Aomori . . ."

"No kidding," I thought. "I'm in Aomori and I just about ran outside naked! Maybe Hokkaido's issuing me a warning not to visit!"

I was sitting in the "relaxing room" after getting changed. The obento from the minshuku was great—fried scallops, yellow pickles called takuan, and rice balls with pickled plums inside. My mind was on other things though. Aside from bears, my next biggest worry was tidal waves. Pictures of the 36 metre high one in July had impressed on me its destructive force. And there I was about to wander down to the coast barely half an hour after a sizeable earthquake. I stared out at "Mount Dread," still hiding under its cover of cloud. The clouds seemed to be in the shape of a laughing face.

"Ha! Ha! Ha!" I thought, readying myself.

The port area of Ohata looked like someone should do it a favour and toss in a match. Weathered wooden shacks looked like they would just crash in with a gentle push.

The main street was livelier. I polished off half a litre of milk at the supermarket while flirting with the check-out girl.

"Does anyone know how long it takes to walk to Shimoburo?" she asked in a loud voice. The ten or so customers in the shop all shook their head. "This gaijin is walking there!"

"What are you walking to Shimoburo for?" a young man asked.

"Well actually, I'm walking to Hokkaido."

Silence. It was at this stage that I realised that I was barely 30 kilometres from the end of Honshu. The major hurdle of Japan's largest island was almost over. I knew I was going to make it. Only a bear or a tidal wave could stop me.

"Actually I'm going to take the ferry to Hokkaido," I finished lamely. The girl looked disappointed.

The lady in the minshuku centre at Shimoburo onsen tut-tutted me.

"Saturday evening and you haven't got a booking! Tut-tut. I don't like your chances. Tut-tut. Well, you might be lucky. Tut-tut. It's such a terrible summer. Tut-tut. I'll see what I can find."

The first place she tried had a spare room, and she even explained that I was a gaijin before asking.

"We're having a rotten summer!" the owner explained. "My kids have only gone swimming twice so far this year. They usually swim every day! I'll send my son up to the onsen to tell them you're coming!" Maybe he thought it would cushion the shock.

I should have taken my sunglasses to the onsen. The floor was bright yellow and the inside of the bath sky blue! A skinny old man with white hair and a big chest complained to me about the state of the local economy.

"This village depends on tourists and fishing. I'm a fisherman. But we get less and less money for our fish. It's OK for me because I'm old, but for a young family . . . and then they raise the locals' price for the onsen from 70 to 100 yen. It's not right," he said loudly so the money collector could hear.

The waitress in the shokudo looked as if she was about to burst. "I'm due in two weeks," she explained.

"When do you expect to finish?" asked her father, the cook. The surprise on my face must have shown. "Don't you remember? I offered you a ride this afternoon, but you said you were only walking! I assume you're walking somewhere!"

"I should be at Cape Soya in three weeks," I said, slightly embarrassed. We shared a pot of sake, the local brew.

"I'm from Shimoburo," he said, "but I ran a shokudo in Tokyo for ten years. After ten years, I thought I'd go crazy. So many people, and everyone in a hurry. That's not living, that's existing. So I came back home. And I'm just about to have my first grandchild," he added proudly. From the look of his daughter, he didn't have long to wait.

At exactly 4:45 am the minshuku shook violently. "Here we go again," I thought, crawling, half-asleep under the door frame. There was a fair bit of crashing and bashing for thirty seconds or so, then back to relative normality. Apart from the fact that everyone was wide awake wondering what would happen next. I thanked my lucky stars I hadn't been camped at the beach. 1993, the year without a summer. The year of typhoons and earthquakes. Good choice Craig! It's no wonder that Shinto, Japan's native religion, stresses harmony with nature. It seemed that every few days, nature wreaked havoc in some part of that rugged land.

I was out the door by seven, intent on making it to Oma in time for the 11:30 ferry. It wasn't a hardship to get up early. Everyone in the little resort town had been awake since the earthquake anyway. Visible damage was minimal, though damage to nerves was much more obvious.

It was cloudy and the road stuck to the coast like glue. Mt Osore was still hiding on my left. Disused tunnels and bridges next to the road told of the work that had been done to build a train line to Oma before World War II. The war had disrupted the effort and it had never been continued, an elderly shop-keeper told me.

"How did you get here?" asked a kid with a new crew-cut. The white skin still showed beneath the black stubble.

"I walked." He thought about it for a while.

"But Japan is an island country!" Smart kid!

My friend from a few days before, the cyclist from Nagoya, came riding up from the opposite direction. He was wearing full wind-proof gear and gloves. I was still in a sports shirt and shorts.

"I was camping in the park next to the ferry terminal in Oma when the earthquake hit," he explained. "I was so scared I just hopped on my bike and rode for high ground. I thought that there was bound to be a tidal wave!"

That made me feel better. At least I wasn't the only one scared of tidal waves.

The lighthouse at Cape Oma, the northernmost point on Honshu came into view, and I knew I was almost there. Honshu was a major milestone. It had taken 65 days to walk from Shimonoseki. My ankle gave a groan of approval as I sat down at the ferry terminal. Little did it know that it still had Hokkaido to go.

"Where did you get this?" asked the bloke at the ticket counter when I handed over my 10% discount ticket.

"From a shokudo in Akita!" I replied truthfully. He took it away, and I could hear the staff having a good laugh as they examined it.

But my ticket was duly reduced from 1000 yen to 900 yen. I had time for a bowl of noodles before getting on the ferry and sleeping all the way to Hokkaido.

I walked off the ferry to meet a friend of a friend. He looked me up and down. At my feet's insistence I had changed my boots for thongs, and having just woken up, was not looking my best. He, on the other hand, was dressed immaculately in dark suit and tie.

"Mr Craig?" he asked, hesitantly.

"Mr Sugiyama?" Yes. Greetings aside, I knew things were going to get tricky.

"Please get in," he said indicating his smart black Toyota parked at the curb.

"Well, actually I'd like to walk if that's OK."

"Walk?"

"Well I've walked from Kagoshima and I don't want to get in a car." Perhaps my friend hadn't explained things to him.

"But it's about three kilometres!" he said.

"That's OK. I've walked nearly 2,500 already." He shook his head, but my stubbornness won the day.

"Follow me," he said, still shaking his head. So for the next three kilometres I followed a black Toyota with its hazard lights flashing through the back streets of Hakodate at five kilometres an hour. It was like having a police escort apart from the fact that Sugiyama-san's car kept blocking traffic and that angry drivers would vent their frustration with sharp blasts on the horn.

I strode along trying not to laugh. Surely it would have been easier to draw me a map.

Sugiyama-san and his friend Terauchi-san were very strong in their condemnation of some aspects of modern Japanese society. They knew I was searching for the "real" Japan and, surprisingly, didn't hold back in their views. We had eaten in a tiny shokudo and were sitting back drinking tea.

"Life in Japan is too good!" remarked Terauchi-san. "Look at that," he said, indicating the table next to us. The customers had left after eating about half their meal. "When we grew up in the early 1950s, it was a crime to leave as much as one grain of rice in your bowl. If we did, we were scolded by our parents. Now, Japan is a rich country. Life is extravagant. People have forgotten their values! Look at that! Those people have left, not even eating their crabmeat! What a waste!"

"Japanese don't seem too concerned with preserving their country," I chipped in. "Garbage lines the roads. I've seen people dumping bags of garbage by the road, graveyards of rusted cars. Even a washing machine in a river that had just been tossed off a bridge."

"That's right. People are concerned only with keeping their private little world clean. Like their apartments, or the inside of their cars," added Sugiyama san. "People will clean their own environment by dumping their ashtrays into the streets! There are too many rights and not enough responsibilities!" This was pretty damning stuff. Not the sort of thing a gaijin hears from a Japanese too often.

"Japanese like everything to be new. That's why TV ads always say 'shinhatsubai'. 'This is a new product'. Anything old is thought to be worthless and just cast aside. Like those cars you've seen. You can't sell an old car, and it costs money to scrap it, so it's easier and cheaper to just park it somewhere and leave it!"

"Small towns are fighting for their survival," said Mr Sugiyama. "People go to cities like Tokyo and Sapporo for work and a big income. They get there and they don't enjoy it. They want to come home, but there's nothing to come home to. In Tokyo, people from Tohoku congregate in bars in Ueno, talking of their homes. Ueno is where the trains from Tohoku arrive. It's as close as they can get."

"That's why small towns want good facilities like schools, public gymnasiums, concert halls and such—to encourage young families to come back home. The best thing a small town can do is encourage big companies to build a factory there. It provides good work and will bring people back. It's better for the companies, as land is cheaper than in Tokyo, and they don't have to pay as much in wages. And it's better for the workers, as they are back in their hometowns with their families, and everything is cheaper."

"So there is incredible competition to attract companies. Towns produce brochures advertising their town and employ people solely to go around big companies asking them to build a factory. The Mayor of a town is like the head of a company. He has to go out and compete to keep his town alive. In Izumo, Shimane Prefecture, they have a marketing expert as Mayor, and it's proven very successful."

"Historically, small towns have relied on either farming or fishing, but both have gone downhill. If we are made to import rice, farming will die. And we have to go further and further afield to catch fish, and we still compete with imports. It's a tough time for small towns in Japan."

It was an interesting conversation. My two new friends were speaking candidly, from their hearts. Any pretence of "public face" was gone, and I was hearing their true thoughts. I was privileged.

"Until the Meiji Restoration of the emperor in the late 1860s, Hokkaido was known as Ezo and was thought of like a foreign country. Hakodate was the capital, but few Japanese ventured north of here. Hokkaido was inhabited by the Ainu."

"But land was scarce in Honshu. The Meiji Government built Sapporo along the lines of western cities and people were encouraged to immigrate. People came for many reasons. Samurai who had lost their elevated status came. Suddenly they had found themselves the same as everyone else and some couldn't handle it. They came here. Released criminals could come here for a fresh start. Farmers traditionally had many children, but only the first son was important. He inherited the land and family responsibilities.

"Younger sons were often cast out, while unneeded daughters were sold. Those sorts of people came here. They came from all over, often settling in an area with others from their district. There is a town near Sapporo called Hiroshima-cho. Its settlers came from Hiroshima. The people in Yakumo came from Nagoya. Those in Date, from Sendai. Many came from Tohoku, northern Honshu.

"Hakodate is close to Tohoku. It was the link with Honshu. We speak Japanese like they do in Tohoku. Short and sharp. Fishermen and farmers don't need to speak nicely like merchants. They just need to get the meaning across. But north of here, everyone speaks standard Japanese. They had to or they wouldn't have understood each other."

In the evening we adjourned to a karaoke bar in downtown Hakodate. It was very plush, and as soon as we entered, a Filipina bar hostess was assigned to pour my drinks and tell me what a hunk of a man I was. But I wasn't about to have any of that.

Her name was Yolanda, and when she stood on a chair, she was exactly the same height as me. In fact, we had a dance like that which just about knocked my hosts out laughing. She had been in Japan for three years and was sending 50,000 yen home a month to support her family. That was big money in the Philippines, she said, and amply supported her three brothers and sisters. But she didn't seem very happy.

I didn't win a prize for singing.

10. TYPHOONS AND EARTHQUAKES

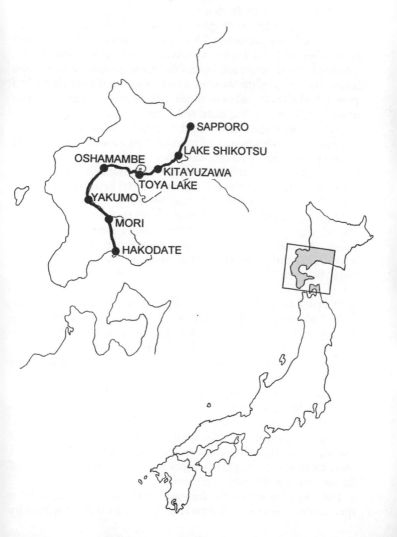

Typhoons are not given romantic names such as "Typhoon Sarah" or "Typhoon Theresa" in Japan. They are simply numbered chronologically through the season. By all accounts, Typhoon 7 was a beauty, wreaking havoc in Kyushu and Western Japan. It had headed out over the Sea of Japan and was clinically dealing to Niigata on its way up the coast.

"Only one or two typhoons make it to Hokkaido each year," commented Sugiyama-san. "And they've usually almost blown themselves out." But Typhoon 7 was on its way. Born in the tropics, typhoons usually approach Japan from the south-east, with Kyushu taking the brunt of the weather attack. Kyushu was having a bad year. It had already had over three times its average rainfall to that time. But "7" was going to hit Hokkaido with a vengeance.

"Ki o tsukete (take care)," said Sugiyama-san as I headed out.

I marched north towards the mountains on a road that ran straight as an arrow. Land was obviously not in as short a supply as in Honshu. It was a four-lane road, and the footpath was twice as wide as some of the roads I had been on! Then a smaller road headed straight for a pass in the mountains.

"I give you ride Sapporo," said a bald taxi driver in English. "No charge!" We had a chat. "That's from the Okushiri earthquake," he said, indicating waves in the footpath, and the gaps, as wide as 20 centimetres between the road and the footpath. "It was pretty bad here!"

"Excuse me, where's the toilet?" I asked in the tiny, single-table shokudo at the foot of the ski area. I had been watching the All-Japan High School baseball tournament on TV with the lady owner, while slurping my noodles and munching boiled eggs.

"It's in the white house next door," she said. "Go in the back door. It's second on the left." I hesitantly did as I was told, and as I had expected, came close to giving the house-owner a heart attack when she found me in her house!

Within two hundred metres of the shokudo, I struck Route 5, the road I was stuck with for the next three days. The traffic was roaring by up the steep grade in low gear, spitting fumes, and I came close to vomiting in the tunnel at the top. It felt like a layer of tar was stuck to the roof of my mouth.

But when I emerged, the view was worth it. Mt Komagatake, a spectacular volcanic cone stood before me, its summit hidden by cloud, and at its feet lay the lakes of Onuma and Konuma, formed when lava flows blocked existing rivers. For the first time on the walk, I had to look for a drink-machine. My mouth was parched and tasted foul, but whereas drink machines virtually jumped out at you on the mainland, none were to be found here. I could see that I would have to adjust my walking technique for Hokkaido.

It was like a different country. The occasional truck passed carrying bales of hay, and farms lined the road. Not paddies, but farms. Cattle were grazing in a few fields. There were even signs advertising land for sale!

A family was selling corn cobs on the side of the road. They had a large stall and were boiling the cobs in a huge pot over an open fire. The daughter, who must have been about ten, was sent off to prepare a couple of fresh cobs for me.

"It's a terrible summer," the father complained. "Hardly anyone is travelling as it's so cold. And no one is stopping to buy corn! Eat as much as you like. It'll go to waste otherwise." He pulled out his four front teeth, inspecting them as we talked. "You're the first walker I've seen this year! Lots of students on bicycles, but no walkers!"

The two ryokan I tried in Mori were full.

"Because of the festival," explained one owner. "Why don't you camp in the park along with all the others? The festival starts in the square outside the station at 7."

The summer festival was a three-day event with a different flavour each night. I had struck the "Modern Music" night, and it was hardly traditional. On one side of the square was a stage, on which a Japanese Elvis Presley look-a-like was crooning into a microphone and swaying around the stage in order to keep warm. He and the big speakers which played his back-up music only seemed to know one song. "Natsu no Matsuri"—"Summer Festival". As he finished each identical rendition he would smooth back his hair and yell:

"One more time, Natsu no Matsuri!"

He was obviously in love with himself.

"Who is that bloke? Is he famous?" I asked the owner of the shop I retreated into to get warm.

"Never seen him before," she said.

There were fifteen teams, each with about thirty members, the men dressed in bright coloured happi coats, and the women in leotards and stockings. The men wore hachimaki headbands, and everybody danced, waving around their plastic fans. They had to dance or they would have frozen to death like most of the crowd who were watching. Actually, the dancers had surprisingly ruddy faces, the result I'm sure of some alcoholic fortification against the elements.

One by one the teams marched up the street, leaving only Elvis shivering in the square, still singing his only song.

"They'll be back in 15 minutes," said the shokudo owner. She was right. Just as I finished my bowl of noodles, the leading dancers reappeared down another street. I went back outside, only to come face to face with a TV camera.

"What do you think of the Mori Summer Festival?" an excited reporter yelled from less than a pace away, thrusting a microphone in my face.

I was so taken aback that the best I could come up with was, "Is this summer?" But the dancers were upon us and I'm sure he couldn't hear me anyway. At least they'd captured me on film. Proof that the Mori Festival was truly an "international" one.

By the time the evening wound down, allowing all the revellers to race home to their heaters, I knew the words to "Natsu no

Modern costumes at Mori's Summer Festival

Matsuri" as well as the crooning Elvis. He was rewarded with a bunch of flowers by a girl in a miniskirt and spent the next five minutes throwing kisses to the crowd. But everyone had already left.

As close as I got to a bear!

Uchiura Bay is a big indentation like a letter "C" in the coastline. It was going to take me three days to walk right around it. Route 5 had no choice but to sit on the coast. Rugged forested hills inland forced it down next to the waters edge, with the railway line. The main road from Hakodate to Sapporo, it had more than its fair share of trucks and cars. I had to be constantly aware of what was going on.

Horror of horrors! The drive-in where I stopped for lunch had a huge stuffed bear outside, standing tall like a human. I didn't really need to worry though. Any bear that would come near Route 5 would have to be totally out of his mind.

It was only mid-day, but the two old men at the next table were well on their way. In fact, they were almost incoherent, giving the waitress a hard time for flirting with me. I was more interested in the TV.

"Typhoon 7 is pounding northern Tohoku and should reach southern Hokkaido sometime during the night," the announcer said.

Pictures from Akita showed the same torrential rains that had soaked me when I was there.

A few kilometres short of Yakumo I turned inland and visited Colonel Sanders' mansion. Yes, that's right, the same Colonel Sanders of Kentucky Fried Chicken fame. I'll bet you didn't know he had a mansion in Hokkaido. It looked as if it was straight out of Kentucky. And not only a mansion, but a huge farm, part of the KFC public relations machine. The road was lined with silver birches, and there were tour buses in the carpark. The restaurant was packed.

I had a coffee with Matsumoto-san, a friend of a friend who was one of the managers. He had just come back from Kenya and a two-year stint as a farm adviser. The view out over Yakumo and Uchiura Bay was superb, although the cloud had built up, and the waves were picking up in size and power.

"Yakumo means 'eight clouds'," Matsumoto san explained. "We have a locals' joke that it's called that because it's cloudy eight-tenths of the time. Like today. But today is different. Typhoon 7 is almost here. A powerful typhoon hasn't reached here for years. I think you should take a day off tomorrow."

Yakumo was split in two. Half the town seemed to be built along Route 5, which hugged the coast, while the other half was around the station, which was, inexplicably, about a kilometre inland. The hills had receded slightly producing a small coastal plain.

A guy in a huge yellow "caterpillar" construction vehicle was earning his stripes, cruising around a driving school practice area with his instructor, on the outskirts of town.

A rusted metal "poster" was riveted to the wall outside, encouraging locals to join the "Self Defence Forces", Japan's version of the "home guard" that is actually one of the biggest armies in the world. According to Article 9 of Japan's Constitution, which was written by an American, General Douglas MacArthur, and his staff after World War II, Japan renounced war "forever" along with the maintenance of "land, sea and air forces, as well as other war potential". That is to say that, legally, Japan cannot have armed forces. In the early 1950's however, it was ruled that Japan had the right to self-defence, and the "Jieitai", the "Self Defence Forces" were established. Funding has generally been kept to 1% of Gross Domestic Product, but since Japan has such a huge GDP, this is a big amount of money.

In the 1950s, 60s and 70s, it suited the USA to have military bases in Japan, as their Cold War enemies, Russia and China were in the immediate vicinity. However, as the American economy declined, Japan forged a huge trading surplus with the USA, and the Cold War ended, and the Americans have clamoured for the Japanese to spend more and more on self-defence. There has also been huge debate in Japan over participation in United Nations Peace Keeping Missions, and as much as possible, Japan has stuck to sending money or medical personnel for such projects.

This particular poster had its paint peeling off, and I couldn't read the telephone number, so I doubt if it had directly led to any increase in defence-spending, an incredibly emotional issue in Japan.

I met "Miss Melons" in her family minshuku, not far from Yakumo Station. She was a bijin and I could see how she'd got her title. No, it's not what you think. She'd been away, living in a melon-growing area, when she'd won her title at a local festival.

The minshuku had a shokudo downstairs, with rooms above, and the shokudo was packed for the evening meal, mostly with family members. I sat with Grandma, who was in charge of her two-year-old grandson, the chef's child. The chef's wife, the child's mother, was waiting on tables, despite being highly pregnant, and Miss Melons, the chef's sister, was racing around, always making sure that I had plenty to eat. She brought me seconds of everything before I'd finished my firsts.

"I think she likes you," said Grandma winking. It had already occurred to me that Miss Melons was ripe. In fact, the customers and even other family members were giving her a hard time for paying me so much attention.

I relaxed in my room with a beer after dinner.

"Do you mind if I come up after work, and practice my English?" she said when she brought up the beer.

"You speak English?"

"Yes. I can serve you, but only beer!" she said in perfect English, laughing.

There was more to Miss Melons than met the eye!

Matsumoto-san from Colonel Sanders' mansion showed up.

"I was so worried about you because of the typhoon. I thought you mightn't have been able to find a place to stay," he said.

"Would you like to stay for a beer?" I asked, slightly reluctantly.

So we sat there and had a strange conversation, Miss Melons, Matsumoto san and I. Matsumoto san had picked up Pidgin English in Kenya, Miss Melons was rather eloquent, and I hadn't spoken English for what seemed like months. So we spoke a mixture of Japanese, English and Pidgin.

"My father had six children so he could have cheap workers!" Miss Melons joked. "We have to work hard, but at least we can drink his beer!" she added laughing. And the bottles kept appearing, courtesy of Ku, Miss Melons' 21-year-old sister, who herself looked like a future candidate for the title.

"Ku! Ku! Come sing with us," slurred a drunken voice out in the corridor.

"I can't, I want to practice my English with the gaijin!" was the reply.

I looked at Miss Melons.

"She can't speak a word," she laughed, a sparkle in her eye.

"But Ku! . . ."

The door slid open and Ku rushed in followed by two sloshed construction workers who were long-term residents. They stopped just inside the door.

"Excuse me, we're studying English," I said in English. Ku looked confused. "Would you like to join us, Ku?" I said, indicating for her to sit down.

"But he speaks Japanese!" one said. "We heard him in the shokudo! And you can't speak English, can you Ku?"

"She speaks perfect English, and I can't speak Japanese," I replied in Japanese.

At this point, Miss Melons' father turned up, probably to find out where all his beer was disappearing to. But I didn't feel bad for drinking it. He was the red-faced drunk who had been poking fun at me in the shokudo at lunch-time!

Typhoon 7 had arrived. There was no doubt about it. The wind was blowing violently outside, though it was only spitting as I had breakfast with Grandma and the slave-driving father. The girls hadn't appeared. The forecast was terrible and the news was full of destruction all over Japan.

"It'll take about an hour and a half to get to Oshamambe," the father said.

"But it's 30 kilometres!" I replied.

"Where's your bicycle?" he asked. I shook my head in despair. It's amazing how things can go in one ear and out the other.

Within 15 minutes of my starting, the rain started pelting down, matching the wind for discomfort. It was a battle just to stay on the road. If I walked on the left, I was blown into the fields. And if I walked on the right, sudden gusts would blow me into oncoming traffic. Not that there was much traffic. The TV had warned against going out unless absolutely necessary. And of course, I was the only idiot out walking.

The hills to the left were covered in cloud, and even above me, the cloud level must have only been a couple of hundred metres. Conditions could hardly have been described as pleasant, but I was enjoying myself in a perverse sort of way. It was me against the elements—and the odd crazy driver. It was Day 84, but I was still happy to take on a challenge. Hokkaido wasn't going to beat me. I felt focussed!

The windows in the shokudo at Kuroiwa were all fogged up. I was absolutely pooped and had only managed ten kilometres! One of the two Hokkaido teams in the High School Baseball Championship was playing on TV, live from Osaka, where it was a perfect day. They were the underdogs.

"Our teams don't get to practice as much as teams in Western Japan. There's still snow on the ground in April," the owner explained. But against expectations, the team from Asahikawa, the place which has experienced the lowest recorded temperature in Japan, scored a couple of early runs and went on to win. My fellow customers were ecstatic. Good news on a foul day.

The rain had relented somewhat, and after a further ten kilometres of battling away I found myself in Kunnei. There was no one on the street, but I wasn't the only customer in the shop.

A bent-over old lady, leaning on a cane was ordering some food for the holiday period.

"My son is coming to visit from Sapporo on the 13th," she said sadly to the old couple running the shop. "He only comes to visit once a year at Obon, with his family. They drive from Sapporo, have lunch with me, then drive back in the afternoon. I always provide them with good food, but they don't stay any longer. I wish they'd stay longer."

Obon is the "Festival for the Dead". Buddhists believe that their ancestors return to earth at this time, and it is traditional for everyone to try and return to their home villages and keep contact with family roots. It is not a National Holiday, but traditionally offices and factories close from the 13th to the 16th of August to let their workers catch up with their ancestors.

It had got even murkier when I ventured back out. Road signs warned traffic to drive slowly because of earthquake damage to the road, but they didn't stop me marching as fast as I could to Oshamambe. It had suddenly become incredibly warm and humid. I knew what was coming.

Just as I entered Oshamambe Station, the clouds burst and the rain came down in buckets. The station was packed with young people, cyclists and motorcyclists who, from the conversations that could be overheard, were all looking for a place to stay. The public telephones were all in use. I only had one chance. I had spotted a small ryokan down a small sidestreet a few blocks back. I gave it a go.

"Excuse me, do you have a room for tonight?"

"Sorry, we're full," said the old lady. I looked around. No shoes. Go for it. I gave her the whole story. 84 days on the road from Kagoshima. Sore feet. My wife's Japanese. Two little sons. I could see a ray of hope. I brought out my family photos. Aren't they cute? Look just like me. Nowhere to stay. Used to sleeping on the floor. Use chopsticks every day. Won't put soap in the bath. Squat toilets are fine. Are you sure you haven't got a room?

"Ah you're lucky. I forgot. We had a cancellation!" she said, handing back my family photos. I signed with relief. "The last gaijin we had couldn't speak a word of Japanese. He was so much trouble we vowed never to have another one. But you're fine. You're just like a Japanese!"

Oshamambe's festival was cancelled. The tiny pink paper lanterns that hung the length of the main street were being blown horizontal by the wind and barely surviving the pouring rain. It was hardly festival weather.

I visited the onsen in my thongs, the backs flicking dirty water up the back of my legs. Two young cyclists from Tokyo were there, their arms and legs blackened by the sun, though where they found it was anyone's guess.

"We're going to sleep in the station," they said. "Though there's not going to be much room. There must be another twenty or so people with the same plans."

I kept my satisfaction to myself.

The ryokan owner bid me farewell at 7:30. It was cloudy and warm, but at least the rain had stopped. Sodden festival decorations hung in the streets, and the only hive of activity was around the station. Thankfully, Typhoon 7 had departed for other parts.

Within ten minutes I had gleefully waved good-bye to Route 5 which headed inland on its way to Sapporo, taking the bulk of the traffic with it. Route 37 stuck to the coast of Uchiura Bay, and I had gone a good three or four kilometres before discovering that I'd forgotten Spot. I'd left him in the brolly rack at the ryokan, and if was too far to go back! My faithful companion, who had protected me for six weeks, forgotten in Oshamambe. That was a well-travelled brolly. He'd done his job well, and I'd forgotten him, leaving myself open to the elements. I had no sword to whip out and stab street signs with, nothing to slice through attacking vegetation, and no protection against invading typhoons. No machine gun to blat away with at similarly-armed children. It was a sad moment. And I'd had plans to leave him at Soya Misaki for a south-bound walker. But no! For a couple of kilometres I even sang "I left my brolly in Oshamambe" to the tune of "I Left My Heart In San Francisco". But there was no one to hear. The waves pounded in and there wasn't a building for ages.

Things looked pretty bleak on my map. Unlike Honshu, where I could bank on a town or a village every 10 kilometres or so, Hokkaido left me doing some careful planning. I couldn't just pass up a shokudo, as, chances were, I mightn't see another one for three hours, and by Murphy's Law, even if I did find one, it was bound to be closed. And of course, my map could mislead me. A station was marked at Asahihama. There's bound to be a shokudo, I thought, but there was only one run-down station building, and nary a house in either direction. Hokkaido was testing me!

Rugged cliffs appeared, and Route 37 started climbing inland. It twisted and it climbed, until surprisingly at the pass, I came across a "Swiss Restaurant" with a Mercedes and a Volkswagen parked outside. It was tucked among the trees, looking very "European" and inviting, but mentally tossing a coin, I took my chances, as it was barely 10:30.

After two sooty hell-holes of tunnels, I took a break in a grass verge to recover. My shoulder had been blackened by the tunnel wall, as had the back of my throat. The sky had cleared and it was hot. Maybe summer had arrived? Ha! Ha!

A car advertising a pachinko parlour in Toyoura raced by for the second time. It had two large loud speakers on top. The driver slowed as he passed me on a particularly steep incline.

"Gambare gaijin san, gambare," he yelled through his loud-speakers. "Keep going Mr Gaijin, keep going!" There was only me to hear.

It made me feel much better!

When I finally found a shokudo, it was packed and I shared a table with eight construction workers. They were burly, happy types, enjoying their lunch break, and their leader took a special interest in me. Respectfully, and appropriately, the others called him "shacho", the term for a company owner or President. He had a big warm smile, white teeth standing out in his suntanned, leathery face.

"You have 'konjo' (guts)," he said. "Good luck! By the way, I've already paid for your lunch."

I could see the town of Toyoura a few kilometres ahead, beyond two or three curves in the road, on the forested slopes down to the sea. All of a sudden a truck spraying insecticide on weeds rounded a corner directly in front of me.

I only had a couple of seconds to think, responding by thrusting out my hand in a motion of "stop". The misty spray continued shooting out the side of the truck, and I had two choices. To jump out in front of the truck or be sprayed from head to foot. I opted for the spray, but within a metre of me, the driver must have hit a stop button and I was saved. I looked up to see him waving, and within a metre of passing me, he must have hit the spray button as the stuff came shooting out once more. Whew!

The town of Toya marked the spot where I would turn inland, leaving the coast. Mt Komagatake, at the southern tip of Uchiura Bay, was clearly visible, only its knobbly top hidden by white cloud. I had followed the Bay from Mori, at its base, and walked nearly 110 kilometres in three days. But there was more to go for day 85.

"There's a fireworks display every night during the summer up at Lake Toya," the noodle shop owner said. "We're not having a festival here tonight." I had asked the same question at the visitors' desk at the station but had only managed to get an unintelligible gurgle out of the lady in charge. "It's only about six kilometres," she said encouragingly. I had already notched up 45 for the day, and my feet were killing me, but it seemed like a good option. Besides, I like fireworks.

"Me handsome Japanese boy!" laughed the bravest of three High School boys in English. "Me handsome Japanese boy!" They were all in the standard black uniform, walking home, despite it being the middle of the summer holidays.

"No you're not. You're at least as ugly as me," I laughed back. "You've been to school today?"

"Judo club," one explained. "We train every day through the summer." And then I was stuck with the same questions as always. The road was climbing steeply, skirting the sides of a sizeable volcano.

"Mt Usu," one of the boys explained. "It last erupted sixteen years ago, the year we were born!"

An old man with a wrinkled face and a scraggly grey beard rode by on a bicycle. I'd met him just as I was entering Toya, and we'd had quite a yarn, walking together for about ten minutes. He was puffing as he struggled up the hill.

"How are you gaijin san?" he asked. "You're going on to Lake Toya? Good idea! The fireworks are pretty, and there are plenty of places to camp. Good luck!"

The boys were stunned.

"Who's that?"

"How do you know him?"

"An old friend!" I explained.

The staff at the "Genghis Khan" restaurant sized me up as a potential record-breaker the moment I walked in. The great Genghis Khan must have been fond of mutton, as his name is synonymous with a BBQ mutton restaurant. Slices of mutton, along with various vegetables such as onions, green peppers and bean sprouts, are brought out, and the customers cook by themselves on a hot plate built into the middle of the table.

I hadn't been able to pass the place by. It had been dark, and I had rounded a corner to see a brightly illuminated sign: "Genghis Khan, Tabehodai, 980 yen." "Tabehodai" is the Japanese equivalent of "all you can eat", and it was in this category that the waitresses thought they'd found a record-breaker. I must have looked hungry. The bets went up when I told them I had just walked from Oshamambe.

But I disappointed them. It must have been the noodles in Toya barely an hour before. No matter how much I tried, I couldn't eat more than three plates of sliced meat, no matter how many times I was asked if I'd like another plate load.

"We've calculated that you've only had 1.2 kilograms of mutton. The record belongs to a student who was cycling around Hokkaido. He ate 2 kilograms, rode all over Hokkaido for a couple of weeks, and then came back and did it again!" one of the waitresses told me excitedly. "He was only small. So when you came in carrying your big backpack, we thought you were bound to break his record."

They gave me a coffee on the house for a good effort, and a ton of encouragement for the rest of the walk.

"Fireworks? Oh yes, there'll be fireworks! They have them every night over the summer. They even had the display last night during the typhoon!"

The surprise intake of meat was having a drastic effect on my system. I wriggled nervously in my seat, praying for control as the couple at the next table prattled on.

"You've walked from Oshamambe! That's marvellous! We've just driven from there. It took us a little over half an hour. How long did it take you?"

Before I could answer, I farted louder than a thunderclap. The wife dissolved into giggles. It was time to go watch the real fireworks at Lake Toya!

The sky was jet black when I topped a rise and finally saw Lake Toya below. The lake is shaped like a huge donut, with Nakajima, the island in the middle, being the hole. Bright lights and tall high-rise hotels marked the town, and all around the lake small clusters of lights were visible. I set about descending in time for the fireworks display, passing carloads of onlookers who planned to watch from high above the lake. They stared at me as if I were a skyrocket!

It was a resort town. Huge hotels lined the waterfront, their well-manicured gardens reaching right down to within a few metres of the lake, with its fleet of tourist boats and docks. Crowds were beginning to gather. Families in matching yukata and geta. Couples hand in hand. All waiting for the display. Hordes of people were boarding the colourfully-illuminated paddle-steamer that would head out onto the lake to disgorge its fiery load into the night sky.

All I could do was collapse on a soft, moistish lawn, take off my boots, and, using my pack as a pillow, relax on my back. The hotel behind me was all of ten stories high, its top floor being a long fogged up window, the onsen.

The carnival atmosphere picked up a few minutes after the paddle-boat headed out into the dark of the lake. An explosion of light and sound signalled the start, and for the next twenty minutes, skyrockets burst high in the sky, raining streams of colours to the excitement of those assembled below. Two small powerboats raced around the main boat, setting off all sorts of "hanabi", "flower fires", as fireworks are known in Japan. I could see the faces of those around me, hear their gasps of approval and the excited chatter.

"That's wonderful!"

"Look at that! It has the shape of a rabbit!"

"Subarashii!"—Great!

"Sugoi!"—Amazing!

Lying there, looking around at the clusters of friends and families, the happy faces, I felt lonely. I wished my wife and children were there to share and enjoy. What were they doing? Enjoying the festive season of fireworks in Osaka, no doubt.

The boat moved down the shoreline in the direction I wanted to go, so I followed it. It carried on until opposite the last big hotel in town, shooting rockets at the stars, and then stopped as suddenly as it had started. The sky was dark again and only the lights from the hotels lit up the foreshore. The crowd quickly dispersed, leaving me alone, wondering where I could pitch my tent. The "No Camping" signs were only in Japanese, and I toyed with the idea of playing the part of the non-understanding gaijin and camping anyway. But it was a warm, clear night, and surely the camping area I'd been told about couldn't be that far off!

Showa Shinzan, the latest addition to the area's volcanoes, loomed high, silhouetted against the night sky on my right. It had erupted in 1943. Its name can be translated as "the new mountain of the Showa period", that being the time that Hirohito was Emperor.

I had left the town far behind, and only the occasional car broke the silence as I trudged along the side of the lake, glad to have my "kumayoke" ringing away on the back of my pack.

I arrived at the campground which was packed with colourful tents after 10. It had been a 58 kilometre day, the longest of the trip, and my feet felt like it!

I managed to find a spot, squeezed between two others, to pitch my tent, before relaxing to watch the pandemonium. Three kids were kicking a soccer ball, uprooting the odd tent peg while being screamed at by their mother. Families were cooking over spitting portable barbecues, and two men were practicing their golf swing, but without clubs—all within a metre or two of where I was sitting. Quite a change from the empty campgrounds of pre-summer vacation times. The noise was deafening.

The family in the tent next door were still out eating and drinking. Holding up a beer can, the father beckoned for me to join them. Just what I needed!

I could be forgiven for thinking I was somewhere in Central Tokyo when a large lady collapsed one corner of my tent by falling on it at 6:30 the next morning.

"Sumimasen," she said. "Excuse me", and carried on with whatever it was she was doing.

Nothing had changed from the night before. The kids were back playing soccer, the clubless golfers back perfecting their swing, and mothers were cooking breakfast instead of the late-night BBQs. The population density in that campground must have been greater than that of Tokyo! Sometime between when I fell asleep after 11, and when I crawled out of my tent at 6:30, someone had managed to erect a bright orange tent so close to mine that I could have pulled out two tent pegs without moving.

An old lady was carting cold drinks around, selling them at each tent as if she were hawking popcorn at a baseball game. She even had the same call.

"Drinks! Drinks! Who would like a drink?"

By 7:30, half the tents had been packed away, and most of the action was in the carpark, where motorbike enthusiasts revved up and inspected each others' "pride and joys", and families tried to stuff piles of gear into small cars, along with the kids. It was like a camper's worst nightmare. I headed for a wash in the lake, where a crowd of kids gathered to watch me do what I assumed everybody else was there to do. Go for a swim.

"Look at that gaijin! Swimming in his underwear!"

"Unbelievable! It's so cold!"

"Incredible! He'll have a heart attack!" I could hear the murmurs. But after my 58km, onsen-less day, the water was cool and refreshing, and I was beyond caring if they thought I was mad.

"Fruit Village," the signs proclaimed. The valley was full of orchards, its rich volcanic soil being used to full potential. Apples, strawberries, melons, nashi and grapes were mixed in with the occasional rice paddy. The footpath was wide under an open blue sky, and only the occasional car came down out of the mountains towards me. It was pleasant walking, but my body was falling apart! The previous day had drained me. The soles of my feet throbbed, and the spring had gone out of my step. And it was 50 kilometres to Lake Shikotsu with not much in-between.

The grey-haired old lady in the run-down shop at Bankei answered my questions sadly.

"No, we don't have an Obon dance here anymore. All the young people have gone. There are only old people left in town, so we don't bother. Festivals are for the young."

My map showed an onsen and a Youth Hostel at Kitayuzawa, barely five kilometres up the road.

"But we have an onsen here in Bankei," she said, indicating the building next door with the paint peeling off.

"How big is Kitayuzawa?" As soon as I asked, I felt bad, and hoped the old lady excused my insensitive questions.

Kitayuzawa was in a narrow valley, alongside a river, with wisps of steam coming out of all sorts of unusual places. A couple were boiling eggs in a rock pool on the far side of the river and the village had a distinctive "hot springs resort" feel about it. It was a sleepy little town, though, and only one shokudo was open. A small log-house-type building, it was perched on a knoll above the road, with only its noren signalling that it was open for business.

But when I entered, I knew straight away that it was a place with character. Ella Fitzgerald's "Mac the Knife" was playing at high volume, and tinted windows made the place dark and inviting. A chubby but attractive middle-aged lady looked up from her sewing, blinking as her eyes adjusted to the glare from outside. "Irrashaimase." Welcome. There was no one else in the place. She turned the volume down.

"That's fine," I said. "I love jazz." She turned it up a notch. I sat at the bar taking it in. The place had been tastefully, lovingly decorated with flowers, a fish tank and jazz posters on the walls. "I'm not going to go far from here today," I thought to myself.

Chikako, the owner, had stacks of jazz cassettes, records and CDs that all looked as if they got regular use. I chose Duke Ellington to follow Ella and settled in with a huge plate of curry, rice and deep-fried pork.

"Not too many customers today?" I asked.

"I'm not too worried if no one comes," she replied smiling. "I just like to listen to the music. Please don't tell my husband though. He thinks I'm working!" We'd hit it off in an instant. There are times when you take an instant liking to someone, and this was one.

"If no one comes at night, I close early, turn all the lights off, and sit here with the volume up!" she said.

"Sounds great! How about tonight?" My feet were feeling better already. She broke into a smile, eyes sparkling. We had found a common passion.

She called the Youth Hostel for me.

"The manager likes jazz too," she explained. "He often comes in the evening too."

I spent the afternoon doing my washing, taking a nap, and re-covering in the Youth Hostel's onsen. It was piping hot, straight out of the ground, and my feet, ankles and knees appreciated the half day off. A 58 kilometre day, followed by one of 15! Inconsistent, but who cares! I didn't. I didn't have far to go.

By 5:30 I was back at Chikako's, sipping sake, writing post-cards and listening to Dave Brubeck. Chikako was sewing cloth juggling balls to sell as souvenirs. We enjoyed each other's company.

"There used to be a railway through here," she explained. "People mostly came here by train. But the line was pulled out when the railways were privatised. Not so many come any more." A familiar story. "But we make enough money out of my husband's shop, so I can just sit here and listen to the music." She put on her favourite Miles Davis CD.

The music, the sake and the company were a great combination, and when I headed back to the Youth Hostel, I felt a completeness within myself.

Had the walk aged me? The manager's wife guessed that I was

50 years old! Maybe a soak in the onsen would take the years off. I tried it.

The Youth Hostel's guests, all 15 of them, came outside for a team photo, before I set out on my 87th day. There was a mixture of cars, bicycles and motorbikes in the car park, but of course, I was the only walker. The young crowd were all on their own private adventures, but all were interested in mine. They sent me off with a rousing, encouraging farewell. The walk was coming to a climax, and I could feel my own excitement building up.

"It's a long way to walk to Shikotsuko," said the man who was washing his car in Otaki.

"That's OK, I've walked from Kagoshima," I replied.

He bowed so low that I could see the bald spot on the back of his head.

"Gokurosama."

The signboard for Safe Driving announced that Otaki had gone 293 days without a road death.

"Let's try for 1000 days!" it encouraged the vacationing race-drivers who hurtled by on that Saturday morning.

I didn't feel so safe though, especially after coming across a dead fox, splattered in the middle of the road, with a wicked grin on its face.

It started to rain while I was climbing steadily in the forested mountains. I reached for Spot, but where was he? Sitting in a brolly rack in Oshamambe! I cursed my stupidity for not re-arming myself when I had the chance. My chances of finding a brolly out in the wild were slim to say the least.

Four cyclists were waiting at the mouth of the tunnel for the rain to stop.

"The forecast is terrible," one moaned. "Not much of a summer, is it?" I couldn't help but agree.

I passed another four pairs of bicycle tourers in the 1.5 kilometre tunnel, one just about coming to grief when he caught sight of me in his headlight and, in shock, went careening off into the far lane, narrowly avoiding a car which honked angrily.

The far end of the tunnel was depressing for two reasons. One was that it was raining so hard that I daren't venture out and had to sit under the tunnel overhang next to a sign. The other reason was that there was a bear painted on that sign! As in "Beware of Bears."

The rain let up for a total of five minutes, during which time I idiotically headed out into the murk, fooled into thinking that the worst was over. It wasn't. But surely it wasn't far to the drive-in I'd been told about. A group of cyclists were struggling up the steep grade as I rapidly descended.

"How far to the drive-in?" I asked.

"What drive-in?" Things were getting more and more depressing. But they can only stay so for so long.

A van pulled over. I waded over to explain that I was walking as the driver wound down his window. Two big dogs were playing in the back seat.

"Quick get in!"

"Thanks but . . ." and then I spotted it. A pink plastic brolly in the front seat.

"Thanks but I'm only walking. Can I buy your umbrella?" I blurted out hopefully. It obviously wasn't the reply he was expecting. He looked at me, then at the pink brolly. It was a cheap 500 yen throw-away type. Just what I was after!

"Sure. Keep it," he said, handing it out the window.

"How much?" I said, reaching for my wallet which was soaked like the rest of me.

"Nothing. Good luck!" He drove off, leaving me thankful for the generosity of a good Samaritan.

I wasn't the only lunatic out in the rain though. When I eventually came to the drive-in I'd been told about, which the cyclists must have missed in the pounding rain, a gaijin couple on mountain bikes turned up too. More crazy Kiwis! And from not far away from my hometown, either! News from home!

The rain had relented when I emerged from another tunnel and was faced with a magnificent view of Lake Shikotsu. A caldera lake, it was formed by the subsidence of land between Mt Eniwa to the north and Mt Fuppushi to the south, volcanoes that on that day reached up into the clouds.

I turned off the main road onto an unpaved, pock-marked road into the forest heading dead north towards Mt Eniwa. My map marked it as a reasonably major route, but the state of the road was shocking, and it looked like bear territory in the dense forest. Within ten minutes I had seen a live fox whose grin was just as wicked as the dead one I'd come across earlier.

I decided it was time to sing. Even if a bear couldn't hear my kumayoke, my singing was bound to scare it off. It's had that effect on women in countless karaoke bars! Every now and then a car would roar by, splashing me with dirty water from the puddles in the countless potholes and giving me a break from bear-scaring.

The road climbed high above the lake, clinging to the mountain side. It was a near vertical drop to the waters below. It skirted the western shore, twisting and turning through the thick undergrowth that hid who knows what. At one stage I could see two fishermen in a boat, far below, staring up towards the road. I stopped singing.

My map showed an onsen at Okotan, on the lakeside at the foot of Mt Eniwa. The air was heavy and humid when I finally arrived, glad to have an escape from the inevitable deluge.

"The onsen?" queried the old lady in the run-down ryokan. "It closed years ago."

"Well, do you have a room for tonight?"

"Sorry, this ryokan is closed too. My husband and I run the cabins and campground. The government closed the ryokan, as they don't want one here in the National Park." I didn't like my chances but I asked anyway.

"How about a cabin?"

"A what?"

"A kebin." I corrected my Japanese pronunciation of this English word taken and adjusted to suit Japanese mouths.

"They're full . . . apart from one where the last guest spilt orange juice all over the tatami. We weren't going to use it tonight but . . ."

I managed to convince her that I didn't care, and the old man, her husband, led me through the trees to a dank, musty little hut just as the rain started. There was no electricity and only the barest of essentials, but I was happy, laughing at my good luck. There was no way that I wanted to spend the night in my tent!

A family, barbecuing under a tarpaulin, had watched my arrival, and a son was sent to invite me to join them. "Genghis Khan", slices of barbecued mutton, was the order of the day. Mutton and sake. A great mix.

"You have such a big body," the uncle said. "Eat! Eat!" I ate as he drank. And then it really started raining. Forked lightning split the sky open, followed by cracks of thunder that seemed to make the earth shudder. Raindrops pounded down and the tarpaulin partially collapsed, sending a torrent of water down the uncle's back. Dulled by sake, his reactions were slow, and he was completely soaked before he realised what was going on. I tried, but couldn't hold back a chortle, which brought on an eruption of laughter from the whole family. We had no choice but to break up the party, racing to our respective huts.

I sat in the doorway of my dilapidated cabin, staring out at one of the most spectacular electrical storms I had ever seen. Lightning lit up everything like a huge camera flash, followed closely by ear-pummelling thunder, and the process would repeat itself within seconds. I thanked my lucky stars I had decided against camping at Bifue, at the south-west corner of the lake. Most of those tents would be afloat. Luck was with me.

It was sunny, windy and cool when I threw the "kebin" door open the next morning. Almost unbelievably, the couple in the cabin next door were frying bacon and eggs over a camp cooker on the porch. The smell wafted over and I was green with envy. My only escape was to go for a swim. It was 6:30, but at the lakeside two fishermen were casting off the dock, and a lone guitarist was singing Bob Dylan with a Japanese accent on the beach. A group was trying to push a car off a saturated lawn, the driver accelerating and cutting up the green grass. They eventually towed it off, but the grass was a mess. They all stopped what they were doing to watch me take a swim.

The road twisted this way and that, following the contours of the mountainside as it climbed and climbed and climbed.

A car flew by heading downhill, with a white-haired old lady in the back seat pointing at me and jabbering excitedly. I didn't think the climb was ever going to end. A shelter-roof protected the road from heavy snowfall in places, and reinforced concrete banks protected it from landslides. But the lack of traffic made me wonder why they bothered.

There was a viewing platform at the pass, looking down over Lake Okotan, a picturesque mountain lake surrounded by deep green forest. Two cyclists in singlets and shorts were resting after climbing the pass from the other side. It had taken them two hours from Sapporo.

"Aren't you cold dressed like that?" I asked, when I noticed them shivering. Stupid question! I was only in a shirt and shorts also.

"You wouldn't be cold with such hairy legs!" one of them answered laughing.

"You'll have no problem getting to Sapporo. We've seen the All Blacks. New Zealanders have much power," added the other.

A big group of mountain bikers rode past, strung out over a couple of kilometres. All were dressed appropriately in helmets, sunglasses and skin tight gear. The leaders, sleek and muscley, showed excellent form. As the pack passed I noticed a change in style and body shape until I got to the last few stragglers, huffing and puffing up the hill. The last two guys were solid overweight types, pushing their bikes, obviously in desperate need of a rest.

"It's our first time," one huffed.

"And our last," the other puffed.

"Have a drink," the first one said, slipping his drink bottle out of the holder on his bike and passing it to me. His face was bright red and he was breathing heavily.

"Have some gum," said the other. "It's at least 20 kilometres to the next shop!" Neither of them seemed too keen to get going, but another biker was sent back to check.

"Oi!" came the yell from up the road. Both groaned.

"Gambatte," they said, trying to remount their bikes.

"Gambatte," I replied back. I had the feeling that they needed the encouragement more than I.

I'd been walking for nearly five hours before I saw the first building of the day. It was a golf club house. Signs advertised snow-mobiling on the golf course during the winter, and opposite the entrance, huge steel swing gates that could close the road lay open. Next came a ski area, and then a stocked fishing pond, surrounded by Sunday anglers. I was getting back to civilisation.

I trudged down out of the mountains into Sapporo, prefectual capital of Hokkaido, site of the 1972 Winter Olympics and Japan's fifth largest city. My body was falling apart, but the prospect of a bath and a day off kept me going.

"Where are you going man?" I turned around to find myself faced with a red-headed Mormon on a bicycle. His suit was immaculate. "I've been here for eight months, but sometimes I find it hard to get my point across," he confided. I wasn't surprised.

By the time I reached my friend's parents' house in Shiroishi, an eastern suburb not far from central Sapporo, I had clocked up 44 kilometres for the day. A bath, a beer, and a feed can do wonders!

After dinner I wandered down to the local "Obon" dance and joined the revellers. The previous night had been rained off, and the locals were taking advantage of the fine weather. Stalls were selling "yakitori" (grilled chicken), beef, noodles, and a wicked mixture of shochu and tea which just about knocked me over. Kids were throwing rings at worthless prizes, firecrackers were banging away, and hundreds of costumed dancers bounced around the central stage in rhythm to a huge taiko drum. A tiger with bobbly eyes tried to make me join in, but my feet weren't up to it. I could only sit and watch. A huge spotlight swirled around the night sky, bouncing light off the broken cloud. I had another shochu and tea.

11. THE FINAL PUSH

As Hokkaido was only colonized in the 1860s, Sapporo, its prefectural capital, is a modern-style city as compared to other cities in Japan. In 1870, the Governor of Hokkaido visited the United States, collected a group of advisers, and set about planning the new city. Consequently, central Sapporo has a grid system of wide roads running north-south and east-west, unlike other cities in Japan which have narrow twisting roads that are almost impossible for the uninitiated to follow.

My friend's mother saw me off with an obento and some salty dried scallops to eat as I was walking. The family had been very kind, but I knew I hadn't lived up to the "gaijin" they had been expecting. My friend had sent a gaijin visitor before. He had played the part perfectly, not speaking a word of Japanese, incapable of getting on a bus by himself, and not used to chopsticks, Japanese food or sleeping on the floor. This was obviously what they were expecting, and when they found that I had done it all before, it took some of the fun out of my visit for them.

It was warm and sunny when I set out on the final leg of my walk. Fluffy white cumulus clouds were pushed along with a gentle breeze, and I couldn't help wondering if summer had finally arrived in mid-August.

I was heading north-east out of town on Route 375, when a car tried to squeeze through a gap between two trucks. All he managed to do, however, was clip the front fender of the truck on his right. The truckie blasted his horn and both pulled over. This will be interesting, I thought.

The driver of the car, sixtyish, with greased-back hair and sunglasses and wearing a track suit, jumped out to inspect his sleek black machine. He knelt down, checking his rear bumper, unprepared for the truckies' onslaught. The younger man, powerful-looking in a cut-off T-shirt, rushed up and shoved him in the shoulder so hard that the driver fell to the ground.

"Bakayaro!! You idiot! What do you think you're doing?" He had the older man by the collar with his left hand, his right balled into a fist like a pistol, cocked and ready for fire. The older man had his arms out, his face contorted with fear.

"Please! Please! I'm in a hurry. I'm sorry."

I thought about crossing the road to break it up, but the truckie looked so angry that he might just have a go at me. And after all, it had been the old man's fault. He probably wouldn't take on any trucks in the future. I kept walking.

"Baka!" I could hear the truckie yelling as I pointed towards Cape Soya.

The wide Ishikari River plain was beginning to narrow. I was getting close to the mountains in the west, and on the eastern side Hokkaido's central mountains were drawing closer. It would take me three days to get to the head of the valley, so I could quite safely put away my map and head straight up Route 275. The valley was full of rice paddies.

"We're having such a bad summer that the rice might not be harvestable," an old man told me. "That would a disaster!"

Shokudo were hard to come by, and on more than one occasion, I was tricked into thinking I'd found one, only to discover that the doors and windows were boarded over. I ended up eating my obento leaning up against a Coke machine on the side of the road. It was the first I'd seen for ages.

The road met the mountains at Tobetsu, turning right to skirt the base of the foothills. Signs for golf courses and ski areas became commonplace. Flat land is such a scarce commodity in Japan that it is simply too expensive to be used for such extravagant means as a golf course. Flat land is used for production, and such play areas are pushed into the hills. Japanese golfers, on seeing a foreign course, often comment about how flat it is, mainly because theirs are so hilly.

I turned off the main road at precisely four o'clock, heading for Nakagoya Onsen at the foot of a ski area carved into the trees.

"Hokkaido corn is delicious. Try some," encouraged an elderly man in a broad straw sunhat who was selling from a shack outside his house. "I grew it myself!" he said proudly. It was very good.

"You can camp at the ski area," he added. "No one will mind. If you need some water, just come and use my tap. There's a shokudo at the onsen."

So I was set for the day. An onsen, a place to camp, a shokudo. All I could need. But it pays to be flexible.

"I was born on Karafuto, or Sakhalin as it is called now," said Toshi san. "When I was a boy we used to climb out a trapdoor in the roof of our house and ski to school. The snow was about six metres high!" A wiry, strong-looking man of about 60, he was impressed with my knowledge of his birthplace, mostly gleaned from my friend at the drive-in in Akita who had also been born on Karafuto.

We were sitting in the sauna at the onsen, taking breaks in the conversation to submerge in the icy cold "mizuburo" for a few seconds at a time.

"My father didn't escape back to Japan with us at the end of the war. He was sent to a Siberian work camp and didn't come home for eight years! When he was released he came back an old man. There was no work he could do, and the government didn't provide any welfare. He died very bitter." I was surprised at his openess considering that the topic obviously pained him. We shared a common love, karate.

"I have been training myself since I was 14," he said. "This walk is part of your training in life. You are very disciplined to have come this far. You have a strong will."

"My wife says I'm stubborn," I replied.

"She's probably right," he laughed.

So I spent my 90th night out at Toshi's house. My plans to camp at the skiground were well forgotten. We drove back to Sapporo in his car, with him promising to bring me back to the onsen the following morning so I could restart from exactly the same spot I had finished for the day.

Needless to say, his family were surprised, but it was a pleasure to talk well into the night without interruptions from a television. His wife even managed to overcome her initial embarrassment and try out the odd phrase from her weekly English conversation class.

Toshi loves motorbikes and had been all over Hokkaido on his favorite black Yamaha. Consequently he had plenty of good advice, marking campgrounds and accommodation houses on my map.

It was overcast and cool when we arrived back at Nakagoya Onsen at 10 the next morning. With a parting wave, Toshi went back into the onsen for a bath, and I headed back to the main road.

"Did everything go all right?" inquired the corn seller who was back in his stall.

"Perfectly," I replied, remembering the corn cob he had given me, still in my backpack.

The old lady wearing No 1 on her front and back was incredibly vicious on the "gateball" ground. She was slightly bent, wearing a white bonnet to shade her face and neck from the sun, and would cackle to herself each time she smashed one of her opponents balls out of the playing area. Similar to croquet, gateball sees teams of players try to mallet wooden balls through little hoops on a usually grassless field. If they hit another players' ball, they get to belt it away from the hoop. No. 1 was particularly nasty and skilled. The rest of her team was sitting and watching, wondering if they'd ever get a turn, smoking and yarning. Her opposition were chasing their big wooden balls to wherever No. 1 had whacked them.

With an exceptionally brutal smack, No. 1 whacked No. 8's ball over so that it stopped at my feet, barely a few metres from the road. I had been watching for a few minutes. The old men who were waiting, waved and pointed at me.

No. 8 came trotting over to get her ball. I picked it up and just as she got close lobbed it to her with a gentle throw. The timing was perfect. She stopped and bowed to me just as the ball left my hand. As if in slow motion, just as she reached the bottom of her bow, the wooden ball conked her right in the middle of the head. The whole group of twelve players burst into laughter. But No. 8 barely winced. She picked up her ball, bowed again, and trotted back to the game.

A worker trimming weeds on the side of the road with a weed-eater made me feel much better by asking if I was a university student.

"But you look so young!" he said. Good news when only a few days before I had been told I looked as if I was fifty!

Tsurunuma Park was just too good to pass up. I had only managed 30 kilometres for the day, half of those in thongs, because of a dull thudding pain in the soles of my feet. But the prospect of an onsen and a cabin in a campground was just too tempting. The camping area was beside a large man-made pond with dock-loads of "swan" and "frog" boats for punters to paddle around in. It was an overcast Wednesday, though, and the "play area" was deserted.

"Why don't you speak English to the gaijin?" a grandfather encouraged his young grandson as we sweated together in the sauna. The boy must have been about ten or twelve.

"But I don't know how to," the boy complained. There were eight of us crammed into the hot little sweat-box.

"Go on, practice your English!" one of the others ribbed him.

"But I can't," he replied.

"Aren't you studying English at school?" I asked him in Japanese. The poor kid just about fell off the seat. The older men just laughed.

The onsen's claim to fame was that it had played host to the great young Japanese sumo wrestlers, Takanohana and his brother, Wakanohana. Their handprints, in red ink, and signatures were displayed ceremoniously in the waiting area.

It was there that I met a young guy from Nagoya. He, with his motorbike, had travelled by ferry to Otaru, near Sapporo, and he had a week to bike all over Hokkaido.

"I've been dreaming of doing this since I was a kid," he said excitedly. "It's a chance to be free. I can just go wherever I like, stay wherever I like." He had a list of towns which provided "Rider Houses" for young cyclists and bike travellers like himself. Accommodation was free in dormitories, and cooking facilities were provided. Hokkaido was out to become a mecca for young adventurers in the summer. Toshi had told me that each town was trying to organize campgrounds where young visitors could stay for minimal cost, in an effort to boost Hokkaido's reputation as an explorers' paradise. I couldn't help but applaud their efforts. Tsurunuma Koen had gone a step further.

"I'm staying in a tree house," he laughed.

"A tree house?"

"That's right. The one next door is empty. Why don't you stay there?"

So I spent the night in a tree house. It wasn't a real tree house, but being high above the ground, it might as well have been. It was constructed of a huge log pole protruding vertically out of the ground for about five metres. About three metres off the ground was a hexagonal platform which formed the floor, and the design from there was in the form of an American Indian tepee, coming to a point at the top of the pole. A steel ladder led to a trapdoor in the floor, and there were even a couple of windows. Basically, it was a wooden tepee about three metres above ground level. And there were six of them in a row!

I fell out of my tree house the next morning to find my new friend cooking up breakfast under a blue sky next to his beloved motorbike. Like all bikes and cycles that had passed me since I'd arrived in Hakodate, it had a bright yellow flag sticking up saying

"Safety Summer Hokkaido!" The authorities were doing a good job.

We shared his canned corned beef and eggs, and my bread and canned fruit to make quite a feast.

"I'm a computer programmer," he said, "But my real love is motorbikes. I work all week, then on Sundays I ride my bike over a hundred kilometres to a friend's bike workshop and repair bikes for free. Then at the end of the day, I ride home."

"Why don't you become a bike mechanic?" I asked him.

"That's what I always wanted to do," he said sadly. "But our economy is in recession and I can't give up a good job. There's too much competition for good jobs."

The valley had narrowed considerably, and the mountains to the west were barely four or five kilometres away. I spotted two gliders swooping high in the cloudless sky, and another being towed to its release height by a grunting little plane, whose buzz could be heard for miles. It was a perfect day. But my feet ached!

The woman in the shoe shop at Shintotsukawa was pleased to see me.

"I've only got one pair of shoes over size 26," she said with great enthusiasm. "They're size 28. I've had them here for years. Nobody around here has big feet. I'll give you 50% off if you buy them. Here they are!"

Cheap white tennis shoes, they looked like they'd fall apart in a week, but if things went according to plan, that's all I had left. My feet were ready to give up, and the shoes I had been wearing felt like only a paper thin layer seperated my sole from the road.

"I'll take them!" I said, despite my feet being size 27. My feet were getting desperate, and the prospect of larger shoes made them feel much better. "Can you throw these out?" I said, handing her my old ones.

"No problems," she replied. I'd obviously made her day. "Domo arigato gozaimashita." Thank you very much.

Most of the traffic turned right over the Ishikari River towards Fukagawa and Asahikawa. I inspected my map while downing a litre of orange juice in a bus shelter. The sun was strong, and while applying some sun-block, I realised that I was still on my first tube. What had happened to that hot Japanese summer?

My map looked pretty bleak with not much marked on it for the next twenty kilometres. I had learnt a few lessons and opted for an early lunch before leaving Shintotsugawa. The shokudo had only just opened.

The primary school at Uryu had a swimming pool that was open to the community. I followed the signs.

"How much is it to swim?" I asked the attendant, reaching for my wallet.

"Well . . . If you've got lots of money, I'll take it, but if not, then it's free," he said winking. "Have you got a swimming cap?"

He lent me his blue one.

"I'm the sports teacher during school time. During the summer holidays I run the pool," he explained. "Please sign the book so that I can prove that you came. We've never had a gaijin here before!"

As expected, the only other swimmers were children, about seven or eight, all wearing bright coloured caps. The sun had been beating down on my arms and the back of my neck all day, making the water cool and refreshing. Of course the kids swamped me with attention, and it was only stern warnings from the teacher that kept them from hanging off my neck.

"You're very good-natured," he said, handing me a glass of cold wheat-tea when I got out. "I would have drowned a couple of them." And then as I prepared to leave, "Please don't forget Uryu." He marked it on my map.

Three policemen with a speed-checking microwave laughed and waved at me as I entered the first hills I had struck since Sapporo. Looking back, I felt slightly embarrassed. The spot where I had chosen to relieve myself behind a bus shelter a couple of hundred metres before was well within their view.

The town of Hokuryu was proud of its sunflowers. Not only did they stand tall and yellow beside the road, they adorned signs and walls all over town. I was on my way to Sunflower World, a new onsen that the swimming pool attendant had told me about.

Three little girls on bicycles latched onto me as I was leaving town.

"Where do you come from?" one asked. They all giggled.

"From Osaka," I replied.

"But you're a gaijin, aren't you?"

"He looks like a gaijin, but he speaks like a Japanese!"

"And his eyes are blue!"

"Yes, yes, I'm a gaijin!" I replied. The little girl in front slammed on her brakes.

"A gaijin! A gaijin!"

The two behind her weren't prepared for the sudden stop, and I spent the next few minutes disentangling bodies and bicycles and trying to stem the crying. It didn't look too good. The gaijin and three sobbing eight-year-old girls. But my escort was intent on sticking to me like glue.

"Did you fly to Japan?"

"Didn't you vomit? My father went on an aeroplane once and he vomited."

The third one was picking sunflowers for me. I only managed to be rid of them when we got to Sunflower World and they ran for the playground. I escaped to the bath.

"We've had a few length-of-Japan walkers in here. They're usually on their fifth or sixth day, walking south from Cape Soya, excited, but complaining of sore feet and blisters," the woman with the brown fishbowl haircut in the shokudo at Hekisui told me. "They all come through Hekisui. But we've never had anyone walking south to north before. And never a gaijin!"

"It's OK," I replied. "I'm from New Zealand. Everything's upside-down there—that's why I'm going south to north. But I've got sore feet too!"

She gave me an exceptionally large helping of curry and turned on the TV.

"Feel free to stay as long as you like. You can camp at the shrine over the road. And there's a 24 hour convenience store on the corner." It sounded like she'd said it all before, but she was friendly and encouraging.

"Good luck," she said with a warm smile as I left at 9.

There was another tent with two bicycles outside beside the shrine. I could hear heavy snoring. "I wonder who's more tired," I thought to myself, "them or me?"

The grass hadn't been mown for ages, making a soft mat below my sleeping bag. I slept well.

Two trucks roared past at 5:30 am, and then my fellow campers made a heck of a racket of greeting the new day. Hardly surprising considering there were two of them in a tent smaller than my little one-man.

"Why don't they try daylight saving over here," I thought to myself for the umpteenth time on the walk. "Surely it would be better to have all this daylight in the evening!" Japan actually tried daylight saving after the war, but it was stopped when it was found that it only made workers slave away for an extra hour each day. They felt that they should still work until the sun went down!

A lone old man was practicing gateball in the park next to the shrine at 5:45 when I eventually crawled out. As with every morning, my body and especially my ankles and feet took five minutes to get back into action. I hobbled around exploring the old wooden shrine while the old man stared.

The girl in the 24 hour convenience shop obviously wasn't expecting me. She miscounted my change twice, giggled, and spent the next twenty minutes watching me eat my obento after I'd flopped onto a seat outside. I cut some thick soles for my tennis shoes out of my sleeping pad, which was getting shorter and shorter, and was ready to hit the road.

It was calm, with a thick layer of fog hanging over the paddies and fields of sunflowers as I headed towards the coast, away from the Ishikari River valley. But I had some good-sized mountains to cross before the sea would come back into view. The tributary valley I was in quickly narrowed, and I was soon climbing in thick forest.

"This road construction is partly paid for by your gasoline tax," the road sign read. "No wonder gas is so expensive," I thought. "There's so much road construction going on!"

There was a drive-in at the pass. "24 Hour Drive-In," it proudly announced to the world by way of a big sign, but there wasn't a sign of life until I put my 110 yen in the Coke machine outside. Seven big dogs burst into life, barking and trying to knock down the fence that they were confined behind. I almost jumped out of my skin.

An old man with no teeth and no hair came out, a cigarette hanging out the side of his mouth. He looked as terrible as my feet felt, squinting out through his thick glasses. He looked at his watch. It was eight o'clock.

"Come in. Come in. Have some tea," he said. The fog was at about tree level and it was cool. Tea sounded great.

"It's all downhill to Rumoi from here," he encouraged me. "It looks like it'll rain about lunchtime, but you should be in Rumoi by then." How he could tell it would rain, I don't know, as the fog was still thick. But I've always been a strong believer in local knowledge.

"Please come back sometime with your family. I'll still be here!" he said as I left, giving me his address.

My tennis shoes were already starting to fall apart and my knees weren't handling the spongy soles too well either. They creaked and groaned for all of the twenty kilometres out of the Rumoi River valley to the coast. Fortunately, the first shop I came across was a bargain shoe shop, and they even had a selection in my size. I played safety-first, going for a pair strong enough to get me to the Cape. Only a week to go.

The sky had cleared. So much for local knowledge. Rumoi was sleepy and hot. A group of oldies were playing gateball in the park, officiated over by a judge wearing white gloves. Far more active were the jet-black crows that were ripping apart a pile of garbage bags.

I could smell the salt of the sea, and the buildings were weather-bleached and dull. Rumoi was a practical town with no time to worry about appearances. At the port, timber was stacked on the docks, below huge oil tanks and towers of cement. The fishing fleet filled the harbour, unmoving in the calm water. It was incredibly humid. I escaped into an air-conditioned shokudo. The High School baseball champs were down to the final eight, capturing the customers' attention on the TV. It was a good reason not to go back out into the oppressive heat.

"You can fill your water-bottle with wheat-tea if you like," the owner said kindly, indicating the water-cooler which I had already half emptied. "You haven't got far to go now!" she encouraged me. She was right!

At the north end of town, in a residential area, the local pool was in heavy use. I could see the various coloured bathing caps bobbing up and down from the roadside. It was too tempting. I didn't need to wait long.

"A gaijin! A gaijin's come to our pool."

"Quick, go and get your brother."

Two elderly men were supervising. The one who took my hundred yen was friendly, while the other wouldn't look me in the eye and kept as far away as possible. The children weren't as restrained. Three little boys came into the changing room to watch, and when I emerged I was swamped by excited children. The pool was full of beach balls, blow-up animals and floating rings. I was treated like a new toy, and by the time I fought my way to the side thirty minutes later, I was totally exhausted. Another group came to watch me get changed, and as I was putting on my new shoes, one little boy asked if I would like to meet his elder sister!

It was good to be back on the coast, a cool breeze blowing in from the sea. Bare, scrubby hills rose inland on my right, and I could see the shoreline stretching due north ahead of me. With my second wind for the day, I strode away, knowing that I was on the final stretch.

Only one shokudo was open in Obira, and when I entered, the only person visible was a three year old boy watching "death and destruction" cartoons on TV. He blinked a couple of times at me before deciding that the TV was much more interesting. So I sat and watched with him. It took a good five minutes for his mother to come out, and when she did, she almost fell over at the shock of seeing me there.

The campground was high on a hill, a couple of kilometres past town. I followed the road as it snaked steeply up, my calves straining at the change in angle. I met a couple of touring cyclists at the top, and together we turned to watch the sun, an exquisite orange fireball, sink to the horizon in the west. It was a perfect setting sun, unbelievably large and captivating. We watched as it inched out of sight, until it completely disappeared for the day.

My new friends, aged eighteen, had cycled the seventy kilometres from Asahikawa and were feeling pains from their first day on the road. As they pitched their tent, I lay out my sleeping mat on the ground, opened a can of beer and relaxed on my back staring at the sparkling stars in the clear sky. Insects and moths whipped around lights at each corner of the ground, and a group not far away were sitting around a campfire listening to rock music. A group from a university in Tokyo, the eight young men had things well organized. The two women members of the party managed to do all the cooking and then clear up all the dishes, while the young men ate and sat around the campfire drinking beer.

My camp friends invited me to join them for dinner, but I was glad I'd had a meal in Obira. Their meal consisted of a packet of instant noodles between them, and a lettuce, which they ate leaf by leaf with salt. Amazed, I cracked another beer. I, at least, had come well prepared.

It grew darker and darker, and before I finally crawled into my tent, I spotted a "nagareboshi," shooting star. Or it might have been a satellite.

The crows woke me up at 5 am. They were cawing loudly to each other and fighting over food scraps around the cooking area. Caw Caw! Caw Caw! Huge black specimens which, happily, were scared enough of humans not to come too close.

My camp mates had about as much trouble taking their tent down as they'd had putting it up the night before. Still, it was their first night out. By the time I was ready to leave, the whole campground was awake, and as I walked out the gates, the 6 o'clock chimes sounded to wake the town of Obira. I'd been hearing such chimes for most of my 94 mornings on the road, but I still couldn't help shaking my head in amazement.

I had 40 kilometres to go to Haboro, and town markings on my map were pretty sparse. It was going to be a long slog straight up the coast under a hot sun. The only people I saw for the first couple of hours were a couple of fisherman and three different groups of cyclists from the Obira campground. They all slowed as they passed me, raised their fists in the air, and yelled either "Gambatte" in Japanese, or "Fight" in English. A more apt translation in such a situation might be "Keep going!"

Buildings were few and far between, and I couldn't believe my luck when I spotted an onsen sign on my map at the fishing village of Onishika.

"Well . . . they've got a bath at the hotel," the gas station attendant said. "But it's not a real onsen. It's not natural hot water but . . ."

But I didn't care. The man at reception told me the same thing. A gaijin arriving for a bath at 9:00 o'clock was obviously a bit of a surprise, but he handled it well.

The huge tiled bath looked out over a sandy beach to the calm blue sea. Hot water spouted out of a golden lion's head at one end, but on close inspection, the setting lost a bit of its perfection. The gold paint was peeling off the lion's nose to reveal white plaster.

"Not many people come here anymore," the receptionist said. "Not since we lost the train line." A familiar story. As I left he handed me a cigarette lighter with the hotel name and address on it.

"Thanks anyway, but I don't smoke."

"Please keep it for your memories," he insisted. I could think of better souvenirs.

I stumbled across a shokudo in a ramshackle house beside the road at Rikibiru. The glass in the front door had been broken and taped up, and the rotting weatherboards looked as if they'd barely last another winter, let alone that summer. But the women running the place were friendly.

"Don't worry about the weather forecast," one said, looking out the window. "It won't rain today."

"We're halfway between Sapporo and Wakkanai, but our weather is always the same as Wakkanai's," said the other.

The TV forecast was predicting rain for Sapporo and sunshine for Wakkanai. Those ladies seemed to know what they were talking about.

"My husband's a fisherman," one explained.

An old man was packing kombu, a black seaweed, which he'd been drying on the footpath. Strips lay out in neat piles, bending and twisting under the hot sun.

"The fences?" he said. "They're to protect houses from the winter wind. It's bitterly cold. Blows across the sea from Siberia, and goes straight through anything." I had been amazed at the roof-high, higgeldy-piggeldy fences that must have been put up by each place's owner. No self-respecting carpenter would ever claim responsibility. They were made of scrap timber and in some cases were tied together with rope. On my left, they were built on the sea side of the occasional building I came across, and on my right they were built smack up against the road-way.

"I pick it myself, dry it, and send it to Sapporo," he explained, indicating the piles of kombu in his garage. "There's not much else to do around here."

Three young guys were looking for awabi, abalone, in knee-deep water below the road. They'd collected quite a pile, and when I asked them what it was they were after, they tossed me up a can of cold coffee.

"Gambatte."

It was a hot day, and as I climbed what I hoped was the last hill before Tomamae, I thought I'd spotted a mirage. Coming towards me was a rickshaw being pulled by two shirtless blokes in wide straw sunhats. Another was pulling a folding baggage carrier with gear on it, while another was struggling under a big blue back-pack. To complete the group was a young guy in a blue happi carrying a big stick.

Fellow-adventurers from Kyoto University

"You've walked from Kagoshima? Unbelievable," they laughed. "We're from Kyoto University, it's our first year. This summer we're pulling the rickshaw from Cape Soya to Hakodate. Next year we'll do it from Aomori to Tokyo, and in our third year, from Tokyo to Kyoto. Do you want a drink?" It was my turn to laugh.

I looked in their rickshaw. They had all sorts of stuff including an ice chest of drinks, camping gear and various articles of clothing thrown about all over the place.

Their sweaty, smiling, encouraging faces perked me up.

"I'm not the only nutter out here," I thought to myself. "These guys are at least as crazy as I am. Maybe I should get a rickshaw for next time."

We cheered each other off with great enthusiasm.

Before I started my walk, a friend had called me a rebel.

"All adventurers are anti-establishment rebels," he said to me.

"If you weren't a rebel, you wouldn't need to go out and do what you're planning to do. You'd just lead a normal life like me. Rebels often lead lonely lives." I'd thought about what he'd said. I'd had plenty of time to think! He was right.

But I'd just met another group of rebels, and the similar attitudes that we held were more than enough to make us immediate friends. A rebel can recognize another rebel, and as long as there are other rebels around, he won't be lonely.

My meeting with the rickshaw boys had provided me with much-needed mental support.

The town of Haboro was protected by a huge concrete penguin on the edge of town. He looked down on all those entering, with a huge sign in English reading "Welcome" at his feet.

The youth hostel was an old wooden building.

"It used to be the primary school in a coal mining town about twenty kilometres inland from here," explained the young bloke in charge. "Demand for coal dropped in the late 1960s, and by the middle of the '70s everyone left. It's been a ghost town since then. Just like out of a movie. There are lots of run-down buildings but nobody lives there. Haboro bought the primary school and moved it here by truck to use as a youth hostel."

The old building had a great feel about it. "I wonder what the kids who were educated in here are doing now?" I couldn't help but think to myself.

I spent the evening playing cards with the hostel manager, a motorbike tourer from Tokyo, and a fourteen-year-old boy who had bicycled all the way from Gifu, near Nagoya. He had been going for 21 days and was making daily phone calls to his parents and to the teacher who had persuaded his parents to let him do it.

"I'm going to fly home," he said proudly. "I've never been on an aeroplane before!" A just reward for a kid who would have bicycled about 1,600 kilometres.

Hokkaido is a rebel's paradise.

"There are thirteen big hills and only one town between Haboro and Enbetsu," the youth hostel man warned me. "It's about 40 kilometres, but don't worry—you won't be alone. The triatholon is on today. It's the longest in Japan: a two kilometre swim, a 192 kilometre bicycle ride and then a full marathon. I've heard that there are 330 competitors. They'll pass you on their bicycles heading north this morning, and again running south sometime this afternoon."

And indeed, the map looked bleak. But it was with great enthusiam that I set out on that cloudy Sunday morning, my 95th day.

Haboro was wide awake, despite the early time, and on each street corner in town, policemen waited with red traffic-directing sticks, and white-T-shirted officials sat on folding chairs waiting to write down the numbers of the competitors as they raced by.

I was half-way up the first of the hills when a police car cruised by, lights flashing, its white-helmeted cops both pointing at me. A few seconds later I heard a loud "wooosh!" over my right shoulder, and the leader flew by, lean and muscular, in a fluorescent skin suit and orange reflective sunglasses. He nodded as he passed.

No. 2 was a good five minutes back, but he flashed past with the same unexpected woosh which made me jump. And then with shorter and shorter intervals came the chasers. Woosh! Woosh! They flew by. Woosh! I had topped the hill and was heading down the other side. Woosh! They flew by with increasing speed.

At the bottom of the hill, on the flat, was the first of the aid stations. About a hundred metres short of the tents was a man with a loudspeaker.

"No. 93, No. 93. What do you want?" he yelled at No. 93, who was flying on a bike with a solid-black rear wheel.

"Banana, drink," he shouted back.

The official put his megaphone to his mouth, turned to the aid station, yelling:

"No. 93, banana, drink!"

I could see frantic activity among the huge crowd at the aid station, and by the time No. 93 got there, he barely had to slow as one girl passed him a banana, and another a drink bottle.

"No. 243, No. 243, what do you want?"

"Sandwich!"

"No. 243 wants a sandwich," the official yelled into his loud speaker, and sure enough, when he got to the tents, he got a sandwich.

I waited for a break in competitors.

"The gaijin who's walking! What do you want?"

"A beer! I want a beer!" The official laughed. He put his megaphone to his mouth.

"The gaijin who's walking wants a beer!" I could hear the laughing from quite a distance.

When I got to the tents, I received a loud applause and a cold beer from an exceptionally cute girl with a big smile, which made my day.

It was total mayhem when the pack arrived. Cyclists were passing the megaphone man at a rate of about three a second and he couldn't take the orders fast enough. The fifty or so girls at the aid station did their best, standing with arms outstretched, just about getting them ripped off as cyclists grabbed at bananas, sandwiches, drink bottles, and pickled plums. Food was flying all over the place as the riders rode the gauntlet of enthusiastic young women. I carried on, hoping for more aid stations.

The pack had passed. A group of twelve elderly people were sitting in chairs on the side of the road, encouraging the stragglers. As I walked up, they gave me a big clap. I bowed deeply. Even bigger applause.

The shape of the competitors had changed. The lean, muscular types were at the front, but down at the back of the field, the squatter, heavier types were struggling. One thing hadn't changed though. The competitors were still in bright, fluorescent outfits, keen to catch the eyes of the onlookers.

A few touring cyclists were mixed up among the competitors. One stopped.

"Are you the New Zealander walking the length of Japan?" he asked.

"Yes." Well, there probably weren't any others.

"I was in Obira last night. There's a Japanese guy a day behind you who's walked from Kagoshima too. He's been hearing about you all the way. He wants to try and meet you, so you can walk into Cape Soya together. He said to tell you he'll be in Haboro tonight."

So I wasn't the only rebel.

I was sitting with another group of elderly spectators when the last cyclist rode by. She was struggling badly, and we encouraged her as best we could. But it was pretty difficult for her. Just as the leader had had a police car escorting him, she had a police car with flashing lights and two bored looking cops within five metres of her backside.

The old man I was sitting next to was having a great time measuring the height of my knees while sitting, as compared to his. The whole crew of oldies cackled away.

"Please don't forget the beautiful old lady of Ariake," the old man joked as I was leaving, indicating his particularly wrinkled elderly wife. They all burst into laughter again.

It was lonely on the road without the competitors. I trudged into Shosanbetsu feeling safe in the assumption that the shokudo was bound to be open. Carloads of support crews and onlookers had been streaming by. Surely it would be the busiest day of their year. I was correct!

The cook winced when he took my order for Genghis Khan. The shokudo was full, and he and his wife were run off their feet. Instead of a frying pan he reached for his keys, donned a motorbike helmet and shot out the door. Everyone looked confused, and as the minutes passed by and no meals were served up, the complaining started. It was a good ten minutes before he reappeared with a small plastic bag full of mutton.

"Yappari, trust it to be the gaijin to order something difficult," I could see the crowd thinking.

"But it's on the menu," I said to myself.

"There's nothing between here and Enbetsu," the cook warned me as I headed out the door.

"Hopefully there'll be some more aid stations," I thought to myself.

I was accumulating a lot of garbage. One set of officials I passed sent one of their members scurrying after me with cookies and a can of beer. Then a carload of supporters stopped to hand me out a vitamin drink. I stuck to my Winnie the Pooh theory, that consuming was better than carrying, but my pockets were full of wrappers, empty cans and bottles.

The same police car was escorting the same leader on his run back down the coast. This time, instead of pointing, the cops saluted me. I saluted back. The leader was looking sharp. As he passed he raised his hand, slapping mine as I responded. A nice greeting, good encouragement.

The next runner was seven and a half minutes back. A strong, strapping woman was in sixth place. She was hardly slim, big muscles rippling in her thighs as she ran, and breasts bouncing, threatening to escape. She was more than holding her position among the males around her and deserved the respect I had for her.

"Gambare," I said as she strode past.

"Thank you," she replied in English, a smile flashing across her face.

The next aid station fed me watermelon and a can of beer. But I missed out on the best deal. Exhausted runners were being toweled down by enthusiastic female volunteers who rubbed their aching legs, encouraging them to keep going. My legs ached too! But there were no volunteers.

More than one runner intimated that he was envious of the beer I was sipping as I wandered up the road. I slapped hands, traded "gambattes" and smiled at each runner as we passed. The bunch had gone by and the stragglers were still struggling. A man as big as a sumo wrestler pounded by, grinning, followed by three middle-aged women in high-cut gear, running together. A skinny little old man with a white sweatband plodded by looking at the ground. Then a tall skinny guy who looked ready to die.

The last aid-station was trying to get rid of the piles of unneeded food. They laughed, describing me as a good "gomibako" or rubbish bin, and sent me on my way with a packful of sandwiches, bananas and drinks.

The last competitor passed me at 4:30, still with well over 30 kilometres to go. It was the same girl who had trailed the field on the bicycle, followed by the same bored-looking policeman, still barely five metres from her backside. I let out an exceptionally enthusiastic "gambare" and could see her face light up at the attention. The only change at the back of the field was that behind the police car was a bus for "dead" competitors, those who had pulled out. Three figures were slumped in their seats, staring glumly at the floor.

And when they had passed, it was just me on the road with eight kilometres to go. Trudging on by myself, lonely after all the company for the day. Battling past banana peels, orange peels, discarded sandwiches and the odd drink bottle. Alone in desolate Japan. The road was straight as an arrow, surrounded by scrub. Nothing except a bus stop. Who could possibly use it?

The campground at Fujimigaoka, high on a hill overlooking Enbetsu, was totally deserted. It was a warm summer evening and not a soul was there, despite the great facilities. Four little log cabins lay tucked under a stand of trees, unused and with their doors unlocked. There was no one to pay, so I just made myself at home.

A couple of hundred metres down the road was a shokudo. Depositing my gear, and donning my thongs, I wandered down for a feed.

"It's the gaijin rubbish bin!" roared a red-faced bald man, one of a group of twelve I recognized as the officials at the last aid station, which had sent me away with a pack full of food and drink. The whole group turned as he pointed, and suddenly I was the centre of attention for a dozen drunken revellers.

"Come and join us! Come! Come! Do you like sake? Good! Good! Please drink!" I had a cup in my hand before I'd sat down. Unfortunately I was placed next to the most red-faced of them all, Mr Kato. He was concentrating on something.

"Me," he said in English pointing to himself.

"Yes, quite correct," I encouraged him.

"Me. . . ."

"Yes."

"Me speak English good!" he blurted out. The crowd roared. He looked incredibly pleased with himself.

"Very good," I praised him. It was going to be a long evening. I knocked back a small cup of sake. The cup was magically refilled before it touched the table. I knocked it back again, and the same thing happened. Fortunately some food arrived. I broke apart my throw-away bamboo chopsticks and was encouraged to dig in. Kato san was watching me.

"Very good bridge!" he said loudly in English, proud of himself once again.

"Pardon," I said, bemused.

"Very good bridge," he insisted pointing at my hand. I was confused, and so it seemed were the rest of the team.

"Hashi ga umai," he said in Japanese. "You're good with your chopsticks." He shrunk with embarrassment as the table erupted with laughter.

"Hashi ga umai! Very good bridge. Ha! Ha! Ha!" the bloke on my left yelled into my ear, slapping me on the back. The veins were standing out in his temples, and I was scared his head might explode from the pressure.

The word for bridge, as in the kind that you walk over a river on, is hashi. The word for chopsticks is also hashi, only slightly differently pronounced. Kato-san had fallen into a trap for young players. He squirmed with embarrassment. It seemed that the rest of the group had picked up his mistake immediately.

Pots of sake were emptied with frightening regularity, and as the crew prepared a final toast before their departure, Kato-san hushed them in order to make a comeback. All were silent. He looked at me and asked in English:

"Will you sleep with me tonight?"

Once again it seemed that everyone understood his mistake. Except for a mystified Mr Kato. The previous eruption of hilarity was minor compared to what spewed forth. It took a full five minutes for everyone to calm down enough so that we could make a final toast of farewell.

On the way out Kato-san redeemed himself by pinching the waitress' bottom and then they were gone, leaving me sitting at the table with two full pots of sake. I had refused Kato's offer and was alone once again. Well, not entirely. The waitresses were giggling at me. I giggled back.

It was so dark outside that I had to follow the white line in the middle of the road back to the campground. Or maybe the sake had something to do with it.

Rain had pelted down overnight, accompanied by awesome lightning and thunder. I had plenty of supplies—cans of coffee and energy drink, sandwiches, bananas and oranges, all courtesy of that last aid station. The Winnie the Pooh theory came to the fore, and when I set out at 7:30 under an overcast sky, I was full.

Enbetsu was having a busy morning. It was the first day back for schoolchildren after summer vacation, and from the stares, it was a fair bet that the walking gaijin was going to get mentioned to the teacher. Two old ladies on the main street must have heard the news. They stood on the sidewalk staring as I approached, passed, and carried on north. I looked over my shoulder a hundred metres up the road, and they were still there, staring.

On the outskirts of Enbetsu were swinging gates that could close the road in winter. It was pretty bleak, with only the occasional farm amongst the low scrubland. I had plenty of time to think about the walker a day behind me. Who was he? How long had it taken him? Which route had he taken?

Over the course of a couple of kilometres I collected three banana peels from the side of the road, leftovers of the triathalon. I ate my last banana, and with the four peels, in a moment of inspiration, wrote a message on the footpath. He would have to take that road too.

"Soya, on the 26th."

It would have been more readable if I'd had a couple of extra peels. But I didn't. I stood back, proud of my effort. Surely he couldn't miss that.

Had I gone completely loopy?

A few kilometres short of Teshio I was in a cattle-farming area. There were barns full of hay and signs for "Registered Holsteins". And the green was green grass, not green paddy fields.

Two bikers in black leathers pulled over for a yarn. It was a father and son team, and I could tell from the licence plates that they'd come from Wakayama, near Osaka. The old man was in his seventies, unshaven, with long grey whiskers, and his son about half his age.

"You've ridden all the way from Wakayama?" I asked incredulously to the old man.

"How do you know?" he asked, surprised. I pointed at the licence plate on his bike.

"You can read that? That's amazing. Yes, we've ridden from Wakayama. It's taken ten days. My backside is sore!"

"Where have you walked from?" asked the son.

"From Kagoshima. This is my 96th day," I replied. "I've got sore feet," I added laughing.

"That's incredible," the old man said. It was at that point that I realised I had almost done something quite amazing. There I was, surprised at the old man's feat of having ridden his motor-bike from Wakayama, when I had walked nearly twice that distance. It was a strange feeling.

Teshio had obviously not adjusted to the loss of its train line six years before. The line was still marked on the map at the edge of town, and when I asked as to the whereabouts of a shokudo, the best answer I got was "beside the station".

It was packed, but I found a seat at a table with some motor-bikers from Kanagawa. I opened my map book to find that I was onto the last page! Not far to go.

The road turned inland. I wouldn't see the coast again until I was almost at my destination. Cattle stared at me as I mooed at them, and outside a small school in the middle of nowhere, a group of oldies were playing gateball. A teacher and one of his young students were cleaning out the bus shelter.

The teacher stared as I walked up, and as with Kato-san the night before, I could see him thinking.

"Are you a passenger?" he asked in English. I was finding those English-speaking northerners awfully confusing. We reverted to Japanese.

"No, there's nothing between here and Horonobe except a drink machine on the side of the road in exactly two kilometres." It was good to know what I was up against.

The drink machine was, as the teacher had said, exactly two kilometres up the road. I could tell because in Hokkaido most roads have markers that count off each kilometre.

The drink machine was bright pink and specialised in "Jolt Cola". Jolt Cola's claim to fame was written in bright yellow on the pink can—"Caffeine x 2". Not being a decaf coffee drinker, I didn't mind. In fact I was feeling like putting something into my body to perk me up and make sure I could make it to Horonobe. I had two cans just to make sure.

The Teshio River is the fourth longest in Japan, and about five kilometres short of Horonobe, I crossed it on a big iron bridge. In fact I almost went swimming in it when a truck driver spent too much time watching me and not enough time concentrating on the road.

Horonobe is tucked in at the base of the central hills, on the central train line linking Sapporo and Asahikawa with Wakkanai, Japan's northernmost city. It was a busy little town and there were three or four ryokan around the station to chose from. In the first I entered, the big-armed lady owner was most hospitable. The genkan was full of slippers, placed so as to welcome the return of her long-term guests, construction workers. I was lucky though. There was one room left.

The daughter acted as if she wanted to be even more hospitable than her mother. She thrust out her blossoming chest, commandeering me to show her where New Zealand was in her atlas. I enjoyed the attention, but was quite happy to be called away to a dinner of scallops and grilled meat by her mother. After all, the daughter was still in her school uniform!

An old man wearing a white hard-hat came in while I was eating breakfast. The regular guests, the construction workers, had already headed out for the day. He started when he saw me.

"This is a very international place you're running," he said to the fat-armed lady. "Is he eating natto?" he added incredulously.

"Watch what you say! He speaks Japanese," she warned him. The old man had somehow folded himself up so that he was sitting cross-legged on a chair. He lit up a cigarette, still wearing his hard-hat.

"Where's he from?" he asked the lady.

"I'm from New Zealand," I broke in. He ignored me.

"Where's that?" he asked her.

"It's near Australia," she replied, proud of her new knowledge. As any New Zealander would, I squirmed at such an explanation.

"What's he doing here?" he directed at the owner. "What's the point?" I thought to myself. I may as well turn off. But it didn't really upset me. I was used to such situations.

The wind was strong as I headed out of town, straight up into the hills on a minor road past the single-chairlift skifield. The main road to Wakkanai headed away to the left, skirting the base of the hills, and I could see it disappearing off on the flat river plain.

The land levelled off to become rolling farmland and low bamboo-like scrub. Only an occasional farmhouse came into view, carefully positioned so as to be protected from the frigid westerly winter winds. Run-down farm buildings seemed to outnumber those still in use. The whole scene was testimony to the harsh climate. Cattle mostly in barns, the land being used to produce enough feed to tide them through the winter.

The only traffic was trucks carrying either logs or bales of hay. And there were no road signs on such a minor road. But somehow I managed to find Tanaka-san's farm, miles from anywhere.

A friend of a friend, Tanaka-san walked the length of Japan in 1977. Born in Tokyo, at the age of 19 he decided to see what his country was all about. A true rebel. He had found his "real Japan", a country he could truly love, in northern Hokkaido. With his wife and four children, he owns his own farm, milking eighty cows twice a day, and battling to survive the winter. Without a TV.

A man with real spirit!

I was made to work for my dinner, but I enjoyed every minute of it. Late in the afternoon, with Tanaka-san's eight-year-old son, I herded the eighty cattle from a large paddock over the road to the milking shed. They all knew where they were going, but I enjoyed it anyway.

"The cattle are in the barn all winter," Tanaka-san explained. "Sometimes there is so much snow that I have to dig my way over to milk them in the morning."

I continued by helping with preparations for winter, splitting silver birch logs until I had cultivated a decent-sized blister on my left hand. It felt good to be physical with my upper body again, after my legs had taken the brunt of the storm for the previous three months. I split the logs, and two high school girls from Tokyo, on their summer vacation, stacked them. They were there for a learning experience too.

The girls were shovelling excrement when I left in the morning under the watchful eye of Tanaka-san's wife. Tanaka-san himself had started milking at 4:30 am despite what must have been a throbbing head from the alcohol we'd consumed until late the night before. The two elder kids had hopped on the school bus that came specifically to pick them up. It had taken them off to study at the local primary school, which had only seven children.

"It'll have two more when our small ones get bigger. Plus there's a family with young children down the road," Tanaka-san said. "But a lot of families have left this area. The winters are tough."

I thought of a couple of news items I'd seen on TV over the previous few days.

The first was about "U-turners" and "I-turners". The "U-turners" described the country person who had gone to Tokyo to live, decided it wasn't for him, and returned to his country area. Apparently, numbers of U-turners were increasing.

"I-turners" were those like Tanaka-san. People born in Tokyo who want to get out. The item said that 10% of young people aged between 20 and 29 in Tokyo were interested in moving to the country. Reasons given were that they could buy land, build a house, and have a better lifestyle. And as my friends in Hakodate had told me, rural areas were going to great pains to attract such people to live with them. Tanaka-san was a long term "I-turner".

The second item was about a girl from Osaka. A successful office lady with good prospects, she had decided to forsake her future in the big city and move to Hokkaido to be a farmer's wife. And she had decided to do this before picking out her farmer. Wives for farmers have been rather scarce in recent years with young women flocking to the cities. The girl's arrival was being considered a coup in the fightback against the drain.

But I doubted if the excrement-shovelling high school girls would return to live. They didn't appear to be too keen on their work.

I wandered for four hours through beautiful nothingness under a warm sun to reach the small town of Numakawa. There was nothing for that twenty kilometres except green paddocks, an empty road stretching far into the distance, and a cool breeze blowing from the west. It was a perfect day. The odd village marked on my map would turn out to be only a small cluster of houses, and I didn't meet a soul until I wandered into Numakawa, except for a solitary band of road workers who were widening the road. I don't know why they were widening the road though. There wasn't any traffic.

Of course, Numakawa's only shokudo was closed. The grocery store was open, though, and I sat on a bench outside in the sun, munching bread and cheese, talking with a motor-bike rider from Osaka. She had a crew-cut, was wearing black leathers, and looked like a rebel too. But at the end of her ten days exploring Hokkaido, she had a nice safe job to go back to in Osaka.

The afternoon, like the morning, was a twenty kilometre hike through sparsely populated farmland. The wind was so strong that it blew my cap off a couple of times. Over the last couple of hours, on a wide flat river plain heading out to the sea, every one hundred metres there was an arrow suspended off a pole, high over the edge of the road, marking the kerb for grader drivers in winter. I was glad it wasn't winter!

Then three or four kilometres short of the coast, I stumbled across a little village which boasted a school and a Japan Agriculture Co-operative shop. Three big-bottomed women packed into their orange uniforms looked at each other when I walked in. Two were faster than the third, quickly finding something important to do. It was a case of "you snooze, you lose," and the third realised that she hadn't reacted quickly enough. She came to the counter, reluctantly.

"Can you tell me where the campground is?" I asked in Japanese. She sighed with relief, and within seconds the other two had come to her aid, smiling and very helpful. Well, as helpful as they could be, considering that none knew where the campground was.

"I've heard of it. It's not too far too far from here," one said, smiling a charming smile, revealing a mouthful of gold. But that didn't do me much good.

Fortunately a customer knew. He proceeded to draw me an intricate map that became more and more confusing. Halfway through his explanation my mind turned off.

"Forget it. I'll camp by the road for my last night just like I did for my first," I thought.

I thanked him for his kindness, smiled a fetching smile at the big-bottomed trio, and headed out the door with my supplies.

The cows followed me down the road, over the fence, in their paddock. They reacted as if they'd never seen a human mooing before—staring, stamping their feet, and mooing back.

I headed straight out towards the sea, and within a couple of kilometres couldn't believe my eyes. There was a sign for the campground, pointing to my right. "Campground 500 metres," it read. But the guy in the JA had drawn such a complicated map!

There were cabins and tent sites at the campground, but the cabins were all locked and the manager had gone home by the time I arrived. Two couples were getting right into the outdoor life outside their cabin. They had rigged up a portable TV, and the men were watching baseball and drinking beer, while the girls slaved over the barbecue. Why had they bothered to leave home?

The only other tenter was an 18-year-old high school drop-out from Tokyo with long brown Afro-hair. It had taken him 40 days to cycle from the capital.

"I'm going to cycle to Okinawa next!" he said proudly. "My father's dead. My mother's worried. And my big brother's disowned me." A rebel if I ever saw one! We got along well.

It was my 98th night out. The last. The occasion wasn't lost on me. The next day I would walk the twenty-three kilometres to Cape Soya, the northern-most point in mainland Japan, and complete what was for me a major achievement. It was coming to an end.

I was mentally prepared as I hit the road at 7:45 am under a clear sky. It wasn't that I was desperate to finish, but rather that that day, the 26th of August, my 99th day out, would be the culmination of months of planning, months of walking, and a seemingly endless amount of focussed concentration. The following day I would be back in Osaka with my wife and children, ready to get back into my reasonably normal life. Nothing would have changed except that I had done it. The game of life would go on. I had won my own little battle against myself and the elements. But life would go on. I knew it. Still, I couldn't help getting excited.

I passed Wakkanai Airport and hit the coast at 8:30, turning right, with 20 kilometres to go. The wind was strong and the waves were pounding in to the sandy beach.

"19, 19, 19, to go," I sung to myself.

"18, 18, 18, to go," as another marker was passed.

At the 17-kilometres-to-go mark, my long-haired rebel friend from the campground passed on his bicycle.

"I'll be waiting at the Cape," he assured me.

I was rounding the long curl of Soya Bay, passing weather beaten houses, fishing nets drying next to the road, and rock gardens that used fishing floats instead of rocks.

"16, 16, 16 to go." The Cape extended out to sea in front of me.

My ankle must have known that something was up as it did a major moan.

One of my sponsors had contacted the media, and at the twelve kilometre mark a TV cameraman in a four-wheel-drive pulled over. I saw him hold up a photograph, look at me, look back at the photo, and nod his head.

"You're the one, aren't you?" he said shaking his head.

"Yes," was the best I could come up with.

"And you've walked all the way from Cape Sata?"

"Yes."

"How many kilometres is that?" he asked, pulling out a notepad.

"About 3,200 kilometres, give or take a bit."

"And how long has it taken you?"

"This is my 99th day!"

"How do you feel at the moment?"

"I've got bloody sore feet!" He was shaking his head.

"Your wife is Japanese?"

"Yes, we've got two sons."

"And she let you do this?"

"I guess she trusts me."

"You're very lucky." He was shaking his head again.

"I know!"

"Well, just keep walking. I'll drive on ahead and film you from various places. You won't know where!"

The fishing village of Soya was about seven kilometres short of the Cape. There was seaweed being dried on the footpath, and for some reason, at the shop, I was charged 95 yen for a 100 yen ice cream.

"Don't forget your change!" said the woman smiling. "Gambatte."

The cameraman had already popped up a couple of times, once in the bushes on my right, and once from between some buildings on my left. He was going for the "natural" look, obviously not trusting my acting ability. He pulled up as I was eating my ice cream on a bench outside the shop.

"Where did you stay each night?" I thought for a moment before answering.

"Well, I had a tent. In good weather I used my tent. I camped on beaches, at shrines, at temples, beside the road, once in a car park! In bad weather, I tried to find places to stay such as ryokan, minshuku, or youth hostels. Some kind people invited me to stay, and I had friends and friends of friends along the way. I stayed in mountain huts, cabins, business hotels, Government lodging houses. I even spent a night in a welfare centre." I had to think a bit more. "And a night in a station." He was shaking his head. "And one night in a noodle shop!"

"A noodle shop!"

"Yes, in a noodle shop. And once in a tree house!"

I needed a leak, but a second cameraman from another TV station had arrived, and they were having fun popping out of all sorts of unexpected places to film me.

And I didn't think my sponsors would have appreciated the publicity created by people watching me having a pee on the side of the road. It was tough, but I held on.

At the four kilometres to go mark, the 4WD flashed by. It had two loud speakers mounted on the roof.

"Four kilometres. You've got four kilometres to go!" yelled the cameramen, waving.

"What did you eat?" asked the cameramen, driving along with his camera pointing out the window, filming me as I walked.

"Anything and everything! You can't be fussy when you're walking!"

"What about the Japanese summer? Wasn't it hot?"

"What summer?" He nodded his head in agreement.

"What were you worried about while you walked?"

"Bears and tidal waves. I can handle earthquakes but I don't like tidal waves. Or bears." I rattled my kumayoke for the camera.

He drove on.

The second cameraman was going for a close-up. He was walking backwards in front of me, bending, with the camera about shin level, looking upwards.

"Were people kind to you?"

"All along the way. Everyone encouraged me. Though some didn't understand why I was doing it."

"Why did you do it?"

"I'm still not sure really!" I could see it coming. He clipped the kerb with his heel, landing on his backside in the middle of the footpath. He saved his camera but must have ended up with a big bruise. I carried on. "I was looking to find the 'real Japan'. I've lived in Tokyo and my wife is from Osaka. But I've always felt that the big cities are not the real Japan." He nodded his agreement.

"I'm from Wakkanai. I know what you mean."

"And I guess I did it because I'm a rebel."

"A rebel?"

"Well . . . I want to live an interesting life. I want to do interesting things. Walking the length of Japan was . . . well . . . interesting!"

"Would you do it again?"

"Hang on. I'll ask my feet."

With two kilometres to go, my two young camp mates from a few days before came riding up, also heading to the cape. They were immediately set on by the cameramen.

"Where did you meet him?

"What do you think of what he's done?"

"Where have you come from?"

I walked on ahead.

"I've got some more questions," the first cameraman said. "Do you have any regrets?"

"That I didn't get to meet the guy who's a day behind me!"

"There's someone else?"

"Yes, there's a Japanese not far behind. I'm not sure how far back, or on which road, but I've heard he's there."

"How many pairs of boots did you use?"

"I went through four pairs."

"What will you do when you reach Cape Soya?" The Cape was in view, about a kilometre away, around a big bay.

"The first thing I'll do is have a beer, then I'll call my wife." The camera man smiled.

"Did you find the 'real Japan'?"

"Yes I think so."

"Where is it?"

"Out there," I said, pointing south.

I strode through the big carpark, past the cars, motorbikes and bicycles, until I was standing at the base of the pointed obelisk marking Cape Soya, the northernmost point in mainland Japan.

The cameramen, the young cyclists, my Afro-haired mate and a few extras were there to congratulate me.

"Well done!" said the first cameraman, handing me a cool can of beer. I popped the top, and holding it aloft, stood in front of the obelisk for photos and filming.

But it wasn't a feeling of triumph that swept over me. It was a feeling of relief.

I had done it. I'd never have to do it again.

I had three cans of beer, called my wife, and walked back out to the road.

I hung out my thumb and the third car that passed picked me up. A new adventure was starting.

I made it! Cape Soya.

Glossary of Japanese Words Used

akachochin	literally "red lantern"—marks a small, cheap drinking establishment
akisame	the period of autumn rains after summer
ashi	a foot or leg
asobi	literally "play"—can be used to describe adult leisure activities
ayu	a type of small fish
bakayaro	"Idiot!"
ben	a local dialect, e.g., Kagoshima-ben
bijin	a beautiful woman
biwa	a loquat, small orange fruit
chashumen	Chinese soup noodles with slices of roast pork on top
chuken	a faithful dog
daigaku	university
dohyo	a sumo wrestling ring, elevated
domo arigato	"Thank you"
ecchi	a pervert
fugu	a blowfish, globefish—poisonous
futon	a combination of bedding, mattress and bed cover
gaijin	a foreigner
Gambatte	"Keep going!" "Good luck!" "Do your best!"
Genghis Khan	Mongolian mutton BBQ, named after the famous Genghis Khan
genkan	an entrance to a dwelling where shoes are removed
geta	wooden clogs
gohan	cooked white rice
gomibako	a rubbish bin, trash can
Goyukkuri	"Take your time!"
gyudon	rice, with shredded beef, onion and ginger
hachimaki	a headband
hanabi	fireworks
happi	a slip-on jacket like a short kimono
hashi	chopsticks
hayane hayaoki	"Early to bed, Early to rise"
Heisei	the period while Akihito is Emperor

hinoki	a Japanese Cypress
hiragana	a 46 character phonetic writing system
hoko onchi	a person hopeless with directions
honne	one's "private face", real feelings
hotaru	a firefly
hotategai	scallops
ika	squid
inakamono	a country person/bumpkin
iwana	a char (fish)
JA	Japan Agriculture—a co-operative that runs all-purpose stores in the countryside
jieitai	Self Defence Forces
jinrikisha	a rickshaw
jishin	an earthquake
karaoke	literally "empty orchestra"—a popular form of entertainment where guests sing their favourite songs to backsound music
kanji	Chinese characters incorporated into the Japanese writing system—not phonetic
katakana	a 46 character phonetic writing system used for words adopted from foreign languages
katsukare	curried rice, with a fried pork cutlet
keyaki	a zelkova tree
kimono	a traditional Japanese costume; also, clothing in general
ki o tsukete	"Take care!"
koban	a police box
koen	a park
kogen	a plateau
kohai	a junior
konjo	guts—as in, "to have guts"
kokuminshukusha	a National Lodging House
kombu	tangleweed (seaweed)
kotsusenso	the traffic war
kuma	a bear
kumayoke	a trinket that warns bears of one's presence
mamushi	a viper snake
manga	comics, cartoons
matsuri	a festival
minshuku	a guest house
misoshiru	bean-paste soup

mizuburo	a cold water bath
mizushobai	"the water trade"—the evening entertainment industry
moshi moshi	"Hello" (when talking on the telephone)
mugicha	wheat tea
mukaezake	"hair of the dog"
nagareboshi	a shooting star
nashi	a Japanese pear
natsu	summer
natto	fermented soyabeans
nebuta	floats used in Nebuta Festival, Aomori
nomihodai	"all you can drink"
Nihon, Nippon	Japan
Nihonshu	Japanese rice wine
noren	a shop curtain that hangs above the door announcing the restaurant is open
nori	seaweed
obachan	Grandmother, old woman
obento	a packed meal
Obon	Festival for the Dead
ohaka	a grave
Ohayo gozaimasu	"Good morning!"
omamori	a safety charm
omiyage	a souvenir
onigiri	a riceball
onsen	hot springs
otosan	Father
Oyasumi nasai	"Good night!"
pachinko	a kind of vertical pinball
rakkyo	a shallot
ramen	Chinese soup noodles
ri	an old measurement—the distance a man with a load can walk in an hour
ryokan	a Japanese-style inn
sake	rice wine
samurai	a warrior
sempai	a senior
sensei	a teacher
sento	a public bath
shacho	a Company President
shigoto	work

shinhatsubai	a new product
shinkansen	the Bullet Train
Shinto	Japan's native religion
shishamo	a smelt
shochu	potato alcohol
shoji	a paper screen
shokudo	a small eating house
Showa	the period when Hirohito was Emperor 1926–1989
soba	buckwheat noodles
subarashii	"Great!"
Sumimasen	"I'm sorry", "Excuse me!"
sumo	Sumo wrestling
tabehodai	"all you can eat"
taifu	a typhoon
taiko	a drum
takuan	pickled radish
tanbo	a rice paddy
tanuki	a badger
tatami	straw matting
tatemae	"public face"
teishoku	a set meal—usually includes miso soup, rice and pickles, along with a main dish.
tetsudo	a railway
tokai	the city
Tokai	the Eastern Seaboard
Tokugawa	the family that ruled Japan from 1600–1867
torii	a Shinto shrine gate
tsunami	a tidal wave
tsuyu	the rainy season
uchiwa	a fan
udon	wheat flour noodles
umeboshi	pickled plums
untenshu	a driver
waribashi	disposable wooden chopsticks
yakiniku	grilled meat
yakitori	grilled chicken on skewers
yakizakana	grilled fish
yakuza	the Japanese mafia
yappari	"Just as I thought . . . !"
yukiguni	snow country

I was kindly helped by the following sponsors:

Japan Airlines

Ansett New Zealand

Japan National Tourist Organisation

Macpac Wilderness Equipment

Canon New Zealand

Mizuno Sports, Japan

Wish Marine, Japan

Shotover Jet, Queenstown

Paradise Promotions, Queenstown

Thank you for your support, and for believing that I could do what I was setting out to do.